The Structure of Atonal Music

The Structure of Atonal Music

Allen Forte

New Haven and London Yale University Press

Originally published with assistance from the Mary
Cady Tew Memorial Fund.

Library of Congress catalog card number: 72-91295
International standard book number: 0-300-01610-7 (cloth)
0-300-02120-8 (paper)

Designed by John O. C. McCrillis
and set in Press Roman type.
Printed in the United States of America by
The Murray Printing Co., Westford, Mass.
Music autography by Carl A. Rosenthal.

Published in Great Britain, Europe, Africa, and Asia
(except Japan) by Yale University Press, Ltd., London.
Distributed in Latin America by Kaiman & Polon, Inc.,
New York City; in Australia and New Zealand by
Book & Film Services, Artarmon, N.S.W., Australia;
and in Japan by Harper & Row, Publishers, Tokyo
Office.

For Sharland

Contents

Preface   ix

Part 1   Pitch-Class Sets and Relations

1.0   Pitch combinations   1
1.1   Pitch-Class sets   1
1.2   Normal order; the prime forms   3
1.3   Transpositionally equivalent pc sets   5
1.4   Inversionally equivalent pc sets   7
1.5   The list of prime forms; set names   11
1.6   Intervals of a pc set; the interval vector   13
1.7   Some properties of interval vectors   16
1.8   Cardinal number and interval content   19
1.9   Non-equivalent pc sets with identical vectors   21
1.10   The subsets of a pc set   24
1.11   Invariant subsets under transposition   29
1.12   Invariant subsets under inversion   38
1.13   Similarity relations   46
1.14   Order relations   60
1.15   The complement of a pc set   73
1.16   Segmentation   83

Part 2   Pitch-Class Set Complexes

2.0   Introduction   93
2.1   The set complex K   93
2.2   The subcomplex Kh   96
2.3   Set-Complex sizes   101
2.4   The closure property   101
2.5   Invariance within the set complex   104
2.6   Similarity relations within the set complex   108
2.7   Set-Complex structures of small scale   113
2.8   Set-Complex structures of larger scale   124

Appendix 1   Prime Forms and Vectors of Pitch-Class Sets   179

Appendix 2   Similarity Relations   182

Appendix 3   The Subcomplexes Kh   200

Glossary of Technical Terms   209

References   213

Index 1   Musical Examples   215

Index 2   Pc Sets in Musical Examples   216

Index 3   General Index   223

Preface

In 1908 a profound change in music was initiated when Arnold Schoenberg began composing his "George Lieder" Op. 15. In this work he deliberately relinquished the traditional system of tonality, which had been the basis of musical syntax for the previous two hundred and fifty years. Subsequently, Schoenberg, Anton Webern, Alban Berg, and a number of other composers created the large repertory known as atonal music.

Despite some recent and serious efforts, which stand in marked contrast to earlier simplistic formulations, the structure of this complicated music has not been well understood. Accordingly, it is the intention of the present work to provide a general theoretical framework, with reference to which the processes underlying atonal music may be systematically described. It is not claimed that all aspects of atonal music are dealt with (an improbable undertaking, in any event); instead, major emphasis has been placed upon fundamental components of structure. For instance, one can deal with pitch and disregard orchestration, but the reverse is not, in general, possible.

Although a good deal of attention has been paid to the iconoclastic nature of atonal music, there has been a tendency to overlook its significance within the art form. This circumstance is unfortunate and should be corrected. One need only remark that among the major works in this repertory are Schoenberg's Five Pieces for Orchestra Op. 16 (1909), Webern's Six Pieces for Large Orchestra Op. 6 (1910), Stravinsky's *The Rite of Spring* (1913), and Berg's *Wozzeck* (1920).

The inclusion of Stravinsky's name in the list above suggests that atonal music was not the exclusive province of Schoenberg and his circle, and that is indeed the case. Many other gifted composers contributed to the repertory: Alexander Scriabin, Charles Ives, Carl Ruggles, Ferruccio Busoni, and Karol Szymanowski—to cite only the more familiar names.

The present study draws upon the music of many of the composers mentioned above. It does not, however, deal with 12-tone music, or with what might be described as paratonal music, or with more recent music which is rooted in the atonal tradition. This is not to say that the range of applicability is narrow, however. Any composition that exhibits the structural characteristics that are discussed, and that exhibits them throughout, may be regarded as atonal.

The book is divided into two hierarchically organized parts. In Part 1 certain basic ideas are introduced and connections between them are developed. In Part 2 the concepts elaborated in Part 1 are brought within the scope of a general model of structure, the set-complex, and a number of musical excerpts are examined in detail. Thus, the exposition begins with elementary aspects of structural components and their relations and proceeds to a consideration of structures of larger scale and greater complexity.

1   Pitch-Class Sets and Relations

1.0   Pitch combinations

The repertory of atonal music is characterized by the occurrence of pitches in novel combinations, as well as by the occurrence of familiar pitch combinations in unfamiliar environments.

1.   Schoenberg, "George Lieder" Op. 15/1

Used by permission of Belmont Music Publishers, Los Angeles, California 90049.

As an example of a pitch combination, consider the chord at the end of the first song in Schoenberg's "George Lieder" Op. 15 (ex. 1). This pitch combination, which is reducible to one form of the all-interval tetrachord, has a very special place in atonal music. It could occur in a tonal composition only under extraordinary conditions, and even then its meaning would be determined by harmonic-contrapuntal constraints. Here, where such constraints are not operative, one is obliged to seek other explanations. Accordingly, in the sections that follow, terminology and notation will be introduced which will facilitate the discussion of certain properties of such combinations. The first task is to formulate a more general notion to replace that of pitch combination.

1.1   Pitch-Class sets

The term pitch combination introduced in section 1.0 refers to any collection of pitches represented in ordinary staff notation. The transposition of G-sharp in example 1 to the staff position an octave higher would produce a new and distinctive pitch combination. Comparison of this combination with the old one would require additional considerations. A simple and precise basis for comparing any two pitch combinations is provided by the notion *pitch-class set.* *

Suppose, for instance, that the chord discussed in connection with example 1 were to be compared with the chord in example 2, which occurs at the opening of Webern's Six Pieces for Orchestra Op. 6/3. By rewriting each chord

*The term and the concept were introduced by Milton Babbitt.

2.   Webern, Six Pieces for Orchestra Op. 6/3

within the smallest possible range and placing the chords in adjacent positions on the same staff it is evident that the second is a transposition of the first (ex. 3).

3.

In rewriting both chords it was assumed that change of register did not affect notation-class membership; E-sharp remained a member of the class E-sharp, A remained a member of the class A, and so on. Thus, the axiom of octave equivalence (which also applies to tonal music, of course) was invoked. In addition, the assertion that the second chord is a transposition of the first implies that the chords are equivalent in a very specific way: by virtue of the operation transposition. This operation will be discussed in section 1.3 and need not be pursued further here.

For the study of atonal music the assumption of octave equivalence by notation class is not sufficiently general. It is necessary to assume, further, that "enharmonic" notes are equivalent (regardless of register). Thus, E-sharp is the same as F or G-double-flat, for example. This does not imply that notation is arbitrary in an atonal composition, but merely that the notion of pitch-class set is independent of any particular notational forms.

4.

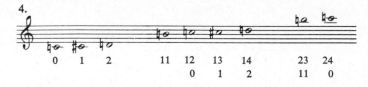

As a consequence of octave equivalence and enharmonic equivalence any notated pitch belongs to one and only one of 12 distinct pitch classes. This can be seen readily if the usual letter-names are replaced by the integers 0, 1, 2, . . . , 11. We then speak of *integer notation,* as distinct from staff notation.

The correspondence of integer notation and staff notation is shown in example 4. The integer 0 has been assigned to C (which is equivalent to B-sharp and D-double-flat, the integer 1 has been assigned to C-sharp (which is equivalent to B-double-sharp and D-flat), and so on until the integer 11 has been assigned to B, completing the octave.* If the assignment procedure were continued, as shown in the example, 12 would be assigned to the second C. But this belongs to the same class as the first C, to which the integer 0 has already been assigned. Indeed, any pitch number greater than or equal to 12 can be reduced to one of the pitch-class integers by obtaining the remainder of that number divided by 12.

A *pitch-class set,* then, is a set of distinct integers (i.e., no duplicates) representing pitch classes. Strictly speaking, one should use the term *set of pitch-class representatives,* but that is unwieldy. In fact, even the term *pitch-class set,* since it is used very often in the present volume, will usually be abbreviated to *pc set.*

A pc set is displayed in square brackets—for example, [0,1,2]. The reader is exhorted to pay attention to this and other notational conventions as they are introduced.

1.2 Normal order; the prime forms

For a number of reasons it is important to distinguish between ordered and unordered pc sets. If, for example, [0,2,3] is regarded as the same as [2,3,0] it is assumed that the difference in order does not render the sets distinct from one another; they are equivalent sets since both contain the same elements. In such case the sets are referred to as *unordered sets.* If, however, the two sets are regarded as distinct, it is evident that they are distinct on the basis of difference in order, in which case they are called *ordered sets.*

To deal with relations between two pc sets it is often necessary to take ordering into account. In particular, it is essential to be able to reduce a set to a basic ordered pattern called *normal order.*† An ordering of a set is called a permutation, and the number of distinct permutations of a set depends upon the number of elements in the set. That number is known as the *cardinal number* of the set. In general, it can be shown that for a set of n elements there are $1 \times 2 \times 3 \times \ldots \times n$ distinct permutations. For example, for a set of 3 elements there are 6 permutations. By convention this series of multiplications is represented by the symbol n! (read "n factorial"). To determine the normal order of a set, however, it is not necessary to consider all of its permutations, but only those called *circular permutations.* Given a set in some order, the first circular permutation is formed by placing the first element

---

*This assignment remains fixed throughout the present volume.
†This is the same as Babbitt's normal form. See Babbitt 1961.

last. For example, the first circular permutation of the set [a,b,c] is [b,c,a].
The next circular permutation is formed in the same way and is thus [c,a,b].
The same procedure repeated once again would produce [a,b,c]. Hence, by
definition, an ordered set is a circular permutation of itself, and, in general,
there are n circular permutations of a set of n elements.

The normal order of a pc set can be determined as follows.* The set must
be in ascending numerical order at the outset and each circular permutation
must be kept in ascending numerical order. This means that 12 must be
added to the first element each time it is placed in the last position to form
the next circular permutation.†

Consider, as an example, the determination of normal order for the pc set
[1,3,0]. The circular permutations of the set, with the addition of 12 to the
shifted element each time is shown in the accompanying table.

		Difference of first and last
A_0	[0,1,3]	3
A_1	[1,3,12]	11
A_2	[3,12,13]	10

By what will be called Requirement 1, the normal order is that permutation
with the least difference determined by subtracting the first integer from the
last. The normal order in this instance is A_0.

In certain cases Requirement 1 is inadequate for the determination of
normal order, in which case Requirement 2 must be invoked. Requirement 2
selects the best normal order as follows. If the least difference of first and last
integers is the same for any two permutations, select the permutation with the
least difference between first and second integers. If this is the same, select
the permutation with the least difference between the first and third integers,
and so on, until the difference between the first and the next to last integers
has been checked. If the differences are the same each time, select one ordering arbitrarily as the normal order. Consider the following example:

A_0	[0,2,4,8]	8
A_1	[2,4,8,12]	10
A_2	[4,8,12,14]	10
A_3	[8,12,14,16]	8

Here, by Requirement 1, both A_0 and A_3 are normal orders.†† Requirement
2 selects A_0 as the best normal order.

The form of a pc set such that it is in normal order (or best normal order)

---

*The procedure to be described is an extension of the one used in Teitelbaum 1965.
†Since 12 is equivalent to 0 in the 12 pitch-class integer system the arithmetic value of a pitch-class in-
teger is not changed by the addition of 12.
†† In this and similar instances the two sets are inversionally related.

and the first integer is 0 is called a *prime form*. A complete list of prime forms for the 220 distinct pc sets is given in appendix 1. Although reference to the list will not be necessary until section 1.5, normal orders will be shown in connection with the examples in staff notation henceforth so that the reader will become accustomed to integer notation and so that certain comparisons (to be explained in the following sections) can be made easily.

1.3 Transpositionally equivalent pc sets

The notion of a pc set in normal order provides a point of departure for the development of certain fundamental procedures which will permit consequential analytical observations about structure to be made.

Let us assume that a significant kind of observation concerns the similarity or difference between two "events," such as pc sets. More precisely, given two pc sets to compare, one might ask: Are they the same, or do they differ? In order to provide an answer a definition is needed. Accordingly, two pc sets will be said to be *equivalent* if and only if* they are reducible to the same prime form by transposition or by inversion followed by transposition. This section is concerned only with transpositional equivalence.

5.   Webern, Five Movements for String Quartet Op. 5/5

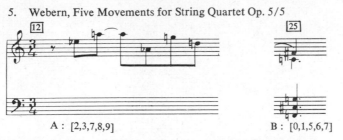

A : [2,3,7,8,9]   B : [0,1,5,6,7]

Copyright by Universal Edition. Permission granted by Theodore Presser Company, sole representative in the United States, Canada, and Mexico.

Consider, as an initial illustration, the two pitch-sets A and B in example 5.† First, we ask whether it is reasonable to compare them at all. They occur some distance apart in the composition, as indicated by the circled measure numbers. The "mode of occurrence" is different in each case: the first is a melodic line, the second a "chord." These differential surface features, however, do not preclude comparison. In fact, the only requirement necessary for comparison is that the pitch configurations be reducible to pc sets of the same cardinal number, and that requirement is met in this instance.

The pc sets (in normal order) labeled A and B correspond to the staff notation of the two configurations. For comparison, it is convenient to align

---

*The logical expression *if and only if* means that two pc sets are equivalent if they are reducible to the same prime form, and if they are not reducible to the same prime form they are not equivalent.

†The attentive reader will notice that a convention has been added, namely the assignment of a symbolic name to the set. This name, an upper case alphabetic character, is followed by a colon.

the integer notation as follows:

$$A: [2,3,7,8,9]$$
$$B: [0,1,5,6,7]$$

Now, the transposition of a pc integer i means that some integer t is added to i to yield a pc integer j. If j is greater than or equal to 12, j is replaced by the remainder of j divided by 12. This is called addition modulo 12, abbreviated to mod 12.

From this it is evident that if pc set A is equivalent to pc set B there must be some integer t which, added to each integer of A will yield the corresponding integer in B. By inspection it is clear that there is such a t and that its value is 10. Here and elsewhere t will be referred to as the *transposition operator*.

Since it is essential that this arithmetic interpretation of transposition be clearly understood, the additions are displayed in the accompanying table for pc sets A and B in example 5.

A   t   B

$$2 + 10 = 12 = 0 \ (\text{mod } 12)$$
$$3 + 10 = 13 = 1 \ (\text{mod } 12)$$
$$7 + 10 = 17 = 5 \ (\text{mod } 12)$$
$$8 + 10 = 18 = 6 \ (\text{mod } 12)$$
$$9 + 10 = 19 = 7 \ (\text{mod } 12)$$

6.   Berg, Four Pieces for Clarinet and Piano Op. 5

A : [0,3,4,7,8,9]

B : [4,7,8,11,0,1]

Example 6 shows the opening clarinet figure in Berg's Op. 5/1 (A) and the opening piano figure in the third piece of the same composition (B). Comparison of A and B reveals that B is transpositionally equivalent to A and that t = 4.

In example 5 (Webern Op. 5/5) two sets which occur some distance apart in the movement were found to be transpositionally equivalent, while in example 6 (Berg Op. 5) two transpositionally equivalent sets were found to occur in corresponding positions at the beginning of different movements of the same composition. These examples are intended to suggest that the operation transposition is of fundamental importance to non-tonal music and that configurations which may be dissimilar in many respects can be, in fact, equivalent at a more basic level of structure. In neither case, however, was an attempt made to further interpret the equivalence relation, since such interpretation requires additional concepts and techniques to be introduced in subsequent sections.

7.   Webern, Four Pieces for Violin and Piano Op. 7/4

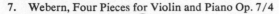
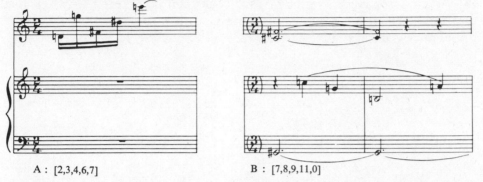

A : [2,3,4,6,7]   B : [7,8,9,11,0]

Example 7 provides a final illustration for this section. The reader can easily determine the value of t for himself by comparing A and B. (Note that B represents the pitch set in the piano part only.)

1.4   Inversionally equivalent pc sets

In the preceding section the process of transposing a pc set A to produce a new and equivalent pc set B was described in terms of the addition (mod 12) of some integer t, called the transposition operator, to every element of A. If we let A be [0,1,2] and t = 1, the process by which B is produced can be displayed as follows:

$$
\begin{array}{cc}
 & T \\
 & t = 1 \\
A & B \\
0 & \rightarrow 1 \\
1 & \rightarrow 2 \\
2 & \rightarrow 3 \\
\end{array}
$$

Observe that every element of A corresponds to an element of B and that the correspondence is unique in each case—that is, some element in B does not correspond to two elements in A. Thus, transposition can be regarded as a rule of correspondence—namely, addition modulo 12—that assigns to every element of B exactly one element derived from A. We will borrow a conventional mathematical term to describe such a process and say that A is *mapped onto* B by the rule T.*

*The mapping is *into*, of course, with respect to the universal set [0,1,2,...,11]. It is not important to draw the distinction at this point.

The notion of a mapping is more than a convenience in describing relations between pc sets. It permits the development of economical and precise descriptions which could not be obtained using conventional musical terms. Its usefulness will be especially apparent as we begin to deal with the process of inversion.

Like transposition, the inversion process can also be described in terms of a rule of correspondence I which maps each element of a set A onto an element of a set B. The inversion mapping I depends upon the fixed correspondence of pc integers displayed in the following table:

$$I$$

$$
\begin{array}{ccc}
0 & \leftrightarrow & 0 \\
1 & \leftrightarrow & 11 \\
2 & \leftrightarrow & 10 \\
3 & \leftrightarrow & 9 \\
4 & \leftrightarrow & 8 \\
5 & \leftrightarrow & 7 \\
6 & \leftrightarrow & 6 \\
\end{array}
$$

Observe that in each case the sum of the integers connected by the double arrow is 12, and recall that 12 = 0 (mod 12). We say that 0 is the *inverse** of 0, 1 is the inverse of 11 and 11 is the inverse of 1, and so on. In general, if we let a' represent the inverse of a, then

$$a' = 12 - a \ (\text{mod } 12)$$

For any set A, therefore, the mapping I sends every element of A onto its inverse, producing a new and equivalent set B. For example, if A is [0,1,2] the mapping is as follows:

$$I$$

$$
\begin{array}{ccc}
A & & B \\
0 & \rightarrow & 0 \\
1 & \rightarrow & 11 \\
2 & \rightarrow & 10 \\
\end{array}
$$

In section 1.3, in addition to equivalence by transposition, two pc sets were said to be equivalent if reducible to the same prime form by inversion *followed by* transposition. The expression *followed by* is easily understood in terms of a double mapping, as illustrated below.

---

*The term inverse is preferred to complement. The latter is reserved for set-theoretic complementation (sec. 1.15).

```
         I      T
               (t = 1)
     A     B      C
     0  →  0  →   1
     1  → 11  →   0
     2  → 10  →  11
```

Here the first mapping I is followed by the T mapping. As a result, 0 in A is sent onto 1 in C, 1 in A is sent onto 0 in C, and 2 in A is sent onto 11 in C.

It is important to observe that whereas transposition does not imply prior inversion, inversion always implies subsequent transposition, even if it is the trivial case t = 0, as shown below.

```
         I      T
               (t = 0)
     A     B      C
     0  →  0  →   0
     1  → 11  →  11
     2  → 10  →  10
```

8. Schoenberg, "George Lieder" Op. 15/6

A : [3,4,7,10] B : [1,4,7,8]

Used by permission of Belmont Music Publishers, Los Angeles, California

Let us consider now some compositional examples of inversionally equivalent pc sets. In example 8, from one of Schoenberg's earliest non-tonal works, the set marked A is inversionally equivalent to B. (The second chord is not equivalent to the other two and will be disregarded for the present purpose.) The mappings by which B is derived from A are:

```
         I      T
               (t = 11)
     A             B
     3  →   9  →   8
     4  →   8  →   7
     7  →   5  →   4
    10  →   2  →   1
```

Here, and in general, inversion of a pc set in normal order produces a pc set in descending order, as is apparent from the fixed mapping on p. 8. Therefore, to compare two pc sets for inversional equivalence, it is necessary to reverse the order of the second. The transposition operator then appears as the sum of each pair of elements, thus:

$$A:[\ 3,\ 4,\ 7,\ 10]$$
$$B:[\ 8,\ 7,\ 4,\ 1]$$

$$\text{sums}\quad 11\ 11\ 11\ 11$$

Before considering another compositional example we introduce a symbolic notation for transposition and inversion which is useful for concisely describing those relations whenever they hold between two pc sets A and B.

Expression	Read as
$B = T(A,t)$	B is the transposition of A at level t
$B = I(A)$	B is the inversion of A

Since inversion always implies transposition, the latter is the same as $B = T(I(A),0)$. For A and B in example 8 we then write $B = T(I(A),11)$ and read "B is the inversion of A transposed at level 11" (or, "transposed with t = 11").*

9. Ives, *The Unanswered Question*

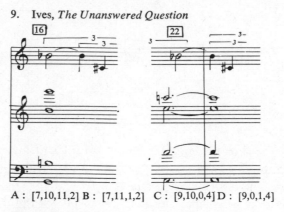

A : [7,10,11,2] B : [7,11,1,2] C : [9,10,0,4] D : [9,0,1,4]

The second illustration from the literature, example 9, is interesting from an historical standpoint since it is taken from one of the early compositions of Ives, *The Unanswered Question* (ca. 1906), and antedates Schoenberg's first atonal composition. The example shows two fragments: the first includes the

*Where it is not essential to use this notation, the form OP_t will be used, where OP is the symbol for the operation and t is the value of t. For example, IT_3 refers to the inversion of some set transposed with t = 3.

initial two notes of the first "question," played by trumpet, together with the accompanying string sonority; the second shows the corresponding music for the second "question."

The trumpet part is the same in both cases, but the accompanying string sonority is different in the second fragment. Examination in terms of equivalent sets reveals, however, that A is equivalent to D and B is equivalent to C. Specifically,

$$D = T(A,2)$$
$$C = T(I(B),11)$$

These relations effectively pair off the sets as follows:

A   B   C   D

10.   Schoenberg, Five Pieces for Orchestra Op. 16/1

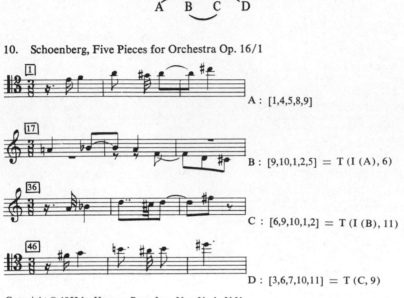

A : [1,4,5,8,9]

B : [9,10,1,2,5] = T (I (A), 6)

C : [6,9,10,1,2] = T (I (B), 11)

D : [3,6,7,10,11] = T (C, 9)

Example 10 shows successive occurrences of the initial theme of Schoenberg's Five Pieces for Orchestra Op. 16/1. The second statement (B), which is rhythmically distinct from the others, is a transposed inversion of the first (A). The succession of mappings is as follows.

$$B = T(I(A),6)$$
$$C = T(I(B), 11)$$
$$D = T(C,9)$$

More will be said about this particular example in section 1.12.

1.5   The list of prime forms; set names

It is convenient to have names for the prime forms so that a pc set can be

referred to without recourse to a cumbersome description of some kind.*
Accordingly, each prime form has been assigned a name consisting of numbers separated by a hyphen. The number to the left of the hyphen is the
cardinal number of the set; the number to the right of the hyphen is the
ordinal number of the set—that is, the position of the prime form on the list.
For example, 5-31, which is the name of both pc sets in example 11 is the
thirty-first set on the list of sets with cardinal number 5 (appendix 1).

11.   Berg, "Altenberg Lieder" Op. 4/2   Stravinsky, Symphonies of Wind Instruments

[9,0,3,5,6]   [11,2,5,7,8]

    To look up the name of a pc set on the list of prime forms it is first neces-
sary to put the set in normal order and then to transpose the normal order so
that the first integer is 0. This operation is shown below for the Berg and
Stravinsky excerpts in example 11.†

	Berg	Stravinsky
normal order	[3,5,6,9,0]	[5,7,8,11,2]
transposed to level 0	[0,2,3,6,9]	[0,2,3,6,9]

Both sets have now been reduced to the same normal order. If this is the *best*
normal order, as described in section 1.3, it will be found on the list of prime
forms. In this case, however, the set is not in best normal order and does not
appear on the list. Therefore it is necessary to take the normal order of the inversion of the set and transpose it to level 0, as follows:

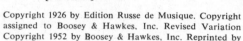

              given normal order
              transposed to level 0   [0,2,3,6,9]

*For example, pc set 5-22 has been described as "a diminished triad with conjunct semitone not only
superimposed . . . but also subimposed" (Perle 1967, p. 228). Ad hoc descriptions of this kind usually
rest upon some analytical interpretations, as in the case cited here.
†The selection of these two excerpts was made only for purposes of illustration and has no further significance.

inversion	[0,10,9,6,3]
ascending order	[0,3,6,9,10]
new normal order	[9,10,0,3,6]
transposed to level 0	[0,1,3,6,9]

The last set displayed above is the best normal order, and the name associated with it on the list of prime forms is 5-31.

1.6 Intervals of a pc set; the interval vector

Thus far, pc sets have been examined from the standpoint of the elements (pc integers) they contain. In addition, equivalence relations based upon transposition and inversion have been introduced, together with some apparatus needed for identifying sets from the list of prime forms. In order to proceed to a more comprehensive study of properties of pc sets and relations between pc sets it is necessary to introduce some additional basic concepts. This section and the three which follow it are concerned with the interaction of components of a set in terms of the intervals (the term is construed in the traditional sense) which they define.

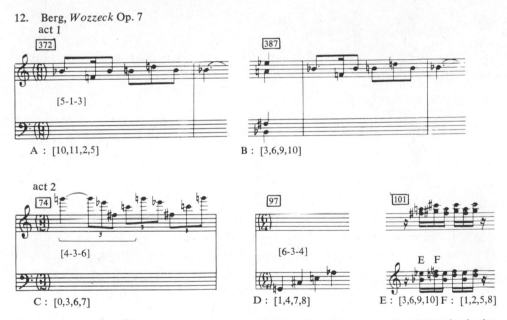

12. Berg, *Wozzeck* Op. 7

Example 12 provides a specific musical reference for the discussion that follows. Here we see six instances of pc set 4-18. Three of these, A, C, and D, are melodic statements. Observe that the intervals between interlocking note-

pairs differ in each case.* This is because a particular linear ordering of a set determines a selection of intervals from the *total interval-content* of the set.†
The three vertical statements of the set (B, E, and F) present all the intervals of the set. This suggests that total interval-content is the more basic and general intervallic property of a pc set. The remainder of this section is devoted to a presentation of some elementary notions which, it is hoped, will render the concept of interval both precise and useful with respect to the study of structures in non-tonal music.

The interval formed by two pc integers a and b is the arithmetic difference a− b. In order not to have to specify that a is greater than b it is assumed that the absolute value (positive value) of the difference is always taken. Thus, for example, the interval formed by 0 and 1 is 0−1 = 1; the interval formed by 5 and 9 is 5−9 = 4. It is not difficult to show that if the intervals between all pairs of pc integers were formed and duplicates were removed there would remain the set [0,1,2,...,11].†† Thus, there are 12 intervals, corresponding to the 12 pitch-classes.

The 12 intervals reduce to 6 *interval classes,* however, by the following defined equivalence.

If d is the difference of two pc integers
then d ≡ d′ mod 12.

In short, inverse-related (mod 12) intervals are defined as equivalent, and as a consequence are paired off as shown below.§

$$0 \equiv 0$$
$$1 \equiv 11$$
$$2 \equiv 10$$
$$3 \equiv 9$$
$$4 \equiv 8$$
$$5 \equiv 7$$
$$6 \equiv 6$$

Each pair thus forms an equivalence class. If we let the integers in the left column above represent the class and, further, omit for practical purposes the class 0, the reduction of 12 intervals to 6 interval classes is completed.

By analogy with the abbreviation for pitch class, pc, the abbreviation *ic* will be used for interval class. Whenever ambiguity might result from use of an

---

*The successive linear intervals are indicated within square brackets as numbers representing interval classes (to be explained below). See Chrisman 1969.

†Ordered sets and order relations are discussed in section 1.14.

††The binary operation-(subtraction) maps S X S *onto* S where S is the set of 12 pc integers.

§The mathematical basis of this partitioning is perhaps best explained with reference to a group-theoretic model. It does not seem necessary to undertake such an explanation here. The partitioning is the traditional one, based upon the symmetrical division of the octave.

integer alone, the prefix pc or ic will make the intended meaning evident.

Among other advantages, the notion of interval class makes the description of total interval-content uncomplicated. Essentially this entails the calculation of intervals between all unordered pairs of pc integers in the given set and the conversion of the resulting numbers to ic integers, where required. As an example, consider the pc integers in A, example 12, and the intervals formed between the first integer, pc10, and the other three.

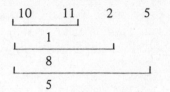

Extending this procedure to the remaining pc integers yields the total number of intervals, six. The entire procedure is diagrammed below.

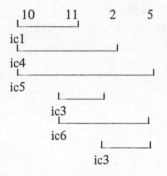

The description of the total interval-content of any pc set is given by its *interval vector*,* which is constructed as follows. Count the number of occurrences of ic1 and write down that number. Count the number of occurrences of ic2 and write that number to the right of the previous number. Continue in this fashion until the number of occurrences of ic6 has been written down. To illustrate, the vector for the set in example 12 is [102111].

The interval vector is an ordered array; that is, the first (left-most) number is always the number of occurrences of ic1, the next number to the right is always the number of occurrences of ic2, and so on. If some interval class is not represented, the entry 0 (zero) should be in the appropriate position in the vector—as in the case of ic2 in the vector of pc set 4–18 given above.

The foregoing explanation should enable the reader to interpret any interval vector, that is, to understand the vector as a representation of the total interval-content of a pc set. Normally, it will not be necessary for the reader to construct interval vectors since these are given in the list of prime forms (appendix 1).

*This array was introduced in Martino 1961.

1.7 Some properties of interval vectors

Although the entire range of pc sets was available to the composers of
early non-tonal music, it would appear that certain sets played a more prominent compositional role than others.* There may be a number of reasons for
this, of course. In many cases, however, the vectors of those sets have special
structural properties, which suggests that the interval content of the set may
have been of primary interest. The main purpose of this section is to examine
in an introductory way three such properties: *unique vector entries, maximum number of some ic,* and *equal or near equal distribution of entries.*

Of the 220 distinct pc sets only 4 have vectors in which each entry is unique:

$$
\begin{array}{ll}
\text{6-1} & [543210] \\
\text{6-32} & [143250] \\
\text{7-1} & [654321] \\
\text{7-35} & [254361]
\end{array}
$$

Since one ordering of 7-35 is the major scale it will not be necessary to demonstrate that it is structurally interesting.† In the non-tonal repertory, however, the set usually occurs in ways which do not readily associate it with the
familiar scale-ordering. As one instance, consider the passage ("Lento occul-
to") from Busoni's Second Sonatina shown in example 13. On the second beat
of the second measure the 7 sounding pitches form 7-35.

13. Busoni, Second Sonatina

7-35 : [7,8,10,0,1,3,5]

With permission of Breitkopf & Härtel, Wiesbaden. From Edition
Breitkopf No. 3828 Busoni, Sonatina seconda.

Pc sets 6-1 and 7-1 are familiar as "chromatic" configurations, as can be
seen from their normal orders, while 6-32 is, in one ordering, identifiable as
the first six notes of the major scale. Here again, these sets occur in singular
ways which tend to dissociate them from traditional tonal contexts. Example
14 shows a vertical statement of 6-32 at the beginning of a composition by
Ives.††

---

*This and any other such comments are not based upon frequency counts but are merely informed
guesses based upon the author's experience with this music.
†See Babbitt's analysis of the intervallic properties of this set (Babbitt 1965).
†† A formation of this kind has often been referred to as a *chord in 4ths.* Terms of this kind are avoided
in the present volume since they are inadequate as structural descriptions and not useful as names.

14.   Ives, *Tone Roads* No. 1

6-32 : [9,11,1,2,4,6]

The four sets with unique vector entries also have another property: each contains the maximum number possible of some interval class. Specifically, 6-1 and 7-1 have the maximum number of ic1, and 6-32 and 7-35 have the maximum number of ic5. Fifty additional sets have the same "maximum ic" property. Among these are many which are prominent in the non-tonal repertory. Some instances are cited in the examples following.

15.   Berg, *Wozzeck* Op. 7
       act 1

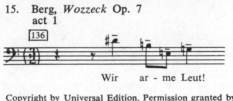

Wir   ar - me Leut!

Pc set 4-19 [101310] is one of two 4-element sets that contain the maximum number of ic4. An instance of this set is the well-known motive from Berg's *Wozzeck* shown in example 15. Some indication of the structural importance of ic4 in the opera as a whole may be provided by the fact that the harmony which closes each act is 8-24, one of the two 8-element sets in which ic4 is maximized (ex. 16).

16.   Berg, *Wozzeck* Op. 7
       act 1

8-24 [464743]

17. Webern, Five Pieces for Orchestra Op. 10/3

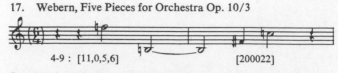

4-9 : [11,0,5,6]   [200022]

There are 27 pc sets with vectors in which ic6 is maximized. Of these, 4-9 occurs frequently. In example 17 this set appears as the initial melodic motive of the movement. Note that the linear statement emphasizes the two occurrences of ic6 within the set.

The third vector property to be discussed has been called equal or near-equal distribution of entries. There is, in fact, only one vector which has equal distribution of entries: [111111]. This is the vector of the all-interval tetrachord, mentioned at the beginning of section 1.0. The term *near equal distribution* refers to any vector in which 4 or more entries are the same. In all, 29 vectors have this property. Two of these are illustrated below.

18. Schoenberg, Five Piano Pieces Op. 23/4

[333321]

The set enclosed in square brackets on the lower staff of example 18 (pc set 6-Z10) has a vector in which the first four entries are the same. This is one of the sets specially marked by Schoenberg in his manuscript.* Note that the disposition of the set here is such that all three intervals of ic4 are given in immediate succession.

19. Stravinsky, *Petrouchka*

[224223]

Example 19 shows the beginning of a well-known passage from Stravinsky's *Petrouchka*. The vector of this set (6-30) also has the "maximum ic" property with respect to ic6.

*See Rufer 1959, p. 23.

1.8 Cardinal number and interval content

In section 1.7 properties of certain interval vectors were explained and illustrated. Assuming that, as one result of the discussion, the reader is now quite familiar with the vector representation, the present section examines certain more abstract structural characteristics of the vector—in particular, those characteristics which are dependent upon the cardinal number of the pc set.

First, it should be evident that the number of intervals formed by a pc set is determined by its cardinal number and that the number of intervals (not the distribution by interval class)* is fixed for all pc sets of the same cardinal number. The arithmetic involved is straightforward, but an explanation may be helpful.

Given a pc set of cardinal number 2 the number of intervals formed is, of course, 1. If an element is added to the pc set, increasing its cardinal number to 3, the new element forms 2 new intervals—one with each of the elements previously in the set. The abbreviated table below shows how the number of intervals increases with progressively larger cardinal number.

Cardinal Number	Number of Intervals
1	0
2	0 + 1
3	0 + 1 + 2
4	0 + 1 + 2 + 3
.	
.	
.	
12	0 + 1 + 2 + 3 + 4 + . . . + 11

Thus, for the general case, if the cardinal number of a pc set is k, the number of intervals n is the sum of all intervals i, for $i = 0$, $i = 1$, . . . , $i = k-1$. Or, $n = \dfrac{k^2-k}{2}$.

Pc sets of cardinal number 1, 11, or 12 are uninteresting from the standpoint of total interval-content, for in each of these cases the vector is fixed with respect to the number of intervals of each class, as shown below.

Cardinal Number	Vector
1	[0 0 0 0 0 0]
11	[10 10 10 10 10 5]
12	[12 12 12 12 12 6]

*With the exception of sets of cardinal number 1, 11, or 12, as mentioned in the second paragraph after this one.

The relation between cardinal number and interval content has some further consequences of general interest. First, the cardinal number of a pc set must be at least 4 in order to enable all 6 interval classes to be represented in its vector. Inspection of the list of prime forms will show that only two sets of cardinal number 4 have a vector with no empty (zero) entry: 4-Z15 and 4-Z29. Second, the vector of any 7-element set has no empty entry—that is, every interval class is represented by an entry greater than 0. Third, the vector of any 5-element pc set contains at least one representative of ic4. This suggests that only the occurrence of more than one representative of ic4 in a set of 5 elements should require analytical attention, all other things being equal. Fourth, the maximum number of empty interval classes for vectors of 5-element and 6-element pc sets is 3. There are, in fact, only two such sets, 5-33 and 6-35, both "whole-tone" formations. The 5-element and 6-element sets with one or two empty vector entries are of special interest, as will be evident in section 1.11, which is concerned with invariance.

One final correspondence of cardinal number and interval content should be discussed here since it has to do with certain absolutes in the universe of interval relations. Specifically, this is the predominance of the odd interval classes (ic1, ic3, ic5) over the even interval classes. Among the pc sets of cardinal 3 through cardinal 9 there are only 31 in which the intervals are so distributed that even classes predominate over odd. Of those sets the majority (18) are of cardinal 5 or 7, another indication that sets of those cardinalities are more refractory than others.

20. Patterns of odd-even intervals

Cardinal number	Number of intervals	Number of even intervals	Number of odd intervals	
3	3	1	2	
		3	0	(3 sets)
9	36	16	20	
		18	18	
4	6	2	4	
		3	3	
		6	0	(3 sets)
8	28	12	16	
		13	15	
		16	12	(3 sets)
5	10	4	6	
		6	4	(8 sets)
		10	0	(1 set)
7	21	9	12	
		11	10	(8 sets)
		15	6	(1 set)
6		6	9	
		7	8	
		10	5	(3 sets)
		15	0	(1 set)

The table, example 20, summarizes the relevant information. Note that for any cardinal number, the number of patterns of even-odd distribution is small. Pc sets of cardinal 6 have four such patterns, while pc sets of cardinals 3 and 9 have only two. Moreover, the canonical instance is afforded by pc sets of cardinal 9, in which there are never more even intervals than odd intervals.

Although the table is set up in a simple manner, some assistance may be in order. The two right-most columns are of greatest importance since they give the patterns of distribution. For example, for any set of cardinal 3 the number of even intervals will be 1 and the number of odd intervals 2, or the number of even intervals will be 3 and the number of odd intervals 0. In the latter category there are only 3 sets.

1.9 Non-equivalent pc sets with identical vectors

In section 1.3 two pc sets were said to be equivalent if and only if they are reducible to the same prime form by transposition or by inversion followed by transposition. Subsequently it was shown that the interval content of a pc set is conveniently represented by an interval vector. As a result, one might conclude that each prime form has a distinct interval vector. This, however, is not the case. For example, the two forms of the all-interval tetrachord, 4-Z15 and 4-Z29, are so constructed that they are not reducible by transposition or by inversion followed by transposition to a single prime form, yet they have identical vectors [111111].

A pair of pc sets, such as those cited above, which have identical interval vectors but which are not transpositionally or inversionally equivalent will be called a Z-related pair.* There are 19 such pairs in all.† In addition to the one of cardinal number 4, there are 3 pairs of cardinal number 5 and 15 pairs of cardinal number 6.

Now, the question of analytical significance arises here. Is it necessary or in some way useful to make the distinction between the pc sets of a Z-related pair? Since they have identical vectors would it not be simpler to select one as a prime form and merely designate the other as a kind of variant?†† A strong case can be made for a negative answer to the latter question. Unless a distinction is made on the basis of fundamental pc set structure, with the identical vector characteristic as secondary, it is not possible to make the necessary and (as will be shown) fruitful differentiation between pitch-class structures and interval-class structures over the full range of the available resources.§ But perhaps the strongest argument for not equating the Z-related

*The "Z" has no special significance. It is merely a descriptor attached to the ordinal number of the set name which serves to identify these special sets.

†These sets were first described in the literature by David Lewin (Lewin 1960).

†† This, unfortunately, was the strategy selected by the author in an earlier study (Forte 1964).

§ Moreover, the members of a Z-related pair are also distinct with respect to subset structure if the cardinal number of the subset is greater than 2. See section 1.10.

sets on the basis of interval content is provided by the musical data with which the present volume is concerned, for there are numerous instances in the atonal repertory in which Z-related pc sets play a primary structural role. Some indication may be provided by the excerpts that follow.

21. Webern, Three Short Pieces Op. 11/1

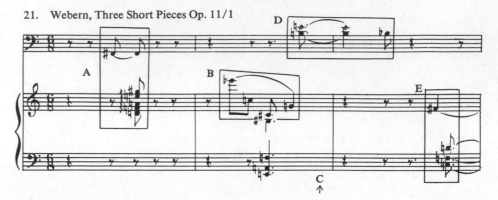

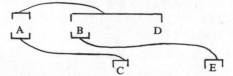

Example 21, taken from the beginning of Webern Op. 11/1, features two Z-related pairs: 6-Z10/6-Z39 and 4-Z15/4-Z29. The sets corresponding to the marked boxes in the example are as follows:

A   6-Z10: [2,4,5,6,8,9]
B   4-Z29: [0,1,3,7]
C   6-Z10: [4,5,7,8,9,11]
D   2-1: [10,11]
E   4-Z15: [0,2,5,6]

The Z-correspondent of 6-Z10, 6-Z39, is B and D combined. A merger of this kind will be written +(B,D) and read "the union of B and D."*

By virtue of the intervallic equivalence of the members of each Z-pair the five lettered configurations are linked in an interlocking pattern, as shown in the diagram in example 21.

*This is ordinary set-theoretic union. For instance, if we write F = +(B,D), this is interpreted to mean that F is the set of all elements that are either in B or in D.

22.   Varèse, *Intégrales*

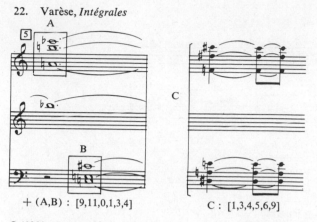

+ (A,B) : [9,11,0,1,3,4]   C : [1,3,4,5,6,9]

In example 22 the 3-element sets marked A and B form an accompanimental sonority which signals the end of the solo passage (middle staff). The set formed by +(A,B) is 6-Z10. The next to last sonority in the composition, marked C in example 22, is the Z-correspondent of 6-Z10, 6-Z39. Factors other than identical interval-content associate the two sets. Observe, for example, that they occur in the same register.

23.   Webern, Six Bagatelles Op. 9/4

6-Z37   [7,8,9,10,11,3]   6-Z4   [4,5,6,8,9,10]

An association of temporally remote events through Z-related sets is also seen in example 23. Pc set 6-Z37 is stated as a continuous melodic configuration at the outset by the second violin. The Z-correspondent, 6-Z4, subsequently is distributed among all four instruments at the close of the movement.

24.   Bartok, Suite Op. 14

5-Z18   5-21

25.   Bartok, Suite Op. 14

5-Z38   5-Z18   5-21

A final instance will serve to complete this introduction to Z-related sets,
and perhaps to indicate the extent to which they characterize much of the
non-traditional repertory. Example 24 is excerpted from the last movement
of Bartok's Suite for Piano Op. 14. It has been somewhat simplified rhythmically in order to show the succession of harmonies clearly. Each beamed pair
is the succession 5-Z18, 5-21, as indicated in the example. These are not the
first occurrences of the sets. Both are introduced in the passage shown in
example 25. There 5-Z18 is preceded immediately by its Z-correspondent,
5-Z38, so that the same intervals are maintained over a two-measure span.

To sum up, it is preservation of interval content, in the absence of transpositional or inversional equivalence, which characterizes the relation between
the two sets of a Z-pair. The Z-related sets have other quite extraordinary
properties (particularly the 6-element sets), and these will be discussed in due
course.

1.10   The subsets of a pc set

The excerpts from Berg's *Wozzeck* shown in example 26 will serve to introduce the notion of a *subset* of a pc set.

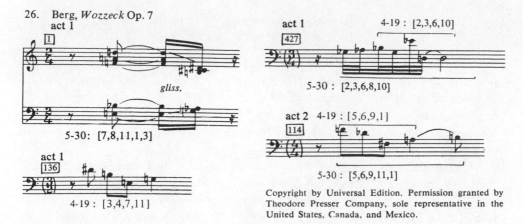

26. Berg, *Wozzeck* Op. 7

act 1

gliss.

5-30: [7,8,11,1,3]

act 1
136

4-19: [3,4,7,11]

act 1
427

4-19: [2,3,6,10]

5-30: [2,3,6,8,10]

act 2   4-19: [5,6,9,1]
114

5-30: [5,6,9,11,1]

Copyright by Universal Edition. Permission granted by Theodore Presser Company, sole representative in the United States, Canada, and Mexico.

In the first of these, taken from the beginning of the opera, we observe that the second set is 5-30. The second excerpt, cited earlier in example 15, is the "Wir arme Leut" motive, which is associated with the protagonist throughout the work. The third excerpt shows another motive associated with the protagonist. This set, which is 5-30 (the same as the set at the opening of the opera), incorporates 4-19 as the last four notes. The reverse situation occurs in the last excerpt in example 26 where the "Wir arme Leut" motive is extended by one note, thus forming set 5-30. In both cases 4-19 is contained in 5-30. Or, equivalently, we say that 4-19 is a subset of 5-30.

Now, if 4-19 is a subset of 5-30, then 5-30 is a *superset* of 4-19. The terms subset and superset represent complementary aspects of what is usually called the *inclusion relation*. In general, for two sets A and B, B is a subset of A iff every element of B is an element of A.* This relation is notated $B \subset A$. As observed above, if $B \subset A$ then $A \supset B$. The latter is read "A is a superset of B." Both notations will be used.

The inclusion relation affords a valuable perspective of the 12 pitch-class "universe" with which we are concerned, and the remainder of this section is devoted to the development of some general concepts and a demonstration of their musical relevance.

Let us begin with the following elementary question: how many subsets does a set of a certain cardinal number contain? As an example, consider the set [0,1,2] and its subsets, listed below.

3 subsets of 1 element:	[0]
	[1]
	[2]
3 subsets of 2 elements	[0,1]
	[0,2]
	[1,2]

*Recall that "iff" is an abbreviation for "if and only if."

1 subset of 3 elements: [0,1,2]
1 subset of 0 elements: [Φ]

The number of subsets of this, and any, set of 3 elements is 8. Two matters perhaps require clarification before we proceed. First, the subsets are unordered. That is, for example, [0,1] is not regarded as distinct from [1,0]. Second, the symbol Φ (phi) which occurs in the last subset on the above list represents the empty or null set. The null set, by definition, is a subset of every set.

As remarked above, the number of subsets of a set of 3 elements is 8, or 2^3. And, for the general case, it can be shown that a set of n elements has 2^n subsets.* Since this number will be large in some cases (for example, $2^9 = 512$) it will be worthwhile to attempt to reduce it, at the same time paying attention to the consequences with respect to subsequent music-theoretical and music-analytical applications.

As a first step we introduce the notion *proper subset*.

X is a *proper subset* of Y iff $X \subset Y$ and
$X \neq \Phi$ and $X \neq Y$.

By dealing only with proper subsets, therefore, and thus excluding the null subset and the redundant duplicate set, the number of possible subsets is reduced to $2^n - 2$.

A further reduction is provided by elimination of the unit subsets, on the assumption that they will not be useful in the study of relations.† The number of subsets then becomes $2^n - (n+2)$. Even with this reduction, however, the number of subsets increases rapidly with increase in cardinal number of the set, as shown in the table below.

n	$2^n - (n + 2)$
3††	3
4	10
5	25
6	56
7	119
8	246
9	501
10	1012

Further reduction is possible, however, and will be approached indirectly through the discussion that follows.

---

*The number 2 is a constant in this situation since the selection of any subset necessarily involves a binary choice, i.e., the elements selected and those not selected.
†Since a binary relation cannot be defined on a unit subset.
††Recall that sets of cardinal number 11 or 12 are not distinct with respect to interval content (sec. 1.6). Sets of cardinal number 2 were excluded from consideration with the reduction of 2^n to $2^n - (n + 2)$.

Having discussed the gross number of subsets for a set of cardinal number n, a reasonable next question is: how many subsets of cardinal number m (m ≠ 0, m ≠ 1, m ≠ n) are contained in a set of cardinal number n? It can be shown that this number is given by the following expression:

$$\frac{n!}{m! \times (n-m)!}$$

The accompanying table* gives the number of subsets of cardinal number m for sets of cardinal number n. Values of n are displayed in the left-most column, while values of m are shown along the uppermost diagonal.

m n	2	3	4	5	6	7	8	9	10
3	3	3							
4	6	4	4						
5	10	10	5	5					
6	15	20	15	6	6				
7	21	35	35	21	7	7			
8	28	56	70	56	28	8	8		
9	36	84	126	126	84	36	9	9	
10	45	120	210	252	210	120	45	10	

The numbers in the table are interesting, for they indicate precisely the scope of the subset universe. In this uninterpreted state, however, they are not especially useful for purposes of analysis and the development of structural theory. For instance, according to the table a 10-element set has 210 4-element subsets; yet, there are only 29 distinct 4-element sets (prime forms). This implies that among the total of 4-element subsets of a set of 10 elements some are multiply represented. Accordingly, given a pc set, we want to know not only how many subsets of a certain cardinal number it contains, but also which subsets it contains in terms of set names.

27. Webern, Five Movements for String Quartet Op. 5/4

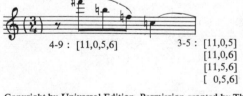

4-9 : [11,0,5,6]   3-5 : [11,0,5]
                                [11,0,6]
                                [11,5,6]
                                [0,5,6]

As an example of what might be called subset saturation, consider the 4-note melodic figure shown in example 27. The four 3-element subsets of 4-9 are reducible to the same prime form, pc set 3-5.

*A modification of Pascal's triangle.

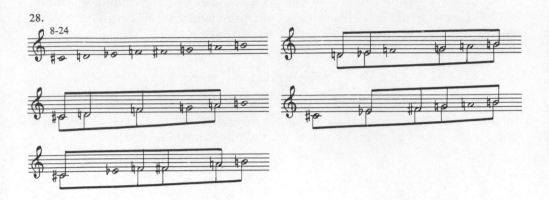

28.

Example 28 provides a larger-scale demonstration of subset analysis, using the two sets from Berg's *Wozzeck* cited at the beginning of the present section, in addition to the 8-element set, 8-24, cited in example 16. The latter occurs at the end of each act of the opera and was described by Berg as a "quasi-cadential chord."* A complete subset analysis would show that the term quasi-cadential is hardly adequate to describe the relation of this chord to the entire work, for it contains many of the sets which dominate the opera as motives. Among these are 4-19 and 5-30 (ex. 26) and 6-34. Two important statements of the latter are shown in example 29.† The three sets, 4-19, 5-30, and 6-34 are each represented 4 times in 8-24, as shown in example 28. Pc set 8-24 is shown in normal order, and aligned below it are the 4 occurrences of 6-34, 4-19, and 5-30. Beams are used to distinguish 4-19 from 5-30; the 6-element set in each case is, of course, 6-34.

29.   Berg, *Wozzeck* Op. 7
      act 2

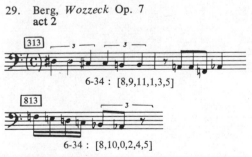

6-34 : [8,9,11,1,3,5]

6-34 : [8,10,0,2,4,5]

*In his lecture on *Wozzeck,* as translated by Redlich. See Redlich 1957.
†Perle has characterized this chord as "the principal referential chord of the work as a whole." (Perle 1967, p. 208). As far as can be determined, however, none of the literature on *Wozzeck* has identified this chord as Scriabin's "mystic chord."

Obviously pc set 8-24 contains many other subsets, including a number of sets that do not occur as motives in the opera. This observation touches upon a general problem that has been (and still is, unfortunately) in the foreground of many attempts to come to terms with atonal music. The problem concerns descriptions of sets in terms of subsets.

A single instance will suffice. The 5-note set labeled A in example 30 (from Berg's Op. 2/3) has been described in terms of the subsets labeled B, C, and D as follows: "Simultaneous mixture of major and minor over the fundamental B produces the 4-note chord B-D-D-sharp-F-sharp (D-sharp incorrectly notated as E-flat), to which the seventh, A, is added."* This description, in terms of a combination of two familiar triadic subsets and a unit subset, is quite arbitrary since no evidence is adduced to show that those subsets are more significant than others. Examples 31 and 32 offer alternative and equally viable descriptions. Notice that the subsets in example 31 are also triadic and that the unit subset is not required. Example 32 uses subsets of different types, and neither is the triadic set.

Descriptions other than the three displayed are possible, of course. The point is that the selection of particular subsets to describe a set usually must involve additional considerations. Among those considerations the notion of invariance plays an important role.

1.11 Invariant subsets under transposition

Given equivalent pc sets A and B, a third set C is determined by the elements that are both in A and in B. This set is called the intersection of A and B, and

---

*Translated from Null 1932.

we write C = ·(A,B). The elements of such a set will be called *invariant pitch-classes** (or simply *invariants* or *invariant pcs*).

33.   Stravinsky, Three Pieces for String Quartet (No. 2)

4-8 : [4,5,9,10]   [3,4,8,9]

Some indication of the function of invariants in non-tonal music is provided by example 33 taken from an early composition by Stravinsky. After the pair A,B has been repeated six times, a contrasting phrase consisting of the set [4,9] is introduced (measure 4), and this is followed by a restatement of the initial pair, as indicated in the example. A and B are transpositionally equivalent forms of pc set 4-8. More specifically, their relation is as follows:

$$B = T(A,11)$$

This value of t applied to 4-8 determines exactly 2 invariants, which, in this instance, form the subset [4,9], and it is that invariant subset which appears in the second phrase (measure 4), as remarked above. The invariant subset thus provides immediate structural continuity between the initial statement of 4-8 and the restatement in measure 6.

The concept of invariance is intimately bound up with the intuitive musical notions of development, change, continuity, and discontinuity. In the case of atonal music invariance is of such elemental significance that it would seem essential to understand its basis, and therefore, in the paragraphs that follow, a systematic examination of invariance under transposition will be carried out.

There is a direct correspondence between interval class and transposition operator such that the number of invariants produced by transposition for any value of t can be ascertained by inspecting the vector entries. Consider, as an example, the prime form of pc set 3-1: [0,1,2]. As shown in section 1.6, the intervals formed by this set can be represented as differences between pairs of operands (pc integers), denoted 0_1 and 0_2 below.

---

*For a detailed discussion of the significance of invariants in 12-tone set music see Babbitt 1960. See also Lewin 1962 and Howe 1965.

$$0_1 \quad 0_2 \quad ic$$
$$1 - 0 = 1$$
$$2 - 1 = 1$$
$$2 - 0 = 2$$

Since there are two intervals of class 1 and one interval of class 2, the interval vector is [210000]. Now, observe the result when the interval class number (ic) is interpreted as a transposition operator (t):

$$0_1 \quad 0_2 \quad ic \qquad\qquad t \quad 0_2 \quad 0_1$$
$$1 - 0 = 1 \quad \rightarrow \quad 1 + 0 = 1$$
$$2 - 1 = 1 \quad \rightarrow \quad 1 + 1 = 2$$
$$2 - 0 = 2 \quad \rightarrow \quad 2 + 0 = 2$$

In every case the conversion of ic to t, indicated by →, and the subsequent arithmetic undo the subtraction, giving back 0_1. In short, 0_1 remains invariant. More precisely, if the value of t is 1, the number of invariants is 2 (pc1 and pc2); while if the value of t is 2, only 1 invariant pc (pc2) is produced. This information can be obtained directly from the interval vector. The entry 2 for ic1 means that 2 elements of the set remain invariant under transposition with t = 1. The entry 1 for ic2 means that 1 element remains invariant under transposition with t = 2. The entry 0 for ic3 means that 0 elements remain invariant under transposition with t = 3, and so on.

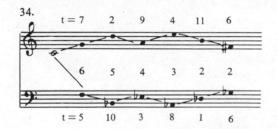

34.

Before generalizing from the foregoing, let us consider another example, pc set 7-35, one form of which is the familiar major scale, as noted earlier.* The transpositions and number of invariants are displayed schematically in example 34. Attention is drawn to two aspects. First, the transposition operators paired off above and below the staff are inverse-related mod 12. Second, 2 invariants are produced when t = 6, yet the vector entry for ic6 is 1. This suggests that inverse-related values of t will always produce the same number of invariants and that the vector entry for ic6 must be multiplied by 2 to obtain the correct number of invariants for t = 6.

---

*The example is borrowed from Babbitt (1965), who also discusses the implications of the unique-vector-entries property of 7-35 with respect to the hierarchical structure of the system of triadic tonality.

It is not difficult to show that inverse-related values of t yield the same number of invariants. The correspondence of ic and t was demonstrated above for two operands 0_1 and 0_2. Since t and t' are equivalent (members of the same interval class), we can let t' replace t as follows:

$$
\begin{array}{cccccc}
0_1 & 0_2 & ic & & t' & 0_1 & 0_2 \\
1 & - 0 & = 1 & \rightarrow & 11 & + 1 = 0 \text{ (mod 12)} \\
2 & - 1 & = 1 & \rightarrow & 11 & + 2 = 1 \\
2 & - 0 & = 2 & \rightarrow & 10 & + 2 = 0
\end{array}
$$

Here the addition of t' gives back 0_2 just as the addition of t gave back 0_1. And, in general, inverse-related values of t produce the same number of invariants. From this it should be evident that when $t = 6$, $t' = 6$ and therefore the number in vector-entry 6 must be multiplied by 2 to give the correct number of invariants.

The foregoing discussion was necessarily somewhat abstract. Before examining some musical examples for invariants it may be useful to set forth some guidelines. With respect to invariants under transposition* there are three cases of special interest: (1) maximum invariance; (2) minimum invariance; (3) invariance involving more than two sets and inverse-related values of t. Whether or not in a particular instance invariants exemplify one of the special cases, it is important to determine their structural significance. That is, the mere occurrence of an invariant subset is of little consequence.

35.   Berg, Four Pieces for Clarinet and Piano Op. 5/1

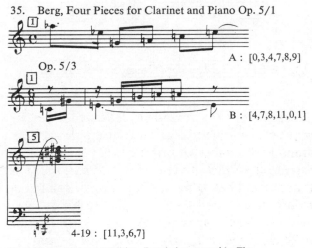

A : [0,3,4,7,8,9]

B : [4,7,8,11,0,1]

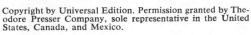

4-19 : [11,3,6,7]

*It is necessary to specify "under transposition" since in many cases more invariants may be obtained under inversion.

36.   Berg, Four Pieces for Clarinet and Piano Op. 5/3

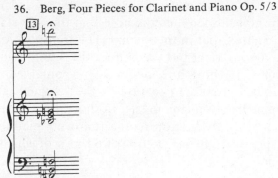

For an illustration of maximum invariance we can return to a composition cited earlier. Berg's Four Pieces for Clarinet and Piano Op. 5. Example 35 shows the opening melodic configurations in the first and third pieces. Both sets are forms of 6-Z44, as indicated. Specifically, B = T(A,4). Since the vector of 6-Z44 is [313431], it is evident that this transposition yields 4 invariants, and that these form the subset 4-19:[0,4,7,8]. Is this invariant subset significant as a structural component of the composition? The answer is affirmative. One occurrence of 4-19 is shown in example 35. In addition, several other important sets in the composition contain 4-19 multiply. Example 36 shows one such set, 7-21, as it occurs at an important formal point in the third piece. Pc set 4-19 is represented 7 times as a subset of 7-21, and no other 4-element set is contained more than 3 times in 7-21.

37.   Stravinsky, *The Rite of Spring*

[7,9,11,0,2,4]

[6,8,10,11,1,3]

An instance of minimum invariance is shown in example 37. The opening bassoon melody returns at rehearsal-number 12 transposed with t = 11. The set, 6-32, is one that has the unique-vector-entries property (sec. 1.7); thus this is the only value of t that will hold exactly one pc fixed, in this case pc11. As one result, the embellished melodic note B in the first statement becomes the main melodic note C-flat in the second. The transposition appears not so much to involve the invariant pc11 as it does the 4-note figure shown in parentheses in example 37. This figure, pc set 3-7, is contained in the transposed form of 6-32 and is a prominent feature of the "Augurs of Spring" section which follows immediately in the music. In short, the transposition effects a specific link from the introduction to the following section. In fact, pc set 3-7 is multiply represented in 6-32 a total of 6 times, of which the set [10,1,3] is only one instance.

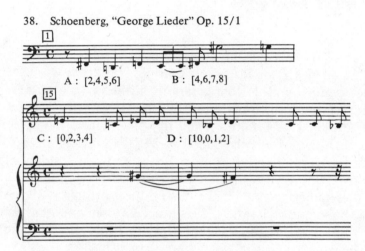

38.   Schoenberg, "George Lieder" Op. 15/1

A : [2,4,5,6]   B : [4,6,7,8]

C : [0,2,3,4]   D : [10,0,1,2]

Used by permission of Belmont Music Publishers, Los Angeles, California 90049.

Example 38 shows a somewhat complicated instance of invariants among more than two sets. First, it is not immediately evident that +(A,B) and +(C,D) are transpositionally equivalent. Specifically, +(C,D) = T(+(A,B),8) and the set-name is 6-2, with vector [443211]. The invariant subset is [2,4], and the transposed set is so ordered that pc4 begins the first 4-note subset C and pc2 begins the second 4-note subset D. The association of the two 6-element sets is strengthened by the statement of [8,6], which belongs to the first, in the accompaniment of the second.

39.   Stravinsky, *The Rite of Spring*

A : [2,3,5,6,9,10]
B : [1,2,4,5,8,9]

The next example of invariants (ex. 39) is of interest since it is a very clear illustration of the occurrence of an invariant subset within a small context and since it highlights the essential nature of equivalent sets in a remarkable musical context. As is evident in example 39, B = T(A,11). The invariant subset [2,5,9] is sustained in dotted half-notes while the remaining elements change. Thus, there is a fluctuation of pitch-class content while interval content remains constant.

It was mentioned earlier that inverse-related values of t produce the same number of invariants. Not only is this true, but it is also the case that inverse-related values of t produce invariant subsets that are equivalent under transposition.*

40.   Schoenberg, Five Piano Pieces Op. 23/2

*This is not true for inversion followed by transposition, and thus is a unique property of the operation transposition.

A remarkable instance of this aspect of inverse-related values of t is shown in example 40.* Three different forms of pc set 9-3 are unfolded in each measure of the passage, and these are labeled A, B, C (measure 18) and D, E, F (measure 19). The transpositional relations in terms of values of t are shown schematically in example 41.

41. Transpositional relations of example 40 in terms of values of t

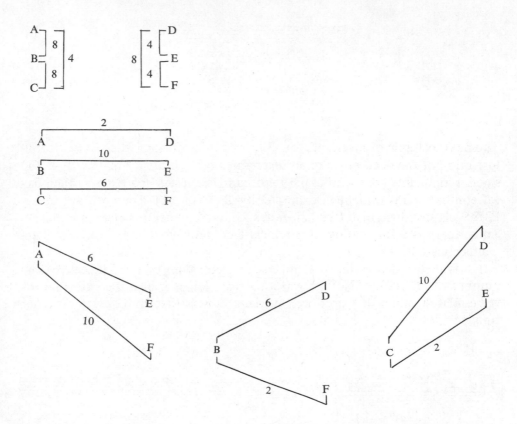

Within the first measure A, B, and C are transpositionally equivalent with values of t = 8 and t = 4. The same situation obtains within the second measure among D, E, and F, except that in this case t has the value 4 twice, corresponding to the double application of 8 in the first measure. As a result of these values of t, pc set 7-21 is held fixed between each of the three pairs of components in measure 18 and between each of the three pairs of components in measure 19.

Inverse values of t also operate between the two measures, as shown in ex-

*Cf. Perle 1968, pp. 49-50.

ample 41. The values 2 and 10 hold pc set 6-2 invariant, while the value 6 holds pc set 6-30 invariant. In the remaining patterns we again find the inverse-related pair 2, 10 and the self-inverse singleton, 6.

Thus, within each measure-pattern only 7-21 remains fixed, whereas between the patterns only 6-30 and 6-2 are invariant. Moreover, neither 6-30 nor 6-2 are subsets of 7-21, and therefore, although there is uniformity over the span of the two patterns due to the use of a single pc set (9-3), there is a specific structural distinction between the pattern comprising each measure and the pattern formed by the adjoining measures in terms of invariant subsets, as determined by the selection of even values of t.

To return now to some general (and final) observations on invariance under transposition, it is perhaps obvious that there remain at least two matters of interest. First, there is the question of complete invariance. That is, for cardinal number n is there some value of t that will yield n invariant pcs? There are indeed some such cases, as one can determine by inspecting the vectors in the list of prime forms (appendix 1).

Three sets of cardinal 4 have values of t that produce complete invariance, hence reduce the number of possible distinct transpositions. In two cases, 4-9 and 4-25, a duplicate form is produced when the value of t is 6. Thus, the number of distinct transposed forms in both cases is 6. Pc set 4-28 produces duplicate forms at three levels of transposition: 3, 9, and 6; consequently, there are only three distinct transpositions.

No 5-element set and no 7-element set is completely invariant under transposition. However, three 6-element sets undergo a reduction with respect to the number of distinct transposed forms. Pc set 6-7 and pc set 6-30 become redundant when t = 6, hence yield only 6 distinct forms under transposition. Pc set 6-20, which produces duplicates when t = 4 and t = 8, has only 4 distinct forms. In all cases the values of t which produce complete invariance may be thought of as effecting a partitioning of the 12 values that t can assume, a partitioning into equivalence classes. Since the number of such classes will always be exactly 1 greater than the number of values of t producing complete invariance (because of the class that contains 0 and represents the non-duplicative forms), we can generalize and state that the number of distinct transpositions of a pc set is 12/m+1, where m is the number of values of t producing complete invariance.

The second of the matters of interest mentioned above concerns values of t which, for a set of cardinal n, yield an invariant subset of cardinal n - 1. Only 29 pc sets are endowed with this capability, and these are displayed in example 42. The invariant relationship can be read from left to right across each row, except for cases in which duples are involved—for example, both 8-24 and 8-21 hold 7-33 invariant. The resulting chains of pc sets are not to be construed as continuous (transitive) with respect to invariance. For example, 8-1 holds 7-1 invariant under transposition, but 8-1 does not hold 3-1 invari-

42.   Invariant subsets of cardinal n-1 for sets of cardinal n

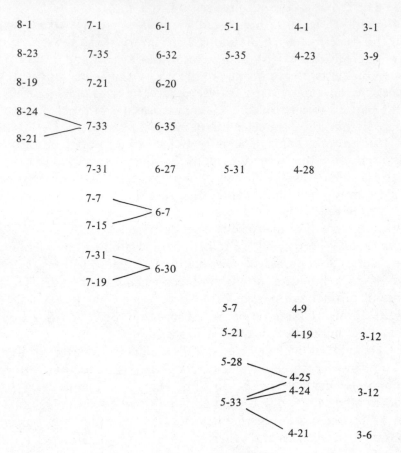

ant under transposition. On the other hand, the sets in each horizontal group are associated in a very significant way: each belongs to the same set-complex. The entity designated by the latter term forms the core of Part 2 of the present volume. As an addendum, it should be remarked that although only five 8-element pc sets hold 7-element subsets invariant under transposition, the 8-element sets in general hold a large number of 5-element and 6-element sets fixed, the only exception being 8-28. It is not surprising to find, therefore, that these large sets play a significant role in atonal compositions.

1.12   Invariant subsets under inversion

The number of invariants under transposition alone is independent of any particular pitch-class representation of a set and is determined solely by the interval content of that set. In the case of inversion followed by transposition, however, the pc set is determinant, hence the situation is somewhat more complicated. Before examining the basis of invariance under inversion let us consider some examples from the atonal repertory.

43.   Schoenberg, *Pierrot Lunaire* Op. 21

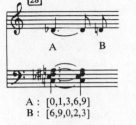

A : [0,1,3,6,9]
B : [6,9,0,2,3]

Example 43 shows the end of the first section of an interlude in Schoenberg's *Pierrot Lunaire*. At this formal juncture in the music the two vertical sets A and B have the same name, 5-31. The only non-invariants therefore are pc1 and pc2, notated on the upper staff. Alignment of the two sets* reveals that B is the transposed inversion of A, with t = 3:

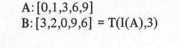

$$A: [0,1,3,6,9]$$
$$B: [3,2,0,9,6] = T(I(A),3)$$

44.   Ruggles, *Angels*

A : [10,11,2,3,6]
B : [10,11,2,3,6]
C : [3,6,7,10,11]

A somewhat similar instance is shown in example 44. The return to 5-21 on the last beat of the measure (B) is the result of an exchange of the upper and lower parts and thus a transposition, with t = 0. The next occurrence of 5-21 (C) involves inversion followed by transposition.

---

*Recall from section 1.4, that comparison of two inversionally equivalent sets requires that the second be reversed.

$$B: [10,11,2,3,6]$$
$$C: [11,10,7,6,3] = T(I(B),9)$$

As is evident, there are 4 invariants.

From the foregoing examples one might assume that the structural effect of inversion is, in general, no different than that obtainable through transposition alone, for in both cases 4 invariants could also have been produced merely by transposition. This, however, is not correct. As a counter-instance, in example 9 (Ives, *The Unanswered Question*) there are two successive occurrences of pc set 4–Z29 and no invariants. Yet the vector of 4–Z29 is [111111], so that transposition for any value of t would yield at least 1 invariant pc. Only inversion followed by transposition (with special limitations on values of t) will result in complete non-invariance in that case.

Let us now consider the structural basis of invariance under inversion followed by transposition. The notion of mapping can be used again here to good advantage. Displayed below is a double mapping of a set S:[0,1,2,3].

S		T(I(S),0)		T(I(S),1)
0	→	0	→	1
1	→	11	→	0
2	→	10	→	11
3	→	9	→	10

For any element a of S, the double mapping first sends a onto a' then onto some element x. Thus, generalizing from the illustration above, the double mapping can be represented as follows:

$$a \rightarrow a' \rightarrow x$$

Since the inverse relation forms fixed pairs from the set [0,1,2,...,11], it is evident that the value of t, which is variable, is of primary concern in the double mapping. We can show that t = x + a, as follows:

(1) Recall that $a + a' = 0$ mod 12 (definition of inverse)
(2) $a' + t = x$ (definition of transposition)
    The latter expression can be modified, without changing its value, by adding a to both sides:
(3) $a + a' + t = x + a$
    Since $a + a' = 0$ we are left with
(4) $t = x + a$

The general problem of interest here is the same one discussed in connection with transposition: given a pc set, what will be the result, in terms of invariants, for some value of t? It is advantageous to approach the general situation by way of the complete invariance case, in which every element of T(I(S),t) is an element of S.

In view of the fact that a + x = t, as shown above, we can reinterpret the problem as that of finding values of x for every element a in S such that a + x = t. Since complete invariance implies that all a and x are in S and since the requirement is that t = a + x, the search can be narrowed to consider the sums of pairs of elements s in S, which will be called the *sums of S*:

$$S_0 + S_0, S_0 + S_1, S_0 + S_2, \ldots, S_1 + S_1, \ldots, S_{n-1} + S_{n-1}$$

where n is the cardinal number of S.*

The prime forms can be used to show that a further restriction can be placed on the sums of S. Since the prime form begins with 0, one can see that t must be in S, for otherwise t + 0 would yield a number not in S, hence fail to meet the complete invariance condition. This implies that we need consider only a subset of the sums of S, namely, the *sums of S in S*.

Accordingly, the problem of finding a value of t that will effect complete invariance reduces to that of finding pairs of operands a,x which sum to t and which exhaust S. An example will clarify. Given S:[0,1,2,3] we ask: is S completely invariant under inversion followed by transposition for some value of t? The sums of S in S are displayed below.

$$0 + 1 = 1$$
$$0 + 2 = 2$$
$$0 + 3 = 3$$
$$1 + 1 = 2$$
$$1 + 2 = 3$$

Clearly, if t = 3 complete invariance will result. The mappings are shown below.

S		I(S)		T(I(S),3)
0	→	0	→	3
1	→	11	→	2
2	→	10	→	1
3	→	9	→	0

Observe that the sums indicate the mappings:

$$t: a \to x, x \to a$$

That is, as a result of the transposition and inversion an exchange takes place between 0 and 3 and between 1 and 2, and of course the total effect is that of a reversal of order of the elements of S.

We shall return to consider the consequences of complete invariance with respect to reduction in the number of distinct inversions that can be generated from any prime form. Now, however, let us consider the situation in which less than complete invariance is possible.

---

*For a set of n elements, n $>$ 1, the number of such sums is $\dfrac{n^2 + n}{2}$.

In such cases t need not be an element of S, obviously, and the number of invariants as well as the mappings can be determined by inspecting the sums of S. For instance, given S:[0,1,2,5] suppose one wished to ascertain what value(s) of t would produce maximum, but less than complete, invariance. This is tantamount to asking which sum is formed the greatest number of times in the sums of S. Inspection shows that 2 is formed by 0,2 and by 1,1. All other sums are represented only once. Thus, when t = 2 the set 4-4 is maximally invariant, with 3 elements remaining fixed.

This example (pc set 4-4) provides an opportunity to make a general comparison of inversion and transposition. Not only does inversion afford fewer invariants than would be available under transposition alone (ex. 9), but it also affords more in a significant number of instances. In the case of pc set 4-4 the maximum of 2 invariants is obtained under transposition alone when t = 1. Under inversion followed by transposition with t = 2, however, 3 invariants can be obtained.

Less than maximum invariance* is obtained from values of t which are not among the sums of S. As in the case of inversional invariance in general, these values depend upon the pc set. For example, pc set 5-5 in its prime form produces 4 invariants under inversion followed by transposition when the value of t is 2. If the prime form is transposed, however, this condition changes, and when t = 2 only 1 invariant is produced.

The preceding material will suffice to provide a perspective on two passages that exemplify the structural application of invariance under inversion over spans of music somewhat longer than those quoted at the beginning of this section.

45. Stravinsky, *The Rite of Spring*

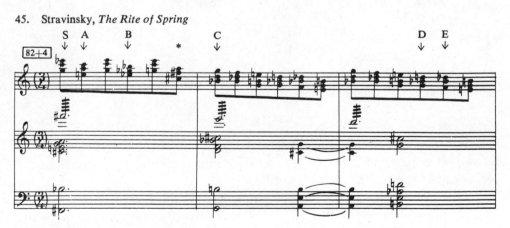

*Less than maximum does not necessarily mean minimal.

In example 45 letters designate vertical sets indicated by the arrows. The 8-element set S, pc set 8-28, which occurs throughout the composition in diverse contexts, has a number of remarkable properties.* Among these is the property that its eight 7-element subsets are all forms of pc set 7-31. It is the five occurrences of the latter that will be discussed.

Set B is a transposition of A with t = 9. Since the vector of 7-31 is [336333], it is apparent that this value of t will yield 6 invariants. The invariant subset (6-27) is then stated at the asterisk, which implies that the entire measure is derived from the 8-element set, 8-28, through the only 7-element subset of 8-28, in which a single 6-element set is held fixed to form the final component. Pc set 7-31 returns at the beginning of the second measure (C) and, in fact, is completely represented by the sonority sustained in half notes. Thus, the first four eighth notes of the moving parts do not change the total pitch content. This changes only on the last quarter note of the measure (to 7-28). A comparison of C and B shows that C = T(I(B),8), producing 4 invariants. Under transposition alone no value of t will produce exactly 4 invariants, and therefore it can be assumed that the inversion here is significant.†

In the final measure quoted in example 45, D is a transposition of C with t = 9 (the value of t in the case of B and A), and again maximum invariance results with 6-27 again the invariant subset. Finally, E = T(I(D),9), with maximum invariance still preserved. Here, however, the invariant subset is 6-Z13, which does not have any special significance in the local context, although it is an important component elsewhere in the music.

The final musical excerpt to be discussed in this section illustrates the role of invariant subsets over a still longer span and indicates the way in which such subsets can be interpreted with respect to Z-related supersets.

Example 46 shows the transitional passage which connects the middle section of the piece to the restatement of the first section, labeled B. For the present, D will be ignored and attention given to A and B. As indicated, they are Z-related and thus have the same total interval-content.†† Further analysis reveals other relations between A and B. Let us consider first the music which provides the immediate connection to B, labeled C_2 in example 46. The set at this point, 4-Z29, occurs twice in A, and, in the case of C_1:[10,2,4,5], forms the invariant subset [2,5] with C_2. The structural importance of those elements is evident in the score. The linking role of 4-Z29 is further substantiated by the two occurrences of that set in B, as shown.

---

*It is also characteristic of much of Stravinsky's other music. Arthur Berger refers to the set as the "octatonic scale." See Berger 1964.

†The invariant subset is 4-28, the complement of 8-28. (The complement relation is discussed in section 1.15.)

††This in itself is of interest with respect to the entire piece, since A is the predominant configuration in the middle section.

46.   Schoenberg, Three Piano Pieces Op. 11/2

Used by permission of Belmont Music Publishers, Los Angeles, California 90049.

Further association of A and B is provided by pc set 4–16, which is formed by the upper voice of A and again as [9,11,4,5]. In B the set is formed by the first notes of the upper voice [8,9,1,3]. One pc is held invariant over all three forms: pc9. (Compare the position of that element in the melodic contours of A and B.)

It remains to explain the segment labeled D. That this is essentially an extension of A is suggested by the continuation of components notated on the lower staff. It is an extension with respect to the components notated on the upper staff as well, for the union of the upper voice of A and the upper voice of D forms 7–Z38, as indicated in example 46. Specifically, it is a transposition of A, with $t = 5$, forming the invariant subset [9,10,2,4], which of course is the same as the upper voice of A taken separately. And, as remarked above, it is precisely this set (4–16) which occurs again as the first four melodic notes in B.

To return to the question of complete invariance and reduction in the number of forms that can be generated from the prime form, it should be evident that if, under inversion followed by transposition, there is one value of t that effects a replication of the prime form, then any (every) inversion is a replica of some transposition of the prime form. In a case of this kind, all the inverted forms of the set are redundant; hence, the number of distinct forms is reduced by 12. A further reduction is determined if the set is completely invariant under transposition alone, as explained in section 1.11. With one exception, all sets that are completely invariant under transposition are completely invariant under inversion followed by transposition. The sole exception is pc set 6–30, which has 12 distinct forms, 6 derived from the prime by transposition and 6 derived from the prime by inversion followed by transposition.*

Although pc sets which are completely invariant under inversion followed by transposition are the exception rather than the rule, their number is quite large. There are 4 such sets of cardinal 3, 15 of cardinal 4, 10 of cardinal 5†, and 20 of cardinal 6. On the list of prime forms (appendix 1) those sets having exactly 12 distinct forms represent the reduction due to complete invariance under inversion (with the exception of 6–30, as noted above).

In section 1.11 the matter of transpositionally invariant subsets of n–1 elements for a set of cardinal n was discussed, and some instances of this special case of invariance have been described in the present section with respect to inversion. An effort will now be made to give a more complete picture of the latter.

It is perhaps not surprising that the overall situation for inversionally invariant subsets of n–1 elements is far more complex than that for transpositionally invariant subsets of n–2 elements, so much so, in fact, that it is not feasible to construct a display of the former corresponding to the illustration provided by example 42. Some notion of the degree of complexity may be obtained by pondering the following counts of sets which either hold some subset (of cardinal –1) invariant under inversion or which are themselves held invariant. Every 7-element set and every 5-element set is involved in this type of inversional invariance. Only 13 sets of cardinal 8, 2 of cardinal 4 (4–Z15 and 4–Z29), and 10 of cardinal 6 are *not* involved.

With the exception of 6–27 and 6–30, all subsets of cardinal –1 held invariant under transposition are also held invariant under inversion. In this respect transpositional invariance is virtually subsumed by inversional invariance—with respect to set types, not, of course, with respect to pc representations of those sets.

The relation between the complete invariance situation and the special situation under discussion is interesting. If a set of cardinal n is completely invariant under inversion, then it holds no subsets of n–2 elements invariant under inversion, with the following exceptions: all sets of ordinal 1 (the chromatic sets), the 4-element and 8-element sets with ordinals 23 and 24, the 5-element and 7-element sets with ordinals 15, 33, and 35, and pc set 6–32.

*Discussed by Howe (1965).
†A curious and refractory situation, first remarked by Lewin (1960), exists between the Z-related sets 5–Z12 and 5–Z36. 5–Z12, which is completely invariant when t = 6, generates only 12 pc sets whereas 5–Z36, for which there is *no* value of t producing complete invariance, generates 24 distinct forms.

47.

Pc set	Invariant subsets under inversion
8-19	7-Z17
	7-22
	7-Z37
7-7	6-7
	6-Z6
	6-Z38
7-31	6-Z13
	6-Z23
	6-Z49
	6-Z50
6-14	5-Z17
	5-Z37
6-Z19	5-Z17
	5-22
6-21	5-8
	5-33
6-22	5-15
	5-33
6-33	5-34
	5-35
6-34	5-33
	5-34

As a final indicator of complexity, example 47 lists the extraordinary cases in which a set holds more than one type of subset invariant. All the sets listed there are amply represented in the atonal repertory.

1.13 Similarity relations

In previous sections considerable attention was given to relations between equivalent pc sets. By definition, each member of a pair of equivalent sets is reducible to the same prime form by transposition or by inversion followed by transposition. In that sense the sets are identical. This suggests that it might be useful to define relations for sets of the same cardinal number so that given two such sets known to be non-equivalent one could determine the degree of similarity between them. The present section, accordingly, is concerned with the development of measures of similarity with respect to certain properties and with the consequences of those measures. Interval content and the inclusion relation play a fundamental role here, and it will be shown that the interaction of pitch class and interval class has interesting implications for the notion of similarity.

48. Ives, *The Unanswered Question*

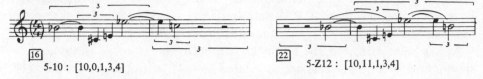

5-10 : [10,0,1,3,4]   5-Z12 : [10,11,1,3,4]

To begin, let us consider the two passages shown in example 48. It is evident that they differ with respect to only one pitch, the last in each case. This means that they share one 4-element subset, namely 4-13:[10,1,3,4]; * This is an instance of what will be called pitch-class similarity. More specifically, we define a similarity relation R_p for sets S_1, S_2 of cardinal number n and S_3 of cardinal number n-1, as follows.

$$R_p(S_1, S_2) \text{ iff } \cdot (S_3 \subset S_1, S_3 \subset S_2)$$

In short, S_1 and S_2 must contain at least one common subset of cardinal number n-1 in order to be in the relation R_p.

This would appear to be a straightforward and useful measure of similarity. Further consideration, however, reveals certain disadvantages. First, to use example 48 as an instance again, pc set 5-Z12 is in the relation R_p to 18 5-element sets (out of 38), while pc set 5-10 is in the relation R_p to 22 5-element sets. Thus, the relation R_p does not seem especially distinctive—at least in this case. And, indeed, it would seem that the relation is distinctive in only a few instances. Every 4-element set is in the relation R_p to at least 11 other 4-element sets, with the exception of 4-28, which has 4 such relations, and 4-9 and 4-25, both of which have 8 relations. The extrema are listed below.†

R_p Extrema

Cardinal number	Maxima	Minima
	4-Z15 (24)	
4	4-Z29 (24)	4-28 (4)
5	5-Z36 (28)	5-33 (9)
6	6-Z11 (31)	6-35 (3)
	6-Z40 (31)	

*In a sketch of this work in the Ives Collection of the Yale Music Library the "question" is, in every statement, B-flat-C-sharp-E-E-flat-B-flat, i.e. the common subset in the final version.
†The R_p relation could be extended, of course, to pc sets of 3 elements. These have been disregarded for the purpose of the present discussion, as have similarity relations between sets of cardinal number greater than 6.

The minima are familiar as "whole-tone" and "diminished" formations, while the maxima are sets with the "Z" property. The Z-correspondent of 5-Z36 is related (R_p) to only 18 other sets, whereas the other Z-pairs displayed above have the same number of R_p relations. The unusual structural discrepancy between 5-Z36 and 5-Z12 was remarked in section 1.12.

As has been indicated, the pitch-class similarity measure R_p is not especially significant since many sets are so related to a large number of other sets. If interval-class similarity is taken into account, however, a considerable reduction is effected.

Example 48 will serve again to introduce the notion of interval-class similarity. If we examine the vectors of 5-10 and 5-Z12 it is apparent that the entries for ic1, ic2, ic4, and ic6 correspond, as indicated by the arrows.

$$\downarrow\downarrow\ \downarrow\downarrow$$
$$5\text{-}10\quad[223111]$$
$$5\text{-}Z12\ [222121]$$

That is, both vectors have two intervals of class 1, two intervals of class 2, one interval of class 4, and one interval of class 6. Two vectors with a four-fold correspondence of this kind will be called *maximally similar,* since there is no case in which a correspondence exists between more than four entries.

Maximum similarity with respect to interval vector encompasses two relations, which will be designated R_1 and R_2. For two vectors V_1 and V_2 to be in the relation R_1, V_1 must contain the same digits as V_2 and four vector entries must correspond, as explained above. For example, the vectors below are in the relation R_1.

$$4\text{-}2\ [221100]$$
$$\times$$
$$4\text{-}3\ [212100]$$

The interchange of entries here, indicated by arrows, distinguishes R_1 from R_2, and in this sense R_1 represents a closer relationship than does R_2. Ex-

49.   Webern, Six Pieces for Orchestra Op. 6/1

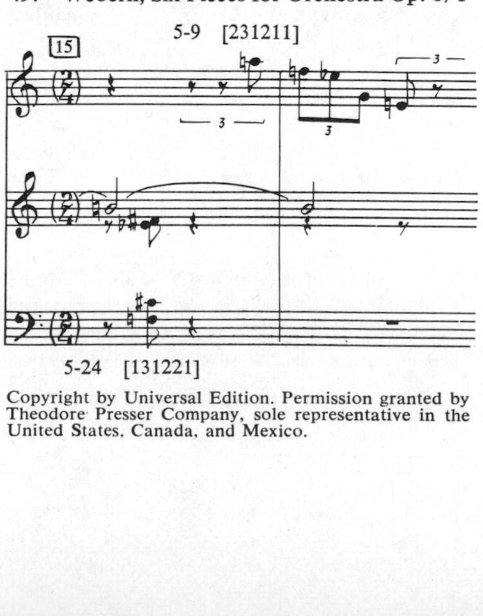

ample 48 provided an instance of R_2. Two sets in the relation R_1 are shown in example 49. Comparison of the vectors of 5–9 and 5–24 shows that interval content remains the same with respect to four interval-classes, while there is a reciprocal change in the case of ic1 and ic5.

50. Schoenberg, *Die glückliche Hand* Op. 18

scene 1

4-2 : [3,4,5,7] [221100]

scene 3

4-13 : [8,11,1,2] [112011]

Used by permission of Belmont Music Publishers, Los Angeles, California 90049.

From the preceding discussion of maximum similarity based on interval content, it follows that vectors are *minimally similar* if no entries correspond. Example 50 shows two configurations from Schoenberg's *Die glückliche Hand*. The first of these occurs at the beginning of the opera, and the second introduces scene 3. As can be seen, the vectors of the pc sets are minimally similar. The relation minimally similar will be represented by R_0

The complete array of similarity measures together with interpretations is summarized below.

Relation	Interpreted as
R_p	Maximum similarity with respect to pitch class
R_0	Minimum similarity with respect to interval class
R_1	Maximum similarity with respect to interval class. Interchange feature.
R_2	Maximum similarity with respect to interval class. Without interchange feature.

It was remarked above that the pc similarity relation R_p is not especially significant taken alone, since by that measure a given set may be similar to many others. When R_p is combined with the ic similarity relations, however, a considerable reduction is effected. Moreover, some unexpected and quite extraordinary relations ensue.

Example 51 is intended to dramatize the situation. On the left is a triangular matrix which displays the relation R_p for sets of cardinal number 4. The relations for any set can be read by traversing the appropriate row and column. For example, for set 4-2 read from left to right on the row designated 2. When the end of the row is reached read down the column. Thus, 4-2 is in the relation R_p to 4-1, 4-3, 4-4, and so on. For the present purpose, however, the specific relations are not of interest. Instead, attention is directed to the matrix on the right in example 51. This matrix displays the compound relation $\cdot(R_1, R_p)$. For instance, the x in row 3, column 2 means that set 4-2 and set 4-3 are both in the relation R_1 and in the relation R_p. This matrix therefore represents a filtering process carried out on the left (R_p) matrix. In numeric terms, of 246 pairs of sets in R_p, only 22 are both in R_p and R_1. If we consider the pairs that are in R_p and in R_1 or in R_2, the count is 66. These sets, which are maximally similar with respect to pitch class and interval class, are displayed in example 52.

In general, then, the relation *maximum similarity with respect to both pitch class and interval class* will be regarded as more significant than pitch class similarity alone or interval class similarity alone. At this junction it seems appropriate to return to the musical excerpts used to introduce the similarity measures in order to determine whether they also exhibit the more significant combination of pc and ic similarity under discussion here. The two sets in example 48, 5-10 and 5-Z12, are in the relation R_p and in the relation R_2, thus meeting the "significance" condition. The two sets in example 49, 5-24 and 5-9, are in R_1 and in R_p. The R_p relation, however, is not explicitly realized, for there are only two pitch classes common to both sets. In cases of this kind involving R_p we will say that the relation is *weakly represented*. The ic similarity relations are, of course, independent of the pc set representation, and therefore are always *strongly represented*.

Example 50 (Schoenberg) deserves separate treatment since it exemplifies one of the extraordinary relations to which passing reference was made above. The two sets, 4-2 and 4-13, are in the relation R_0. They are also in the relation R_p. Thus, they are minimally similar with respect to interval class and maximally similar with respect to pitch class. In this instance R_p is weakly represented.*

The number of pairs of sets related both by R_0 and by R_p is quite small. Some indication is given by the matrix in example 53.† In all, 13 pairs of sets have the dual relation, and 19 distinct sets are involved. Seven belong to two pairs each: 4-5, 4-7, 4-9, 4-12, 4-Z15, 4-25, and 4-Z29.

The compound relation symbolized $\cdot(R_0, R_p)$ is not unique with respect to

---

*The sets are so ordered, however, that the common subset, 3-2, occurs as the first 3 pitches in each.
†Matrices (lists) of similarity relations are provided in appendix 2.

sparse matrix representation. Another such interesting combination is the one in which two sets are maximally similar on the basis of interval content, but minimally similar by the pitch-class measure R_p. If we let the symbol – represent logical negation ("not"), the combination just described can be written $\cdot(+(R_1,R_2), -R_p)$. Example 54 presents the matrix of that combination for sets of cardinal number 5. Example 55 provides a musical instance. The first of the three chords shown is R_2 similar to the second but not R_p similar. (The third chord is in none of the defined similarity relations to the others, and will be ignored here.) A further illustration is provided by example 56. Pc sets 6-16 and 6-9 are in R_1 but not in R_p, with the result that melody and "accompaniment" are at once similar and dissimilar.

51. R_p for sets of cardinal 4

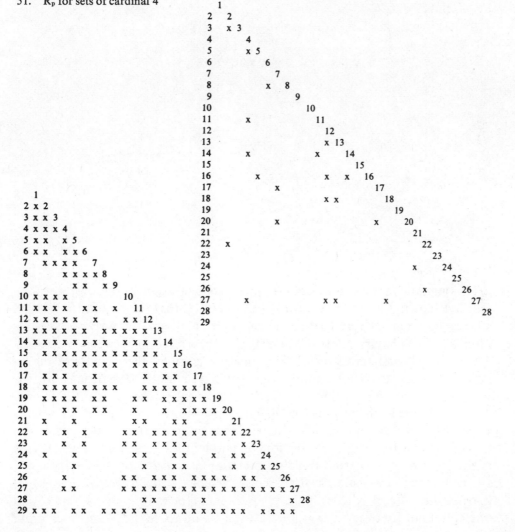

52.   ·(R$_p$, + (R₁, R₂) for sets of cardinal 4

```
 1
 2 x 2
 3    x 3
 4    x x 4
 5      x 5
 6        x 6
 7      x      7
 8        x x    8
 9          x  x 9
10              10
11  x   x        x 11
12    x            12
13              x  x 13
14    x          x      14
15    x x        x x x    15
16      x x  x    x  x x 16
17        x            17
18            x x  x  x 18
19        x    x        x  19
20        x        x  x  x 20
21                    21
22  x          x  x        22
23                    x 23
24                  x      24
25                  x  x 25
26            x        x      26
27      x      x x x x      x        x 27
28                            28
29      x      x x x x  x  x            x
```

Turning now to some important ramifications of a general nature, it will be recalled that the notational form R$_s$(a,b) signifies that the relation R of type s holds between set a and set b. In elementary mathematics a relation of this kind is called a binary relation, since it specifies a relation between two terms. The set of all first terms of a binary relation is called the domain of the relation, and the set of all second terms is called the range. Relations have certain defined properties, three of which are relevant to the present discussion. A relation is said to be *reflexive* if for every a in its domain R(a,a) is true. If R(a,a) is true for no a in the domain, the relation is *irreflexive.* A relation is *symmetric* if for every a in the domain and b in the range, whenever R(a,b) is true, R(b,a) is also true. Finally, a relation is *transitive* if for every a,b,c, where b and c are elements of the range, whenever R(a,b) is true and R(b,c) is true, then R(a,c) is true. If the relation holds for at least one a, one b, and one c, but not for every a, b, c, the relation is said to be *non-transitive.* From

53. $\cdot(R_0, R_p)$ for sets of cardinal 4

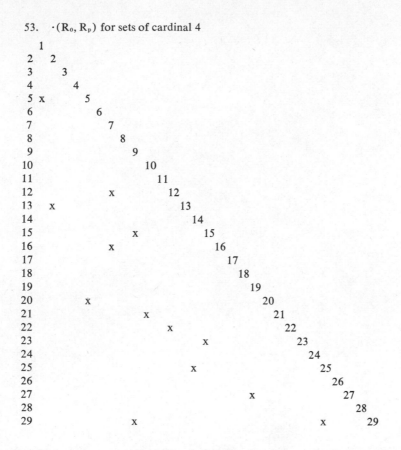

this it should be apparent that R_0 is irreflexive (since a vector will never be minimally similar to itself), symmetric, and non-transitive. The latter property can be verified by inspecting the matrices in appendix 2. The relation R_1 is irreflexive (since, although a vector will always be identical to itself, the interchange feature cannot be realized), symmetric, and non-transitive, while R_2 is irreflexive, symmetric, and non-transitive. The pitch-class similarity measure R_p, is reflexive, symmetric, and non-transitive. Thus, to sum up, all the relations are symmetric and non-transitive. One is reflexive (R_p) and the other three are irreflexive.

While the symmetric property is reflected in the triangular shape of the matrices, the non-transitive property is not so explicitly represented. This is not to suggest that the latter property is of no interest. In fact, those cases in which transitivity holds are of special structural significance since they represent an extension of the particular relation beyond the scope of a single pair of sets to form a collection of interrelated sets. A collection of this kind will be referred to as a *transitive n-tuple,* or simply a transitive tuple.*

Tuple is the generic term. A particular case might be, for example, a triple, a quadruple, etc.

54. $\cdot(+(R_1, R_2),-R_p)$ for sets of cardinal 5

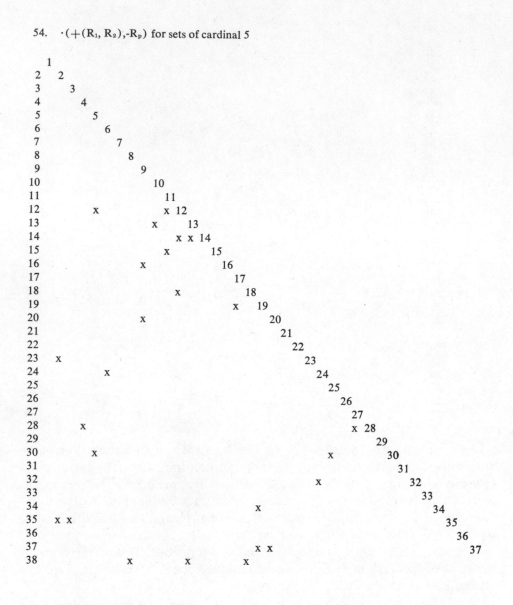

With but a single exception, the number of transitive tuples is not large. These are summarized in example 57. The exception mentioned is not shown: the 80 transitive tuples for R_0 among the hexachords.

These transitive tuples have a number of interesting features, only one of which will be alluded to here, namely, the varying degree to which sets are members of tuples. Among the R_1 quintuples of cardinal 6, for example, pc set 6-Z23 occurs only once, whereas pc set 6-30 is a member of each.

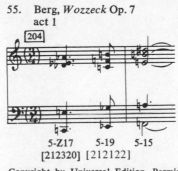

55.   Berg, *Wozzeck* Op. 7
      act 1

5-Z17   5-19   5-15
[212320] [212122]

A compositional instance of a transitive tuple is shown in example 58. The relations R_1 and R_p are transitive over the three 6-elements sets shown there. These three sets occur in many forms throughout the work, such that the final statements here constitute a kind of summation. Notice that R_p is strongly represented only between 6-Z49 and the first occurrence of 6-Z50. The common subset is, of course, 5-32. It should be pointed out that the three hexachords belong to a transitive quintuple, as can be ascertained from example 57.

56.   Webern, Five Pieces for Orchestra Op. 10/4

6-16

6-9

Some additional excerpts will serve to close this section and to indicate some further ramifications of the similarity measures. Example 59 shows a familiar passage from *The Rite of Spring* in which the vertical "dimension" consists of forms of only two sets, 4-18 and 4-27. These two sets are in the relation

57. Transitive tuples

Pc sets of cardinal 4

R₁
*4-4, 4-11, 4-14
4-7, 4-17, 4-20
*4-12, 4-13, 4-18, 4-27

Pc sets of cardinal 5

R₀
5-2, 5-20, 5-33
5-2, 5-30, 5-33
5-2, 5-32, 5-33
5-6, 5-23, 5-33
5-13, 5-23, 5-33
5-16, 5-23, 5-33

R₁

5-4, 5-26, 5-29
5-5, 5-25, 5-30
5-6, 5-24, 5-32
5-9, 5-16, 5-20
5-10, 5-13, 5-14
5-Z12, 5-Z18, 5-19
5-Z12, 5-19, 5-Z38
*5-13, 5-26, 5-30
5-Z18, 5-19, 5-Z36
*5-19, 5-Z36, 5-Z38

R₂

*5-2, 5-3, 5-4
*5-11, 5-Z17, 5-Z18
5-11, 5-Z18, 5-Z37
5-11, 5-21, 5-Z37
*5-11, 5-Z37, 5-Z38
*5-23, 5-27, 5-29

Pc sets of cardinal 6

R₁

6-Z10, 6-Z11, 6-Z24
6-Z11, 6-Z24, 6-Z39
6-Z11, 6-Z39, 6-Z46
*6-15, 6-16, 6-31
*6-21, 6-22, 6-34
6-Z13, 6-Z23, 6-Z28, 6-Z29, 6-30
6-Z13, 6-Z28, 6-Z29, 6-30, 6-Z45
6-Z13, 6-Z29, 6-30, 6-Z45, 6-Z49
6-Z13, 6-30, 6-Z45, 6-Z49, 6-Z50
6-Z23, 6-Z28, 6-Z29, 6-30, 6-Z42
6-Z23, 6-Z29, 6-30, 6-Z42, 6-Z49
6-Z23, 6-30, 6-Z42, 6-Z49, 6-Z50
*6-Z28, 6-Z29, 6-30, 6-Z42, 6-Z45
6-Z28, 6-30, 6-Z42, 6-Z45, 6-Z50
6-Z29, 6-30, 6-Z42, 6-Z45, 6-Z49
6-30, 6-Z42, 6-Z45, 6-Z49, 6-Z50

R₂

*6-8, 6-9, 6-Z11
6-9, 6-Z11, 6-Z12
*6-14, 6-15, 6-Z19
*6-14, 6-16, 6-Z19
*6-14, 6-Z19, 6-31
*6-14, 6-31, 6-Z44

*also R_p transitive

58. Scriabin, Sixth Piano Sonata

A   4-9 : [1,2,7,8]
B   6-Z50 : [7,8,11,1,2,4]
C   6-Z50 : [1,2,5,7,8,10]
D   6-30 : [2,4,5,8,10,11]
E   5-32 : [7,8,11,1,4]
F   4-Z15 : [7,8,11,1]
G   6-Z49 : [4,5,7,8,11,1]

R_1 and in the relation R_p. Since the relation R_p is weakly represented throughout let us give attention to the way in which R_1 is expressed in the music. Comparison of the vectors of 4-18 and 4-27 shows that they differ with respect to ic1 and ic2. At every occurrence of 4-18 the interval which distinguishes it

59.   Stravinsky, *The Rite of Spring*

4-27   4-18 4-27 4-18 4-27   4-27   4-18

from 4-27 is formed by the outer voices. With only one exception the interval which distinguishes 4-27 from 4-18 also occurs in the outer voices. Thus, the similarity relation is expressed as a prominent structural feature of the passage.

60.   Webern, Four Songs Op. 12/4

Rₚ	• (R₁,Rₚ)	• (R₂,Rₚ)
4-5,4-21	4-5,4-16	5-8,5-Z18
4-16,4-21		5-3,5-4

Example 60 displays similarity relations for the opening section of a song by Webern. As in the Stravinsky example (ex. 59), R_p is weakly represented. The similar sets are paired off, with 4-16 following 4-5 in the accompaniment, 5-Z18 (first vocal phrase) following 5-8 in the accompaniment, and 5-3 (upper voice of the accompaniment in measures 4 and 5) matched by the second vocal phrase. Apart from this, however, the similarity relations are not immediately evident at the surface level, as in the Stravinsky example discussed above, which suggests that they may represent a secondary aspect of structure. Example 61 shows a sketch-like representation of the opening measures of Scriabin's Seventh Piano Sonata which will suffice for the present purpose. Note that a partial repetition of the opening succession begins in measure 5. This is, in fact, a transposition of the opening succession, with t = 2. This

61. Scriabin, Seventh Piano Sonata Op. 64

(a)

6-Z49
[4,6,9,10,0,1]

5-16

6-Z19
[1,2,5,6,8,9]

(b)

6-Z13
[9,10,0,1,3,4]

6-Z24
[9,10,0,1,3,5]

6-34
[3,4,6,8,10,0]

transposition produces minimal invariance in each case. In addition, R_p is weakly represented, and thus pitch-class invariance is not a significant structural feature here.

In the entire composition a relatively small number of sets is utilized, and those shown at (a) are prominent throughout. At the end of the composition (b), sets other than those shown at (a) are introduced. Comparison of the two passages in terms of similarity relations provides some illumination. The two hexachords which dominate the first section, 6-Z19 and 6-Z49, are in the relation R_p and in the relation R_0. The same relations hold between the two successive pairs of hexachords in the final section. Moreover, 6–Z13 is in the relation R_p and in the relation R_1 to 6-Z49. These similarity relations are summarized in the graph, example 62.

62.   Similarity relations between parts a and b in example 61

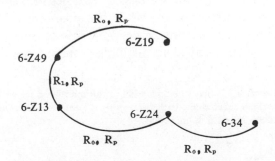

R_0, R_p

6-Z19

6-Z49

R_1, R_p

6-Z13

6-Z24

6-34

R_0, R_p

R_0, R_p

The R_p relation is strongly represented in two cases. The common subset between 6-Z13 and 6-Z49 is 5-16:[9,10,0,1,4]; the common subset between 6-Z13 and 6-Z24 is 5-10:[9,10,0,1,3]. In the first of these, then, we find an explicit structural link, since 5-16 occurs as a set in measure 4 of (a).

63.   Ives, Second String Quartet

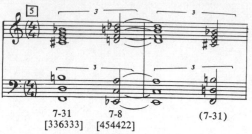

7-31   7-8   (7-31)
[336333]   [454422]

The close of the first phrase of Ives's Second String Quartet is shown in example 63, a striking instance of the extreme fluctuation in interval content that is described by the relation R_0. In this case, one might assume that the choice of sets was not fortuitous, since 7-8 is in R_0 and in R_p with only one other 7-element set, namely, 7-31, which precedes and follows it in this cadential context—although, admittedly, R_p is weakly represented here.

1.14 Order relations

Up to this point little attention has been given to relations of order among pc sets. In part this is because the unordered set is a more elemental concept, and in part it is because in atonal music ordering is by no means such a universally and systematically applied transformation as transposition or inversion.* Nonetheless, order relations are of considerable significance, and it is important to develop some theoretical mechanisms so that they may be interpreted in specific instances.

Let us begin with a simple example of ordering, example 64. Here we see that B is a reordering of A, with the result that two pcs in B (pc9 and pc0) retain their positions with respect to A, while the positions of the other two (pc5 and pc11) are reversed. Before proceeding, notice that the ordered sets here are displayed in such a way as to distinguish them from unordered sets,

---

*It will be recalled from section 1.2 that when we speak of an unordered set we simply mean that the order in which the elements occur is not regarded as a significant property. The term ordered set means, conversely, that order is regarded as important.

64.   Stravinsky, *Two Poems by K. Balmont* (No. 1)

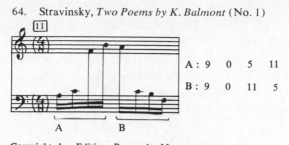

A: 9   0   5   11

B: 9   0   11   5

namely with a space separating the numbers. This notational convention will be employed whenever ordered sets are represented (as distinct from the bracketed representation used for unordered sets). In example 64, then, we have a specific instance of the reordering, or permutation, of a set. A permutation (the term was introduced in section 1.2) is usually defined as a 1–1 mapping of a set onto itself, and it is evident that this is the situation here. However, for reasons that will become apparent shortly, it is essential in the case of pc sets in atonal music to regard a permutation as a reordering that follows transposition or that follows inversion followed by transposition. In example 64, therefore, we have a reordering that follows the transposition of A, with $t = 0$.

65.   Webern, Cello Sonata 1914

A: 5   2   6   3

B: 0   11   3 2

C: 3 5 6 2   D: 11 10 8 7

A more complicated series of reorderings is shown in example 65. There B is a transposition of A, with t = 9, C is a transposition of B, with t = 3, and D is a transposition of C, with t = 5. As a result of this series of transpositions, C has the same pc content as A and therefore the two sets can be compared to determine the amount of rearrangement that has taken place. By inspection we see that only pc6 remains fixed in C with respect to its position in A. Since all the sets are transpositionally related, there is no reason why we cannot compare any pair for order relations, just as we compared A and C. That is, A transposed with t = 0 would have yielded 5 2 6 3. Similarly, A transposed with t = 9 would have produced 2 11 3 0. We can now compare the latter set with B for reordering:

$$2\ 11\ 3\ 0$$
$$0\ 11\ 3\ 2$$

It is now evident that B compared with what will be called the *ordered transposition* of A represents a specific kind of rearrangement: two elements remain fixed with respect to position, while two interchange.

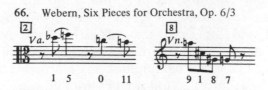

66.   Webern, Six Pieces for Orchestra, Op. 6/3

2   8
   Va.   Vn.

   1   5   0   11   9 1 8 7

67.   Webern, Five Movements for String Quartet Op. 5/5

12   17

   3   9   8 7 2   11   5   4   3 10

Instances of ordered transposition are given in example 66 and example 67. Notice, especially in the excerpt from Webern's Op. 6/3, that the correspondence of order is not matched by other correspondences—for instance register and rhythmic pattern.

Ordered inversion (followed by transposition) is shown in example 68. The notion of an ordered inversion, comparable to an ordered transposition, introduces an additional complexity, for it is necessary, because of the double

68.   Schoenberg, "George Lieder" Op. 15/2

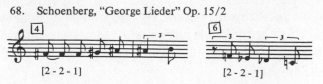

Used by permission of Belmont Music Publishers, Los Angeles,
California 90049.

mapping, to compare three sets. Here, even more than in the case of transposition alone, it is clear that one cannot make a direct comparison of pc content except where complete invariance is possible, as discussed in sections 1.11 and 1.12. What is preserved in the case of ordered transposition and ordered inversion, however, is the *interval succession,* the sequence of intervals formed by adjacent pcs. Once again, pitch class and interval class afford an interesting and useful dichotomy.

An interval succession is shown as a sequence of numbers separated by hyphens and enclosed in square brackets, as in example 68. Although the interval succession provides a useful picture of the order relations between two forms of a set, there is a still more concise representation, which will be called the *basic interval pattern,* abbreviated, with the reader's indulgence and in the interest of economy, to *bip.*

69.   Schoenberg, Five Pieces for Orchestra Op. 16/2

Copyright © 1952 by Henmar Press Inc., New York, N.Y. Reprint permission granted by the publisher.

Example 69 will serve to demonstrate the notion of bip. Three forms of pc set 5-4, marked A, B, and C, are unfolded in this passage. Listed below are the ordered pc sets, the interval successions, and the basic interval patterns.

		bip
A: 8 4 3 2 5	[4-1-1-3]	1134
B: 10 1 9 8 7	[3-4-1-1]	1134
C: 0 3 11 10 9	[3-4-1-1]	1134

From the above the reader can easily infer that the basic interval pattern is merely a normalization of the interval succession, such that the numbers of the latter are grouped together in ascending numerical order without intervening spaces or hyphens. The resulting reduced pattern informs us that the overall successive interval content of the three forms A, B, and C is the same.

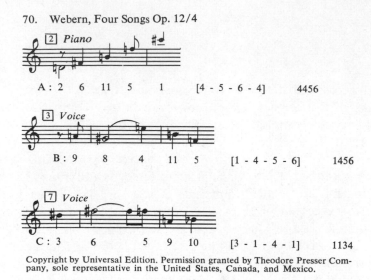

70.   Webern, Four Songs Op. 12/4

A: 2   6   11   5   1   [4 - 5 - 6 - 4]   4456

B: 9   8   4   11   5   [1 - 4 - 5 - 6]   1456

C: 3   6   5   9   10   [3 - 1 - 4 - 1]   1134

Let us now compare some additional bips. Example 70 displays three forms of pc set 5–Z18, as they occur in different locations in Webern's Op. 12/4. Evidently the bip of the second form (B) resembles the first to a considerable extent, since the digits 4, 5, and 6 are shared by both. Moreover, the interval succession 4–5–6 is common. The bip of the third form (C), however, resembles that of the first hardly at all, and it resembles that of the second only with respect to the digits 1 and 4.

71.   Webern, Six Songs Op. 14/1

A: 0   11 6 5 8   9   [1 - 5 - 1 - 3 - 1]   11135

B: 7   4   8   5   11 10   [3 - 4 - 3 - 6 - 1]   13346

Example 71 offers an even more extreme instance of divergent ordered sets, in this case forms of pc set 6–Z13. There is no correspondence of interval succession whatsoever, and only one common digit in the bips. This divergence is dramatically represented in other aspects of the two configurations as well: articulation, register, rhythm, and, of course, timbre.

Thus far interval succession and bip have been emphasized rather than pitch class. The main reason for this is that in atonal music, as distinct from 12-tone music, our main concern is with sets ranging in size from 3 through 9 elements. Thus, except for the case of complete invariance, in which a transposition or inversion maps the set onto itself (permutes the set), it is not possible to compare two forms of a set directly in terms of pitch-class reordering; reference must always be made to intermediary forms of the set. If, however, we wished to measure the amount of rearrangement in terms of repositioning of the elements (pcs) rather than in terms of a change in bip, Babbitt's notion of order inversion provides the most effective means.*

By order inversion is meant the order reversal of a pair of elements in B with respect to their relative positions in A. As an illustration, consider the two forms of 6–Z13 shown in example 71.

$$A: \quad 0 \ 11 \ 6 \ 5 \quad 8 \quad 9$$
$$t = 11: \ 11 \ 10 \ 5 \ 4 \quad 7 \quad 8 \qquad \text{(the ordered transposition)}$$
$$B: \quad 7 \quad 4 \ 8 \ 5 \ 11 \ 10 \qquad \text{(the reordered form)}$$

We now inspect every pair in the ordered transposition of A and ascertain if the relative position of the elements of the pair is preserved in B. If it is not, we count one order inversion. For example, pc11 precedes pc10 in the ordered transposition and in B. However, pc11 precedes pc5 in the ordered transposition, but pc5 precedes pc11 in B. Therefore, an order inversion has taken place. Continuing in this way for all pairs, we count 12 order inversions. Although this is a large number of order inversions it is not the maximum number. The maximum would occur only if B were the retrograde ordering of A. For cardinal 6 this number is 15. And, in general, the number of possible order inversions is the same as the number of unordered pairs of elements, which is a function of the cardinal number of a set (and the same as the number of intervals in the set).

The number of order inversions is associated with permutations in a systematic way, and there is a correspondence between the number of order inversions and the number of permutations represented by a particular permutation class. For example, there is always exactly one permutation that yields 0 order inversions, there is always exactly one permutation that yields the maximum number of order inversions, and there are always n–1 permutations

*Babbitt 1960.

(where n is the cardinal number of the set) that yield exactly 1 order inversion.

However attractive these systematics might be, it is claimed here that order inversions do not reflect adequately change in interval succession or in bip, and that the bip represents a more general and more useful measure of change in ordering. As a demonstration, recall that A and B in example 70 were seen to be more cognate with respect to bip than B and C, while C resembled A hardly at all. A count of order inversions does not reflect these differences, as summarized below.

Set	forms	Number of Order Inversions
A	B	4
B	C	5
A	C	5

The reason for this is perhaps obvious: rearrangement of pitches may or may not affect the succession of intervals. Thus, there is no simple correspondence between order inversions and bip.

72.   Berg, *Wozzeck* Op. 7
       act 2

Marie :   Bin ich ein schlecht Mensch?

Marie :   Ich bin doch   ein schlecht Mensch.

Copyright by Universal Edition. Permission granted by Theodore Presser Company, sole representative in the United States, Canada, and Mexico.

There remain several important aspects of order relations to be discussed. First, it should be apparent that subsets may be compared for order relations. Example 72 shows pc set 4-19 as a subset in two transpositionally equivalent forms of 5-26. The two subsets have the same bip and are, in fact, retrograde-related. The correspondence between the two textual-dramatic situations is self-evident.

Consideration of ordered subsets may also be extended to similarity relations in case of R_p. That is, given A and B in R_p, are they so ordered that the common subset forms the same bip, or has some change in ordering been effected?

The universe of bips is an interesting one and one that can only be explored in a preliminary way in the present context. There are at least two fundamental questions to be addressed. First, how many distinct bips can be derived from a particular pc set? Second, what are the bips associated with a particular set? The following discussion is concerned only with the first of these basic questions, for reasons which will become obvious.

In the determination of the number of bips it is not difficult to guess that the cardinal number of the pc set plays a primary role. Accordingly, let us consider in some detail the case of sets of cardinal 4.

If each permutation of a set of 4 elements produced a unique bip, the total number of patterns for each such set would be 4! = 24.* However, each permutation of the set has a retrograde image that yields a duplicate bip, and therefore the maximum number of bips cannot exceed 12.

Now, it might appear that bips are determined by the total interval content of the set, since they represent a selection from that content. This, however, is not the case. For example, the bip 123 is among the bips of 4-Z15, but not among the bips of 4-Z29, yet both sets have the same interval vector. The reason for this becomes evident when we consider the dyads that form the intervals of 4-Z29:

icl ic2 ic3 ic4 ic5 ic6

pc
dyads: 0 1 1 3 0 3 3 7 0 7 1 7

If we attempt to construct the bip 123 beginning (arbitrarily) with icl, we have available only the dyad 0 1 (or 1 0). To obtain ic2 we introduce the dyad 1 3 (or 3 1). The result, either way, is a pair of intersecting dyads:

$$0\,\overline{1\,3}$$

or

$$\overline{3\,1}\,0$$

Now, however, it is impossible to obtain ic3 since the adjacency 0 3, the only dyad that will yield ic3, is inaccessible. Hence, the bip 123 cannot be completed in this way, nor could it be completed beginning with any ic of the triple.

For pc sets of cardinal 4, then, a bip is formed by a dyadic triple, in which two of the dyads are disjoint, and exhaust the pc set, while the remaining dyad intersects in one pc with each of the disjoint dyads, as shown below.

$$
\begin{array}{cc}
0 & 1 \\
1 & 4 \\
4 & 6
\end{array}
$$

---

*We need not be concerned with transposition and inversion here, since these operations obviously would not affect the number and types of bips for any set.

This general situation follows from the definition of interval succession (interlocking dyads).

Any 4-element set consists of 6 unique pc dyads. These, in turn, combine into 3 pairs of disjunct dyads. For pc set 4–Z15, for example:

$$\begin{vmatrix} 0\,1 & 1\,4 & 0\,4 \\ 4\,6 & 0\,6 & 1\,6 \end{vmatrix}$$

The intervals formed by these dyads are shown below.

dyad	a	b	c	d	e	f
pcs	01	46	14	06	04	16
ic	1	2	3	6	4	5

Now, as remarked above, the interval patterns of a 4-element set are formed by combining a pair of disjunct dyads and a dyad which intersects in one pc with each member of that pair. From the display of disjunct pairs above it can be seen that one pattern can be obtained by combining the disjunct pair a,b with the intersecting dyad c. Another pattern is obtained by combining the disjunct pair a,b with d. Continuation of this procedure yields $4!/2 = 12$ (possibly distinct) bips. These are listed below in terms of their constituent dyads.

a+b+c	c+d+a	e+f+a
a+b+d	c+d+b	e+f+b
a+b+e	c+d+e	e+f+c
a+b+f	c+d+f	e+f+d

If we let the letters in the above display represent intervals it is clear that the maximum of 12 distinct bips is formed if and only if each interval represents a unique interval class. For the 4-element sets this condition is met only by the two all-interval tetrachords, 4–Z15 and 4–Z29. In all other cases there is a reduction determined by the number and placement of dyads that form duplicate intervals.

As an example of the reduction of the maximum of 12 distinct bips, consider the dyads of pc set 4–5:

dyad	a	b	c	d	e	f
pcs	01	26	02	16	12	06
ic	1	4	2	5	1	6

Each combination of dyads will produce a distinct bip, except for a+b+f, which will produce the same bip as e+f+b, and except for c+d+a, which will produce the same bip as c+d+e. The reason, in both cases, is that a = e. This, of course, is only a partial explanation. A complete explanation of the basis of reduction for 4-element sets, as well as for sets of other cardinalities, would require a more complicated formal apparatus. The main point is that the number as well as the types of bips is not an obvious property of the total interval content of a pc set, but is determined by the pc structure of the set as it imposes restrictions on the formation of linear intervallic successions.

73. Counts of basic interval-patterns*

Pc sets of cardinal 4

    3: 4-28
    4: 4-24
    6: 4-1, 4-6, 4-9, 4-19, 4-21, 4-23, 4-25
    8: 4-2, 4-3, 4-7, 4-8, 4-10, 4-17, 4-20, 4-22, 4-26
  10: 4-4, 4-5, 4-11, 4-12, 4-13, 4-14, 4-16, 4-18, 4-27
  12: 4-Z15, 4-Z29

Pc sets of cardinal 5

  11: 5-33
  18: 5-1, 5-35
  22: 5-8, 5-Z17, 5-21, 5-22, 5-34, 5-Z37
  26: 5-15
  27: 5-13, 5-26, 5-30
  28: 5-2, 5-Z12, 5-23, 5-31
  29: 5-7
  31: 5-11
  32: 5-Z36
  33: 5-3, 5-5, 5-14, 5-27
  34: 5-9, 5-24
  36: 5-4, 5-29
  38: 5-19, 5-28
  39: 5-Z18, 5-Z38
  40: 5-6, 5-10, 5-16, 5-20, 5-25, 5-32

Pc sets of cardinal 6†

  17: 6-35(a)
  37: 6-20(a)
  64: 6-1(a), 6-7(a), 6-32(a)
  72: 6-8(a)
  75: 6-21(i), 6-22(i), 6-34(i)
  78: 6-14(p)
  79: 6-Z37, 6-Z48
  80: 6-Z28
  82: 6-Z45
  93: 6-2(i), 6-33(i)
  95: 6-Z29, 6-Z42
  98: 6-Z6, 6-Z38
101: 6-Z19, 6-Z24, 6-30(i), 6-Z39, 6-Z44
103: 6-15(i), 6-31(i)
104: 6-Z4, 6-Z26
105: 6-16(i)
107: 6-9(i), 6-Z17, 6-Z36, 6-Z47
112: 6-Z10, 6-Z46
113: 6-Z13, 6-Z23, 6-27(i), 6-Z49, 6-Z50
116: 6-Z11, 6-Z40, 6-Z41
117: 6-Z12
118: 6-Z3, 6-Z25
125: 6-5(i), 6-18(i), 6-Z43

* In each case the number of bips is followed by a colon.
† The small letters in parentheses designate combinatorial properties as follows: a—all combinatorial, p—prime combinatorial, i—inversion combinatorial.

There is a considerable range of differences among pc sets with respect to melodic fecundity measured in terms of the number of bips associated with each. This information is summarized in the tables in example 73. Some comments on that illustration follow.

With regard to the 4-element sets it is hardly surprising to find that 4-28 has the smallest number of bips, 3. Most of the 4-element sets lie between the two extremes represented by 4-28 and the two all-interval tetrachords. From the standpoint of usage in the atonal repertory, it is interesting to observe that the group with 10 bips seems to be favored. Similarity relations among sets with the same number of bips are of some interest here. For instance, the group with 10 bips exhibits a large number of similarity relations, all of types R_1 and R_p.

The sets of cardinal 5, as might be expected, show a greater range of differences than the sets of cardinal 4 with respect to number of bips. Here at the top of the list, hence most meager, is 5-33, the "whole-tone" formation, while at the bottom we find a number of familiar sets, among them 5-10 (see Schoenberg's Op. 23/3, which uses only one of the 40 possible bips) and 5-32 (see Stravinsky, *The Rite of Spring*). Note also that whereas 5-Z18 and 5-Z38, a Z-related pair, have the same number of bips, 5-Z12 has 28 bips, while 5-Z36, its Z-correspondent, has 32. Here again we find a significant number of similarity relations among sets with the same number of bips. Those with 27 bips form a transitive triple for the relations R_1, R_p, and every set in the group with 40 bips is in R_1, R_p with at least one other set in the same group.

As for the hexachords, again we find the whole-tone formation at the top. At the bottom of the list, and therefore richest in melodic resources, are 6-5, 6-18, and 6-Z43, all multiply represented in the atonal repertory. It is interesting that only three pairs of Z-related hexachords are in the same group: 6-Z6/38, 6-Z19/44, and 6-Z11/40. The others vary with respect to number of bips. Notice, for instance, that 6-Z4 has 104 bips while 6-Z37 has only 79.

Similarity relations abound within the groups. For example, those with 75 bips comprise a transitive triple with respect to R_1, R_p. Those with 113 bips, excluding 6-27, comprise a transitive quadruple with respect to R_1, R_p and 6-27 is in R_2, R_p with every other set in the group.

As a matter of record, the special combinatorial properties are indicated in example 73.* The all-combinatorial hexachords preempt the first four positions in the list, a fact which reflects their very special attributes, while two of the three at the bottom of the list are inversion combinatorial. Among the singletons, notice 6-14, the unique prime combinatorial hexachord, and 6-Z12 (Schoenberg's Op. 19/6).

*As defined by Babbitt (1961). See also Martino 1961.

It was stated earlier that there are two fundamental questions concerning bips. We have dealt with the first of these, albeit somewhat perfunctorily. Although the second question will be bypassed, it may be of interest to discuss briefly an offshoot: given a particular bip, in how many ways can it be formed? This is equivalent to asking how many permutations correspond to a particular bip, and that number can be interpreted as an index of uniqueness.

Here again there is a wide range of differences within and among the pc sets. For instance, for pc set 6-20 the bip 13445 can be formed in 72 ways, while the bip 11133 can be formed in only 6 ways. As another example of extremes, in the case of pc set 6-21 the bip 12344 can be formed in 44 ways, whereas the bip 11222 can be formed in only 2 ways. There is, however, one fixed and perhaps obvious property of all these numbers: they must be even, since any permutation has a retrograde image that will yield the same bip.

A few concrete examples will provide some perspective. Two orderings of pc set 6-34 were shown in example 29. The first of these produces bip 22234, which can be formed in 10 ways, the second produces 12222, which can be formed in only 2 ways. Thus, the second ordering is more unique than the first. Both orderings are special if compared to the bip 23445, which can be formed in 44 ways.

Three orderings of pc set 5-Z18 are shown in example 70 producing bips 4456 (4 ways), 1456 (4 ways), and 1134 (2 ways). However, pc set 5-Z18 does not exhibit divergences as extreme as those of some of the other sets. For example, there are 24 other bips (of the total of 39) that can be formed in only 2 ways. We conclude that bip 1134 is not especially distinctive.

As a final example here, consider example 71, which shows pc set 6-Z13 and two bips: 11135 (8 ways) and 13346 (12 ways). Both patterns lie somewhere in the middle range with respect to uniqueness, since a number of bips can be formed in only 2 ways and several can be formed in as many as 16 ways.

74.   Stravinsky, Cantata (Ricercar No. 2)

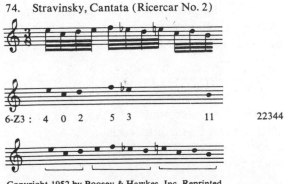

6-Z3 :   4   0   2   5   3   11   22344

The question of repeated pcs and order relations is a somewhat vexing one, and it is necessary to set some guidelines. Immediate repetition of a single pc or of a group of ordered pcs does not affect the order relations of the total sequence, since such repetitions merely comprise an interruption or enlargement of the complete pattern. With one exception, to be discussed below, all other repetitions of the non-consecutive type effect a segmentation. Specifically, if a repetition occurs at order position m, then a new segment begins at position m – 1. (As an instance of this see example 69, measure 1.) Thus, the sequence shown in example 74 does not lend itself to analysis as an ordered set, as that term is understood in the present discussion.* In order to be able to refer to the general basis and background of ordered sets it would be necessary to reduce the succession or to deal with its ordered subsets, as shown in example 74. Neither alternative seems plausible in this instance.

75. Berg, "Altenberg Lieder" Op. 4/3

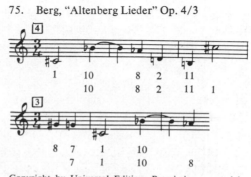

The exception regarding repeated pcs mentioned above occurs when the last pc of a sequence is the same as the first. This kind of repetition closes the sequence and effects an interlocking of identical patterns. In the language of permutations the result is a circular permutation. Example 75 shows an instance of such an ordered formation. Note that this exception might be construed as effecting a segmentation (from right to left) and therefore lose its status.

It must be emphasized that these restrictions on non-consecutive repeated pcs do not imply at all that a pitch sequence containing such repetitions cannot be examined in terms of order relations. As a final and quite extraordinary example of melodic structure and bips consider example 76.† This is an ex-

*See Babbitt 1964.
†Also discussed in Babbitt 1964.

76. Stravinsky, Three Songs from William Shakespeare (No. 1)

cerpt from the complete vocal line, which, in its entirety, is constructed in the manner indicated. A single tetrachord, pc set 4-2, forms the atomic component of the line. Successive disjunct forms of the set are indicated below the stave. Each of these has the same interval succession, [4-2-1]. Interlocking with these are the successions [1-2-4] indicated above the stave. Both, of course, reduce to bip 124. Corresponding to the change of stanza in the text is the change in interval succession to [2-1-1].

A great deal more could be said about order relations and about the melodic resources of pc sets as represented by bips. However, the scope of the present section is thought to be commensurate with the relevance of such relations to the repertory of atonal music.

1.15 The complement of a pc set

The set of 12 pitch-class integers comprises the universal set U, the set of all elements from which sets of cardinal number less than 12 are drawn. The selection of a set of n elements from U effectively divides or partitions U into two sets: the set of n elements selected and the set of 12 − n elements not selected. If, for example, M designates a set of 4 elements selected and N designates the remaining set of 8 elements not selected, then M is said to be

77. Webern, Four Songs Op. 12/4

A : [3,7,8,9]	(4-5)	$\overline{A}$=+(B,C)	(8-5)
B : [10,0,2,4]	(4-21)	$\overline{B}$=+(A,C)	(8-21)
C : [11,1,5,6]	(4-16)	$\overline{C}$=+(A,B)	(8-16)

the *complement* of N with respect to U and N is the complement of M with respect to U. These relations are written

$$M = \overline{N}$$
$$N = \overline{M}$$

and the reference to the universal set is understood, by convention.

The intuitive notion of complementation is uncomplicated and straightforward. The musical ramifications, however, are nontrivial and somewhat complex, as will be shown. This is especially the case for atonal music, where the complement relation plays a fundamental structural role.

To begin, let us return to a passage used as an illustration in a previous section and examine it for the complement relation. The component sets, designated A,B,C, comprise a partitioning of U, as shown in example 77. The complement of any one set is then formed by the union of the other two, as indicated. Of a number of additional observations that might be made, two will suffice. First, notice that the complement of 4-5 is 8-5, the complement of 4-21 is 8-21, and the complement of 4-16 is 8-16. The direct correspondence of ordinal numbers is due to the arrangement of the list of prime forms, and greatly facilitates reference to complementary pairs. Sets of cardinal 6 are an exception and will be discussed below. Second, this is an instance of complementation in a local context of short span.

78.   Schoenberg, Five Piano Pieces Op. 23/3

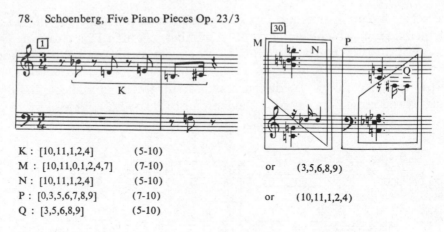

K :	[10,11,1,2,4]	(5-10)		
M :	[10,11,0,1,2,4,7]	(7-10)		
N :	[10,11,1,2,4]	(5-10)		
P :	[0,3,5,6,7,8,9]	(7-10)	or	(3,5,6,8,9)
Q :	[3,5,6,8,9]	(5-10)	or	(10,11,1,2,4)

In contrast to example 77, example 78 shows the complement relation in operation over a longer span of music. The first part of the example indicates the thematic figure K, which reduces to pc set 5-10. In the closing passage (measure 30) there occurs a development of that set and its complement 7-10. This consists of the two mosaic formations shown in the second part of example 78. The second of these, designated P, is the complement of K. Within P is the subset designated Q, which is pc set 5-10. Notice that Q and K share no pitch classes; the condition of minimal invariance is unique in this situation, for there is only one value of t which produces no invariants under inversion followed by transposition.* Let us now consider the formation designated M. This also reduces to pc set 7-10 and contains 5-10 (N). N in this case is the same as K, however.

The latter observation suggests a significant extension of the complement relation, one which is consistent with the definition of equivalent sets (sec. 1.2): if N is equivalent to K and M is the complement of N, then M must be equivalent to the complement of K. Thus, for the general case, given a set A we will designate as $\overline{A}$ any set reducible to the same prime form as $\overline{A}$. In short, we accept as the complement not only the literal pc complement, but also any transposition or any transposition of the inversion of the complement. Indeed, for example 78 the values of t indicate concisely the reciprocal relations underlying the two segments represented there. These are summarized below.

$$M = T(I(\overline{K}),7)$$
$$N = K = T(K,0)$$
$$P = \overline{K} = T(\overline{K},0)$$
$$Q = T(I(K),7)$$

When comparing a set with its complement it is necessary, of course, to perform the operation of complementation upon one of the sets and then to determine the prime form. For this purpose it is more convenient to use the least cardinal number. This is shown in example 78 where pc set 7-10 is represented in two ways: by its actual pc content enclosed in brackets in the usual way, and by the pc content of its complement (literal) put into normal order and enclosed in parentheses. The latter notation will occasionally be used as a convenient alternative in subsequent sections.

As a practical consequence of the complement relation it is never necessary, for purposes of set identification, to deal with sets of cardinal number greater than 6. To identify a set of cardinal 9, for example, one need only discover the three missing pc integers, determine their prime form, and consult the list of prime forms for cardinal 3.

In the course of the preceding discussion reference was made to conditions determining invariant subsets. This was done in order to indicate that the complement relation is not to be regarded as an isolated aspect of structure. On the contrary, the concepts of complementation, invariance, and inclusion are closely associated, and more comprehensive analytical-descriptive observa-

*See Perle 1968 for a discussion of other aspects of the passage from measure 30 to the end of the work.

tions will necessarily take their interaction into consideration. For example, one should not overlook the fact that in example 78 there is a subset held invariant between M and P, namely, [0,7]. This invariant subset appears to have some special significance since no transposition of 7-10 will yield fewer than 3 invariants and only one value of t applied to the inverted form produces exactly 2 invariants (which always form ic5).

79. Stravinsky, *The Rite of Spring*

(a)

7-32 : [7,8,10,11,1,3,4]   5-32 : [3,4,7,9,0]

(b)

Example 79 presents another instance of the complement relation over a longer span of music. Pc set 7-32, a fundamental structure in the composition, occurs at no. 13, the beginning of the "Augurs of Spring." Its transformed complement occurs later in the music at no. 121, at the beginning of "Evocation of the Ancestors." Evidently the connection between these two remote points was originally intended to be more literal, for the sketches of the "Evocation of the Ancestors"* begin with the music shown at (b).

A somewhat different situation is shown in example 80. At no. 14, pc set 7-16 is presented in the configuration shown. The transformed complement, 5-16, occurs at no. 47 and is a focal component of the subsequent passage,

*Sketchbook of *The Rite of Spring* (Stravinsky 1969, p. 73).

which completes the "Jeu du rapt." At 47 + 12, 5-16 is again stated, this time with the additional notes E and E-flat (strings, tremolo). As indicated in the example, these additional notes form 7-16. Notice that here, as in example 78, a set contains its complement. The significance of this relation for the general case will become evident as we proceed.

80. Stravinsky, *The Rite of Spring*

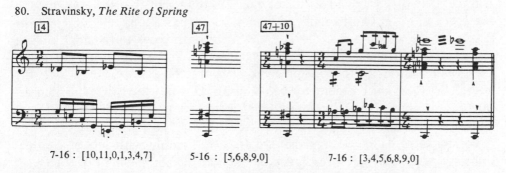

7-16 : [10,11,0,1,3,4,7]   5-16 : [5,6,8,9,0]   7-16 : [3,4,5,6,8,9,0]

The preceding examples suggest that the complement relation is an important structural feature over a broad range of non-tonal music. This is perhaps due to a particular property of the relation, which will now be examined. Here, again, the dichotomy of pitch class and interval class provides a useful perspective. Since the complement of a set may be transposed or inverted—thus affording a variety of pitch-class correspondences—it would appear that a more fundamental property, in the sense of an invariant correspondence, should be sought in the interval vector.

Compare, for example, the vectors of 5-35 and 7-35:

$$5\text{-}35 \ [032140]$$
$$7\text{-}35 \ [254361]$$

Observe that, with the exception of the entry for ic6, each entry in the vector of 7-35 is greater by exactly 2 than the corresponding entry in the vector of 5-35. This invariant correspondence, which might be described as a proportional regularity of interval-class distribution, is a general property of complement-related pc sets. To be more specific, the arithmetic difference of corresponding vector entries for complement-related sets is the same as the difference d of the cardinal numbers of the sets, with the exception of the entry for ic6, in which case d must be divided by 2 (since 6 is its own inverse mod 12).* As a practical consequence, given the vector of S, the vector of $\overline{S}$ can

*This extraordinary property was first documented by Milton Babbitt, with reference to the special case of 6-element sets.

easily be determined. For instance, given the vector of 4-Z15 add 4 to each entry from ic1 through ic5 and 2 to the entry for ic6, thus:

$$4\text{-}Z15 \quad [111111]$$
$$8\text{-}Z15 \quad [555553]$$

In view of this intervallic proportionality it seems reasonable to regard the complement of a set as a reduced or enlarged replica of that set. As shown in the previous examples the replication may occur over a long temporal span or it may occur within a small local context; in both cases a particular kind of structuring is effected. In addition, examples 78 and 80 illustrate still a further ramification of the complement relation, the situation in which the complement of a set is contained in the set. This indicates that the complement is a special subset (or superset) of a set. Some implications of this are considered below.

To simplify, let us assume that we are dealing only with sets of cardinal number greater than 6. Thus, it is possible that the complement of such a set could be a subset of that set. The following rather remarkable fact can then be recorded: with only one exception every set contains its complement at least one time.* Here, as elsewhere, the extrema are of interest. These are summarized below for sets of cardinal 7, 8, and 9.

Maxima	Minima
7-21 (6)	7-Z12 (0)
7-33 (6)	
8-19 (8)	8-28 (2)
9-5 (13)	9-1 (7)
9-8 (13)	9-6 (7)
	9-9 (7)

An instance of 8-19 is shown in example 81, at the close of the composition. The complement relation partially explains this otherwise enigmatic closing sonority, for 4-19 serves as "cadential harmony" elsewhere in the movement (in measures 7 and 14, not shown here). In order to dramatize the multiple representation of 4-19 in 8-19, example 81 displays in notation the 8 forms. Of these only one occurs in the previous music. The untransformed complement of 8-19:[2,3,6,10] occurs 4 times, however, which renders the pitch-class aspect of the complement relation more significant than it might otherwise be in this context.

In connection with example 81, it is also interesting to observe that the vertical formation at the beginning contains 4-19 only once. Thus, the two final notes, G-sharp and E, bring in 7 forms of 4-19.

*7-Z12 does not contain a subset 5-Z12; i.e., 5-Z12 cannot be mapped into 7-Z12 under inversion or transposition. See Forte 1964.

81. Stravinsky, Three Pieces for String Quartet (No. 3)

8-19 : [4,5,7,8,9,11,0,1]   4-19 subsets

[4,5,8,0]   [8,9,0,4]   [0,1,4,8]

[0,4,7,8]   [4,8,11,0]   [9,1,4,5]   [1,5,8,9]   [5,9,0,1]

Discussion of the complement relation in the case of hexachords has been avoided up to this point since it requires special treatment. Of the 50 6-element pc sets, 20 are self-complementary. For example, the complement of 6-1 is 6-1. In short, any hexachord not of the "Z" type (sec. 1.9) is its own complement. The complement of a Z-hexachord, however, is its Z-correspondent. For example, the complement of 6-Z3 is 6-Z36. This remarkable situation has a number of significant consequences for substructures of atonal music, one of which will be explained in the ensuing discussion. First, however, example 82 shows a passage from *Wozzeck* in which a Z-related pair of hexachords occurs in succession. In this instance the second hexachord is also the literal pitch-class complement of the first.

82. Berg, *Wozzeck* Op. 7
     act 3

6-Z17 : [0,1,2,4,7,8]

Marie: Wie der Mond roth auf - geht!

6-Z43 : [3,5,6,9,10,11]

Wozzeck: Wie ein blu-tig Ei - sen!

The notions of inclusion and invariance associate naturally with that of complementation, as was suggested earlier. Likewise, the similarity measures (sec. 1.13) take on a new dimension when combined with the complement relation. In particular, a general extension of the intervallic similarity measures can be made to any pair of sets whose cardinal numbers are inverse-related. According to the definitions of the intervallic similarity relations R_0, R_1 and R_2 given previously (sec. 1.13), for distinct sets S_1 and S_2 of the same cardinal number,

$$\text{if } R_i(S_1,S_2) \text{ then } R_i(\overline{S}_1,\overline{S}_2) \quad [i \text{ has the value } 0,1,2]$$

We observe that the second part of this expression is trivial in the case of cardinal number 6, and accordingly extend the definition of intervallic similarity measures to include sets with inverse-related cardinal numbers. Again, for distinct sets S_1 and S_2 of the same cardinal number,

$$\text{if } R_1(S_1,S_2) \text{ then } R_1(\overline{S}_1,S_2)$$

This extension permits comparison of sets, for instance, of cardinal numbers 7 and 5, as shown in example 83.

83.   Scriabin, *Two Poems* Op. 63/1

7-26 : [9,10,0,1,2,4,6]   7-26 : [0,1,3,4,5,7,9]   5-33 : [5,7,9,11,1]

In accord with the extended definition,

$$\text{since } R_0(5\text{-}26,5\text{-}33) \text{ then } R_0(7\text{-}26,5\text{-}33)$$

With respect to intervallic distribution over the three phrases shown in example 83, the first two are equivalent, while the last represents maximum differentiation compared with its predecessors.

A somewhat more complex situation can be seen in example 84. Four of the sets are interrelated by R_1 or R_2, as summarized below.

$$R_2(5\text{-}Z38,5\text{-}16)$$
$$R_2(5\text{-}Z38,7\text{-}32)$$
$$R_1(5\text{-}16,7\text{-}32)$$

84. Stravinsky, *Three Poems* (No. 2)

5-Z38 : [1,2,3,6,9]   6-Z36 : [0,1,2,3,4,7]

5-16 : [5,6,8,9,0]   5-Z38 : [1,2,3,6,9]   8-13 : [7,9,10,0,1,2,3,4]   7-31 : [9,10,0,1,3,4,6]

A 7-32 : [0,1,3,5,6,8,9]   B 7-32 : [6,7,9,11,0,2,3] C 7-32 : [3,4,6,8,9,11,0]

Pc set 7-31 has no R_1 or R_2 relations whatsoever, and its occurrence here has to do with the composition as a whole: it is the first and last compositional set in the work. In passing it should be remarked that 5-31 occurs three times as a subset of 7-32—more than any other subset of 7-32.

The three successive occurrences of 7-32 in example 84 deserve mention here since they involve inverse-related values of t and maximum invariance.*

	Invariants	
B = T(A,6)	[0, 3, 6, 9]	4-28
C = T(B,9)	[3, 6, 9, 11, 0]	5-31
C = T(A,3)	[0, 3, 6, 8, 9]	5-31

*An editorial correction has been gratuitously supplied by the present author in the final measure of example 84, viz., the sharp sign above D. Otherwise the pc set is 7-34, which has no contextual significance.

Observe that the invariant subset produced by the inverse-related values of t is 5-31, the complement of the initial and terminal sets in the composition, as remarked above.

Perhaps the most interesting as well as strongest association of complementation and invariance is to be seen in those few cases in which a pc set is capable of holding its complement invariant under transposition or inversion (or both) for one or more values of t. These are summarized in example 85.

Some aspects of example 85 will now be familiar to the reader. For instance, under transposition alone the values of t are always inverse-related. And in the case of cardinal 6 the invariant subset is improper. Indeed, this would always be so unless a pair of Z-related hexachords were involved, and that circumstance is impossible, as we know.

It should be pointed out that of the sets that hold their complements invariant under inversion followed by transposition all are all combinatorial except for 8-6 and 7-8.*

85.   Pc sets which hold the complementary subset invariant

Under transposition		Under inversion	
8-1	4, 8	8-1	3, 11
8-6	4, 8	8-6	0, 4
8-9	2, 10, 4, 8	8-9	1, 11, 5, 7
8-10	4, 8	8-10	1, 5
8-13	4, 8	8-23	7, 11
8-23	4, 8	8-28	0, 3, 6, 9, 2, 5, 8, 11
8-28	1, 11, 2, 10, 4, 8, 5, 7	7-1	4, 8
7-1	2, 10	7-8	6, 10
7-2	2, 10	7-22	6, 10
7-4	1, 11	7-34	2, 6
7-7	1, 5, 7, 11	7-35	4, 8
7-8	2, 10	6-1	6
7-9	2, 10	6-7	2, 8
7-13	4, 8	6-8	7
7-22	4, 8	6-20	1, 5, 9
7-23	2, 10	6-32	9
7-24	2, 10	6-35	0, 2, 4, 6, 8, 10
7-26	4, 8		
7-29	5, 7		
7-30	4, 8		
7-34	2, 10		
7-35	2, 10		
6-7	6		
6-20	4, 8		
6-30	6		
6-35	2, 4, 6, 8, 10		

*See Martino 1961.

This brief section has endeavored to demonstrate the important role played by the complement relation in structuring music over both short and long time-spans. The natural association of complementation with invariance, inclusion, and intervallic similarity has also been indicated. The association of complementation with inclusion is of special significance, and the reader's attention is drawn to three examples in which the complement is explicitly "embedded": example 78 (Schoenberg), example 80 (Stravinsky), and example 81 (Stravinsky). These point to the concept of the set complex, which is to be developed in Part 2.

1.16 Segmentation

In Part 2 the notion of pc sets and relations will be given considerably greater scope through the concept of the set complex. Before taking this step, which will involve some systematic abstractions, it is necessary to give attention to a fundamental and more immediate analytical process, the process of *segmentation.* By segmentation is meant the procedure of determining which musical units of a composition are to be regarded as analytical objects. Whereas this process is seldom problematic in tonal music, due to the presence of familiar morphological formations (harmonies, contrapuntal substructures, and the like), it often entails difficulties in the case of an atonal work. The purpose of the present section therefore is to set forth some procedural guidelines and to illustrate some basic types of segments that the analyst should take into account.

For the purpose of the present discussion the term *primary segment* will be used to designate a configuration that is isolated as a unit by conventional means, such as a rhythmically distinct melodic figure. For the most part such segments are indicated by some notational feature, for example, by a rest or beamed group, and offer no novel problems. Similarly, chords, in the sense of vertical groupings, and ostinato patterns are not difficult to identify as primary segments. There is no need to illustrate these familiar events here.

As suggested in the foregoing, the main problems in determining segments arise in those situations in which notational or other clues do not adequately reveal structural components. The general neglect of this problem area is probably due to a widespread, but unstated, assumption that atonal music is structured, if at all, only at the most obvious surface level. It is hoped that the present discourse will show that assumption to be untenable as well as unfruitful.*

One segmentation procedure that is often productive may be described as *imbrication*: the systematic (sequential) extraction of subcomponents of

---

* Schoenberg's music is especially refractory, since his segmentation methods are "concealed" to a large extent. See Forte 1972.

some configuration.* An instance of linear imbrication is shown in example 86.

86.   Schoenberg, "Lied ohne Worte" from Serenade Op. 24

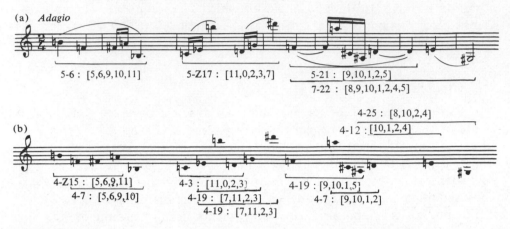

By permission from Wilhelm Hansen, Musik-Forlag, Copenhagen.

At (a) the long melodic line has been divided into segments on the basis of slurred groups of notes and rhythmic patterns. At (b) the results of a systematic imbrication are shown. In this case subsets of cardinal 4 have been extracted, moving sequentially from left to right. (Cf. ex. 76.) Now, whether this technique provides useful information about the music in this case is a question that cannot be answered without reference to other components not shown here. In short, this is merely an illustration of what is essentially a pre-analytical technique.

Imbrication represents an elementary way of determining the subsegments of a primary segment. Also of potential interest are segments that are formed by the interaction of more than one primary segment. These will be called *composite segments.* A composite segment is a segment formed by segments or subsegments that are contiguous or that are otherwise linked in some way. Like other segments a composite segment has a beginning and an end, both of which may be determined in several ways—for example, by an instrumental attack or by a rest.

As an initial example of a composite segment, consider example 87.† While

---

*See Gilbert 1970 for a detailed and systematic treatment of imbrication, with emphasis on trichordal subsegments.

†In fact, composite segments have been used in the illustration of previous technical material. See, for instance, examples 7, 13, 19, 21, 23.

87.   Schoenberg, Five Pieces for Orchestra Op. 16/1

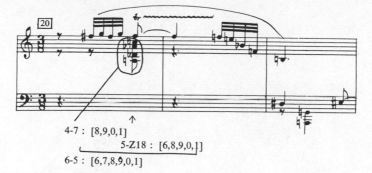

4-7 : [8,9,0,1]

5-Z18 : [6,8,9,0,1]

6-5 : [6,7,8,9,0,1]

the primary segments are easily recognized, an additional step is required in
order to obtain the composite segment consisting of the first two notes of
the melody and the accompanying chord. Since the set thus formed is equivalent to that formed by the upper voice taken alone it may be assumed to be
of significance.

We will now examine one excerpt from a long work and one short work
from the standpoint of segmentation procedures. These compositions are
quite dissimilar in style, texture, and so on, and the segmentations differ
correspondingly.

The first sample is drawn from the "Procession of the Oldest and Wisest"
(Cortège du sage) part of Stravinsky's *The Rite of Spring*, a complicated
passage employing the full resources of the orchestra. Example 88 provides
a condensed score from which the percussion has been omitted. In the interest of graphic clarity the instrumentation is only partially indicated.

The main linear components are displayed separately in example 89. Of
these, the principal melodic-thematic element is the tuba line, and the set
which it forms is, as shown, 5-Z36. Accompanying the tuba line are the lines
marked Vn.1 and Tpt. The illustration thus summarizes in sketch fashion the
interaction of those melodic components. The groupings indicated by brackets
are not arbitrary, but are determined by repeated patterns in the accompanying lines. As a result of these groupings three large sets are formed. The last
of these, pc set 10-3, would probably be omitted from consideration in a
complete analysis, but the other two are significant. Pc set 9-11 and its complement play important roles in the work as a whole, and 4-3 appears to be
at least of local significance since it is embedded in its complement. Considered separately, the two accompanying lines form segments and sets as
shown at (b) in example 89. In particular 6-Z28 is interesting since it occurs

88. Stravinsky, *The Rite of Spring*

elsewhere in the work and has an important role in the last movement ("Sacrificial Dance") together with its complement.

89.   Linear components of example 88

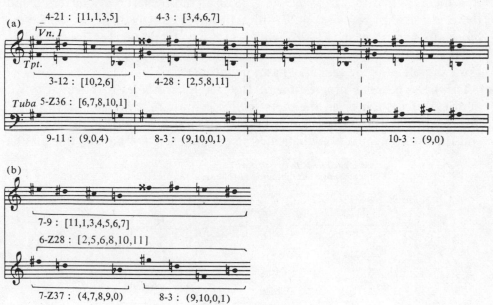

Segments formed by the remaining two combinations of these three lines yield additional sets that should be taken into account in a complete segmentation, but which need not be discussed here. Instead, let us examine some additional segment-types represented in the Stravinsky excerpt.

The part marked Ob. in example 88 consists of nine tetrachords, representing types 4-25 and 4-9, as shown in example 90. This component combines with the theme (tuba) in the following way: whenever the focal note of the theme, G-sharp, occurs it forms pc set 5-28 with one of the tetrachords of type 4-25. Otherwise the Ob. part blends with the metrical succession of segments to which we now direct attention.

90.

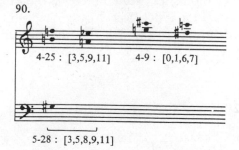

One of the more obvious features of this section is the dyad G-sharp-D in the lower register which is repeated on each quarter note. This fixed element suggests that ic6 is of special importance in the music, and indeed it is. If we examine the string parts alone on each quarter note of the first measure it is apparent that they carry pc set 4-28 on all but the last two quarters, where there is a change to pc set 4-27. In addition, each pair of pc set 4-28 combines to form (trivially) 8-28, while each pair of pc set 4-27 combines to form 8-18. Pc set 4-18 is a fundamental tetrachord in *The Rite of Spring*. For example, it is the cadential harmony at 58+5.

The homogeneous progression of the string harmonies is reflected in the metrical succession of all the parts—which is quite remarkable in view of the diverse linear components shown in example 89. This metrical segmentation and the resulting pc sets are indicated in example 91. On all but one of the

91.   Stravinsky, *The Rite of Spring*
       Vertical composite segments at rehearsal number 70

m.1:
        5 - 31   6 - 30   6 - 30   6 - 27   5 - 31   6 - 30
             8 - 28   8 - 28   9 - 10

m.2:
        7 - Z38   7 - 31   6 - 27   6 - 30   6 - 30   6 - Z28
             8 - 18   8 - 28   9 - 10

m.3:
        5 - 31   7 - 28   7 - Z38   8 - 12   (5 - 31   6 - 30)
             8 - 28   12 - 1   (8 - 28)

quarter notes the vertical segments form sets of cardinals 5, 6, or 7. Notice the complementary pair 5-31/7-31 and the occurrence of 6-Z28 and 7-28 among these, sets also formed by the composite segments displayed in example 89 and example 90. On the half notes sets of cardinals 8 or 9 are formed—8-28 and 8-18 again—with the exception of the 12-note set on beats 3 and 4 of the last measure. This is due to the 8-note set on beat 4, which serves to accent the end of the phrase in the tuba line. Beats 5 and 6 of the last measure begin the repetition. Notice that although the sets are the same as those formed on beats 1 and 2 of the first measure the string parts are distributed differently.

92.

6-Z28 : [2,5,6,8,10,11]

Example 92 provides a final demonstration of the extent to which the passage is structured. The component marked Tpt. in example 88 forms, in fact, an independent and significant set, 6-Z28, as shown.

To sum up, two basic types of composite segments were illustrated by the foregoing examples: combinations of primary linear segments and vertical groupings through the entire texture. Segments of the latter type may not always be significant, but in this case they appear to be so because of the correspondences between horizontal and vertical formations.

93.   Webern, Five Pieces for Orchestra Op. 10/4

Although at first glance the short Webern composition in example 93 seems to be simpler than the Stravinsky excerpt it offers some problems with respect to segmentation. It is not difficult, however, to identify the primary segments, and subsegments of those, as shown in example 93. A word of explanation is in order here concerning the A section. Pc sets 4-7 and 3-4, as subsegments of the initial melodic configuration 6-16, are determined by rhythmic pattern, whereas the two 5-element subsegments are not. The latter are justified contextually, as will be evident in the sequel.

The next step is to determine the composite segments. Since the composition divides into three sections, separated by rests in all parts, we begin by determining the entire pc content of each section. Additional composite segments are then determined by the systematic adjoining of pitches from left to right (imbrication) as well as by grouping according to cues provided by the primary segments. For example, the slurred group E-flat-D played by the trumpet in measure 2 signals the beginning of a composite segment whose pc content is 5-20. Another occurrence of this set has already been shown in example 93 with the first five notes of the melodic line, mentioned above.

Similarly, the composite segment determined by the last five notes of C yields a pc set (5-6) of the same type as the last five notes of the opening melodic line. The complete results of this step are shown in example 94.

94. Composite segments

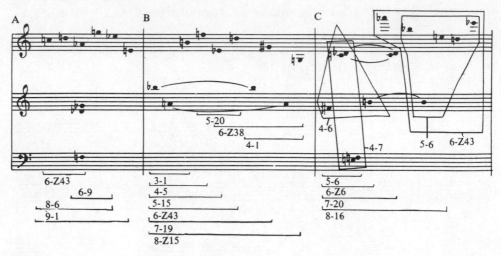

Although the question of contextual criteria for segment determination will be discussed more fully below, it might be pointed out here that a systematic segmentation procedure such as that outlined above may often produce units that are of no consequence with respect to structure, and therefore that editing may be required. For example, in section C of this composition a total of 22 non-duplicative segments are determined by attacks and releases involving rests.

The Webern composition under consideration here provides an opportunity to point out a basic type of composite segment. As a rule a composite segment will not extend across a vertical rest—that is, a silence in all parts. This does not mean, however, that some elements of a composite segment may not be separated by rests. As an instance, observe the segment in section B, with pc content 6-Z38. The dyad E-flat-D is separated from the dyad G-sharp-G by rests, yet they are linked together by B-flat-A, and the three dyads combine to form a composite segment.

The complete segmentation of the Webern composition yields a total of 21 pc set names. Some sets are represented more than once within a section—as 3-4 in A and 5-6 in C—and some sets occur in more than one section.

Only one set occurs in all three sections: 6-Z43.* An additional regularity is seen in the complement-related pairs, of which there are four. Notice, for example, that 6-Z38 in B is followed by its complement 6-Z6 in C, thus affording an immediate structural link between the two sections. Nevertheless, there are some apparent anomalies, such as pc set 4-12 in B, which has no counterpart elsewhere in the music. The significance of the large sets of 8 and 9 elements is also not immediately evident.

From the two samples that have been discussed it can be inferred that a general result of the segmentation process is a temporal stratification or layering in which some constituents are over (or under) others, while still others may intersect in some common subsegment. In a very specific sense, the amount of stratification provides a measure of the complexity of a particular work or passage. And in the determination of composite segments we find a natural analogy to the set-theoretic operations of union and intersection over pc sets.

During the foregoing presentation several references have been made to *contextual* criteria for segment determination. The term contextual here is intended to cover decisions concerning segmentation which involve references to the local context of the candidate segment or which involve references to non-local sections of the music. It seems virtually impossible to systematize these in any useful way. Certainly, however, recurrence is a commonly invoked criterion. If a particular segment forms a set that is represented elsewhere in the music, it is probably a legitimate structural component. On the other hand, a segment that forms a set that occurs only once may have its own *raison d'être*.

Since the largest context to which reference can be made is that provided by the entire composition being analyzed, the sets and relations which it unfolds provide variable contextual criteria that may be used to refine the segmentation process. As sets are identified and relations are revealed, it is usually not difficult to make judgments concerning significance. The most effec-

95.   Schoenberg, Three Piano Pieces Op. 11/2

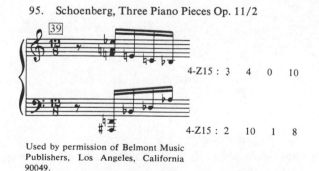

4-Z15 : 3   4   0   10

4-Z15 : 2   10   1   8

Used by permission of Belmont Music
Publishers, Los Angeles, California
90049.

*The reader may wish to satisfy himself that 5-15 in B and 5-15 in C have the same bip.

tive basis for these judgments is provided by set-complex relations (to be set forth in Part 2). These relations, properly interpreted, will often point out sets of lesser significance which would be more correctly replaced by a super-set or further decomposed into component subsets. Judgments of this kind will be amply demonstrated in the analyses presented in sections 2.7 and 2.8.

As a final comment on the matter of contextual criteria, it should be said that knowledge of a particular composer's way of composing (as distinct from familiarity with some superficial aspects of style) provides guides for segment determination. For instance, Schoenberg often conceals the main structural components of his music behind primary configurations. In example 95, for instance, two transpositionally equivalent forms of pc set 4–Z15 are juxtaposed in a way that is not immediately obvious.

96.   Schoenberg, Three Piano Pieces Op. 11/2

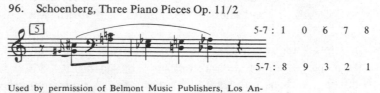

5-7 : 1   0   6   7   8

5-7 : 8   9   3   2   1

A similar, but perhaps more transparent, situation is shown in example 96, where two inversionally equivalent forms of pc set 5–7 are unfolded simultaneously. In contrast, Stravinsky rarely does this, and the themes and harmonies at the surface level of the music interact to form other levels of structure. More sophisticated techniques of segmentation will reveal more about the music in both cases, however. Even an apparently simple melodic structure such as that shown in example 97 exhibits a more intricate and unifying substructure just below the surface level.

97.   Stravinsky, Symphonies of Wind Instruments

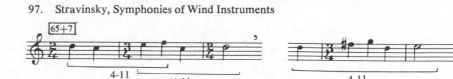

4-11   4-11   4-11

Perhaps the most important aspect of segmentation introduced in the present section is that having to do with large composite segments. Such segments are of considerable import and open a dimension of structure that is believed to have been totally disregarded in studies of atonal music.

2 Pitch-Class Set Complexes

2.0 Introduction

In the sections of Part 2 that follow, the concepts introduced in Part 1 will be brought within the purview of the set complex, which provides a comprehensive model of relations among pc sets in general and establishes a framework for the description, interpretation, and explanation of any atonal composition.*

The earlier sections necessarily deal with some abstract materials in an effort to construct an adequate and—it is hoped—lucid framework for the analytical applications made in the final two sections.

As will be shown, the set-complex model has a number of interesting and novel implications for many aspects of structure, not the least of which is form. It is impossible to explore all of those implications fully in the present context, and in that sense all of Part 2 may be regarded as merely an introduction to the universe of set complexes.

2.1 The set complex K

The notion of a set complex can be approached directly and conveniently by way of a musical example (ex. 98).

98. Webern, Five Movements for String Quartet Op. 5/4

6-5 : [11,0,3,4,5,6]

As indicated by the vertical arrow, the pc set sounding at the end of the passage is 6-5. Every pitch class stated in the music up to that point is represented in that final set. That is to say, every set stated previously is contained in the final set.

From example 98 it might be assumed that the set complex is associated with the inclusion relation (sec. 1.10) and, indeed, that is the case. However,

---

*The notion of the set complex was first introduced by the author in 1964. The present treatment includes a large number of refinements and extensions. See Forte 1964.

the concept of the set complex is dependent, in addition, upon the complement relation. The following discussion develops the necessary general aspects.

99.   Complementation and inclusion

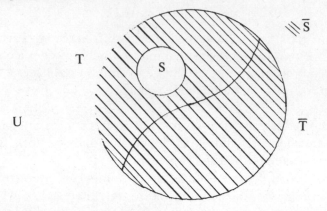

The complement relation is associated with the inclusion relation in the following specific sense. Consider two sets, S and T, where S is a subset of T. This being the case, then the complement of T is a subset of the complement of S. In conventional notation this is written as follows:

$$S \subset T \text{ iff } \overline{T} \subset \overline{S}$$

It is not difficult to prove this for the general case, and the diagram in example 99 will suffice to indicate the structural situation. There the large circle delimits the universal set of 12 pitch-classes, and the curved line partitions the space into T and $\overline{T}$. $\overline{S}$ is then represented by the area not in S, and $\overline{T}$ is clearly a subset of $\overline{S}$.

It is this natural association of inclusion and complementation that provides the basis for the set complex. This aggregate is designated $K(T,\overline{T})$ in full notation, but since the specific name of $\overline{T}$ can be determined from T (with the exception of the Z-related hexachords) the shorter notation $K(T)$ will usually suffice. This is read "the complex about T." In the formal definitions that follow, the symbol # designates cardinal number. For example, # (X) is read "the cardinal number of (the set) X." Logical *or* is represented by | and is to be construed as inclusive, unless indicated otherwise. Logical *and* is represented by &. The Greek letter ϵ (epsilon) stands for "is a member of." Thus, $S \epsilon K(T)$ signifies that S is a member of the set complex about T. The formal definition of set-complex membership follows.

Preliminary conditions on # (S) and # (T):

1. $2 < \#(S) < 10 \ \& \ 2 < \#(T) < 10$
2. $\#(S) \neq \#(T) \ \& \ \#(S) \neq \#(\overline{T})$

Then,

$$S/\overline{S} \; \epsilon \; K(T,\overline{T}) \; \text{ iff } \; S \supset\subset T \; | \; S \supset\subset \overline{T}$$

The compound symbol $\supset\subset$ is read "can contain or can be contained in." $S/\overline{S}$ is read "S and its complement."

Some comments on the definition may be useful. First, and perhaps obviously, the relation determined by the definition of set-complex membership is symmetric. And whereas condition 1 above is arbitrary (simply omitting sets of cardinal 2 and 10 from the set complex), condition 2 is a logical extension of the condition which is necessary for sets of cardinal 6 to sets of the remaining cardinalities (3,9,4,8,5,7), therefore rendering the definition general.

The condition attached to the inclusion relation here, "can contain or can be contained in," is important since otherwise there would be a contradiction of ordinary set-theoretic definitions in subsequent formal expressions. This condition effectively brings into play the transformations *transposition* and *inversion*. A simple example will perhaps clarify. Suppose we have two pc sets, as follows:

8-18: [0,1,2,3,5,6,8,9]
7-3: [0,1,2,3,4,5,8]

We wish to determine if 7-3/5-3 ϵ K(8-18, 4-18). The reader can verify for himself that 7-3 cannot be contained in 8-18—that is, it cannot be mapped into 8-18 under transposition or inversion for any value of t. However, the complement of 8-18 maps into 7-3 under inversion with t = 0:

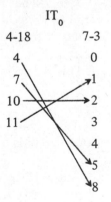

Here we have taken the literal complement of 8-18, but this is not necessary, of course. Any form of 4-18 can be mapped into any form of 7-3. Similarly, 5-3 can be mapped into 8-18:

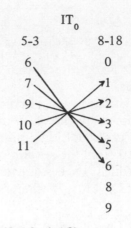

And therefore 7-3/5-3 ϵ K(8-18, 4-18).

2.2   The subcomplex Kh

In many cases the rule of set-complex membership yields aggregates of considerable size. For instance, K(3-1) contains 94 sets. This suggests that analysis in terms of K-structure may sometimes require additional refinement of the set-complex concept in order to provide significant distinctions among compositional sets. Examination of a particular composition, for example, might yield the information that every 4-element set represented in the work belongs to K(3-2). Yet K(3-2) is but one of seven set complexes about sets of cardinal 3 which contain *all* 4-element sets.

Further difficulty may be foreseen in the possible absence of what will be called the *reciprocal complement relation*. As an example of this consider the fact that while 3-1 ϵ K(8-3), 3-1 $\not\subset$ 4-3. That is, the set-complex relation between 3-1 and 8-3 does not extend to the complement of either set, and the relation therefore lacks completeness with respect to the universal set, as represented by the complement relation. Reduction to a useful and significant subcomplex is evidently needed. This is provided by the following definition of the subcomplex Kh.*

$$S/\overline{S} \ \epsilon \ Kh(T,\overline{T}) \ \text{i f f} \ S \supset\subset T \ \& \ S \supset\subset \overline{T}$$

The reader will undoubtedly notice that this definition differs from the definition of K only with respect to &.

From the previous discussion it should be evident that this definition produces 4 relations for any S and T that satisfy it, because

$$S \subset T \ \& \ S \subset \overline{T} \ \text{i f f} \ \overline{T} \subset \overline{S} \ \& \ T \subset \overline{S}$$

---

*The letter h has no special significance, but merely serves to identify this particular subcomplex.

This is what is meant by the *reciprocal complement relation.* To give a specific example,

$$3\text{-}1 \subset 4\text{-}1 \ \& \ 3\text{-}1 \subset 8\text{-}1$$
$$\text{hence} \ \ 8\text{-}1 \subset 9\text{-}1 \ \& \ 4\text{-}1 \subset 9\text{-}1$$

The relation Kh is symmetric, of course, as is evident from the reciprocal complement relation.

At this juncture the reader's attention is directed to appendix 3, which contains the lists of the subcomplexes Kh. Observe that the reciprocal complement relation permits the complexes to be displayed concisely. Just as $\overline{S}$ is implied whenever the set S heads a list, so the appearance of any name T as a member of the complex about S implies that $\overline{T}$ is also a member of that complex. For convenience, however, the names of Z-related hexachords are given in full.

100.   Schoenberg, Six Short Piano Pieces Op. 19/6

101. Schoenberg, Six Short Piano Pieces Op. 19/6
Set-complex relations

	9-4	3-7	3-9	8-1	4-4	8-Z15	4-23	7-4	7-5	7-6	7-Z12	7-24	7-28
8-1	K	K	K										
4-4	Kh	Kh	K										
8-Z15	K	Kh	K										
4-23	K	Kh	Kh										
7-4	Kh	Kh	K	Kh	Kh	K							
7-5	Kh	K	Kh	Kh	K	K	K						
7-6	Kh	Kh	K	K	Kh	Kh							
7-Z12	Kh	Kh	K	K	K	K	K						
7-24	Kh	Kh	Kh	K	K	K							
7-28	K	Kh	K			Kh							
6-Z12	Kh	Kh	Kh	K*	K	Kh	K	K*	K*		K	K	K*
6-22	Kh	Kh	Kh			Kh						Kh	
6-34	Kh	Kh	Kh			Kh						Kh	Kh

* The asterisk attached to K indicates that the inclusion relation holds. This is used in case of a single Z-type hexachord.

102. Pc sets 3-7 and 3-9 in 5-24 and 7-24

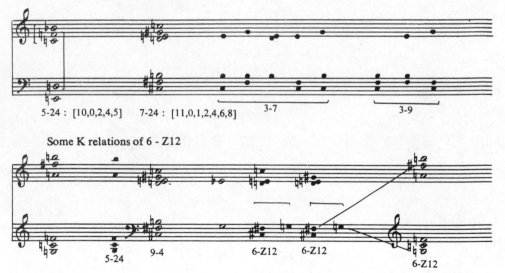

5-24 : [10,0,2,4,5]   7-24 : [11,0,1,2,4,6,8]   3-7   3-9

Some K relations of 6 - Z12

5-24   9-4   6-Z12   6-Z12   6-Z12

103. Set-complex sizes (Kh)

Cardinal 3

20	40	43	44	62	63	64
3-12	3-1	3-6	3-10	3-3	3-2	3-8
	3-9			3-4	3-7	
				3-5		
				3-11		

Cardinal 4

4	8	10	12	13
4-28	4-9	4-25	4-1	4-8

14	20	24	25	26
4-3	4-19	4-4	4-2	4-5
4-6		4-14	4-12	4-11
4-7		4-18	4-13	4-Z15
4-10			4-22	4-16
4-17			4-27	4-Z29
4-20				
4-21				
4-24				
4-26				

Cardinal 5

7	9	10	11	13
5-Z12	5-1	5-15	5-8	5-6
	5-35	5-Z17	5-34	5-10
		5-22		5-16
		5-33		5-20
		5-Z37		5-25
				5-32

14	15	16	17	18
5-3	5-2	5-4	5-9	5-13
5-5	5-Z18	5-11	5-24	5-26
5-7	5-19	5-29		5-30
5-14	5-23			
5-21	5-28			
5-27	5-Z36			
5-31	5-Z38			

cont'd.

Cardinal 6

7	9	10	11	13	15	16	17
6-35	6-20	6-Z4/37	6-Z6/38	6-7	6-Z10/39	6-1	6-Z3/36
		6-Z13/42			6-Z19/44	6-Z12/41	6-Z25/47
		6-Z23/45			6-Z24/46	6-Z17/43	
		6-Z26/48				6-32	
		6-Z29/49					
		6-Z29/50					

19	20	21	23	26	28	31	30
6-30	6-8	6-Z11/40	6-27	6-2	6-21	6-5	6-15
				6-14	6-22	6-9	6-16
				6-33	6-34	6-18	6-31

Before continuing with a discussion of some of the important general (and abstract) aspects of set complexes, it seems appropriate to demonstrate some of the concepts introduced thus far by examining in terms of K and Kh a composition from the atonal repertory. This also provides an opportunity to introduce some convenient graphic means for displaying set-complex relations.

Example 101 is a table that shows the relations K and Kh for the sets indicated in example 100. The stepped shape of the table reflects the fact that sets of the same or inverse-related cardinal number are not compared. Thus, for example, to read the relations for 8-1, proceed left to right across the row to the end, then continue with the column labeled 8-1. The entry at the intersection of any column and row gives the relation between the sets named at the head of that column and row. An empty entry signifies that the sets are neither in K nor in Kh. (Obviously, S ϵ Kh(T) implies S ϵ K(T)).

From the table it is evident that 5 sets are in the relation K to all (possible) others: 9-4, 3-7, 3-9, 8-Z15, and 7-24. The complement of only one of these, 7-24, is represented as a segment, however, and therefore reciprocal complement relations are of minimal significance in the piece. Example 102 shows occurrences of 3-7 and 3-9, the prominent trichords in the work, in 5-24 and in 7-24. The 5 occurrences of 3-7 in 7-24 are exceeded only by 6 occurrences of 3-8 (which is not a compositional component here).

Pc set 6-Z12, which is a kind of motto for the composition, is in the relation K to all but one other set. Example 102 displays some of these relations. Note especially the motive F-sharp–G in the two forms of 6-Z12 in 9-4 (measure 8), which remains invariant in the subsequent statement of the motto.

2.3 Set-Complex sizes

An interesting and important property of a set complex is its size. There is, in fact, a considerable range of sizes, as can be seen in the counts summarized in example 103.

Before commenting on these, it is appropriate to introduce a useful term, the term *nexus set*. Prior to this, statements such as $S/\overline{S} \in Kh(T,\overline{T})$ have been used. We will now refer to T (or, alternatively, to $\overline{T}$) as the nexus set and say that S and $\overline{S}$ belong to the set complex *about* T. Exactly 114 sets qualify as nexus sets.

Returning now to example 103, notice that the largest Kh is that about 3-8, while the smallest is that about 4-28. As remarked several times before, pc set 4-28 and its complement 8-28 are sets with special attributes. Pc set 5-Z12 is likewise a set with special characteristics, and it is not surprising to find it as the nexus set of the smallest Kh among the nexus sets of cardinal 5. It is, however, surprising that Kh (5-Z12) is the only set complex entirely lacking in hexachords.

For nexus sets of cardinal 5 and cardinal 6 maximum size is attained by three set complexes in each case. With the possible exception of 5-26, all these nexus sets are exclusively characteristic of the atonal repertory.

It will be seen that several of the Z-related pairs are nexus sets of the smaller Kh and that none occupy the higher positions on the list. In all cases the size of a Z-hexachord complex is radically affected by the reduction from K to Kh, due to the requirement symbolized by the logical operator &.

Since correspondences among various general structural features are always welcome, one would hope to find some in the case of Kh sizes. Unfortunately, however, there is no simple correspondence between, for example, the size of a Kh and the number of bips associated with its nexus set, nor is there a simple correspondence between the size of a Kh and the combinatorial properties of its nexus set.

2.4 The closure property

We know, of course, that the set-complex relation holds between every component of the set complex and the nexus set. This section is concerned with the set-complex relations within the set complex, among its components. This is of interest because if every member of some set complex were in the set-complex relation with every other member, that set complex would be a self-contained and highly structured unit. If the members of some set complex are only in the set-complex relation to the nexus set and there are no internal set-complex relations, then that set complex is effectively isolated from other set complexes. The property under consideration here will be called the *closure property*.

The question of closure can be formulated in terms of transitivity. We wish to determine the truth of the following assertion:

$$\text{If } A \in Kh(B) \ \& \ B \in Kh(C) \text{ then } A \in Kh(C)$$

In accord with the symmetric property, the foregoing can be rewritten as follows:

$$\text{If } A \in Kh(B) \ \& \ C \in Kh(B) \text{ then } A \in Kh(C)$$

In case this is not true, we may then wish to know whether the closure property holds for K, that is,

$$\text{If } A \in Kh(B) \ \& \ C \in Kh(B) \text{ then } A \in K(C)$$

In considering these questions it will be convenient to deal only with the least cardinal numbers of nexus sets and components. Also it is necessary to recall that the inclusion relation is transitive:

$$\text{If } X \subset Y \ \& \ Y \subset Z \text{ then } X \subset Z$$

Now, let us consider first an arbitrary set complex about a nexus set T of cardinal 3. For every $S \in Kh(T)$, the following inclusions determine membership:

$$S \supset T \ \& \ S \subset \overline{T}$$

This is obviously because the possible cardinal numbers of S are 4, 5, and 6, as stipulated above. Accordingly, the transitive property of the inclusion relation provides no general information about transitivity within the complex with respect to Kh or with respect to K, and we can only assume that K and Kh are non-transitive for all components of a set complex about a nexus set of cardinal 3.

Proceeding now to the case of Kh about a nexus set of cardinal 4, it may be helpful to display a particular example. Representative members of each cardinality for Kh(4-3) are shown below·*

$$3\text{-}3 \subset 4\text{-}3 \ \& \ 3\text{-}3 \subset 8\text{-}3 \text{ hence } 8\text{-}3 \subset 9\text{-}3 \ \& \ 4\text{-}3 \subset 9\text{-}3$$
$$5\text{-}10 \supset 4\text{-}3 \ \& \ 5\text{-}10 \subset 8\text{-}3 \text{ hence } 7\text{-}10 \subset 8\text{-}3 \ \& \ 4\text{-}3 \subset 7\text{-}10$$
$$6\text{-}Z3 \supset 4\text{-}3 \ \& \ 6\text{-}Z3 \subset 8\text{-}3 \text{ hence } 6\text{-}Z36 \subset 8\text{-}3 \ \& \ 4\text{-}3 \subset 6\text{-}Z36$$

---

*Recall that $S \subset T$ iff $\overline{T} \subset \overline{S}$.

From this it is apparent that

(1) 3-3 ⊂ 4-3 & 4-3 ⊂ 5-10
3-3 ⊂ 4-3 & 4-3 ⊂ 7-10
Hence 3-3 ⊂ 5-10 & 3-3 ⊂ 7-10
and therefore 3-3 ∈ Kh(5-10,7-10)

(2) 3-3 ⊂ 4-3 & 4-3 ⊂ 6-Z3
3-3 ⊂ 4-3 & 4-3 ⊂ 6-Z36
Hence 3-3 ⊂ 6-Z3 & 3-3 ⊂ 6-Z36
and therefore 3-3 ∈ Kh(6-Z3,6-Z36)

(3) No general statement can be made concerning the
relation between members of cardinal 5 and cardinal 6.

To sum up, for Kh about nexus sets of cardinal 4 all members of cardinal 3 are
in the relation Kh to all members of cardinal 5 and cardinal 6.

Transitive relations for Kh with nexus set of cardinal 5 are illustrated below
for Kh(5-35):

3-6 ⊂ 5-35 & 3-6 ⊂ 7-35 hence 7-35 ⊂ 9-6 & 5-35 ⊂ 9-6
4-26 ⊂ 5-35 & 4-26 ⊂ 7-35 hence 7-35 ⊂ 8-26 & 5-35 ⊂ 8-26
5-35 ⊂ 6-32 & 6-32 ⊂ 7-35

From this it can be ascertained that

(1) 3-6 ⊂ 5-35 & 5-35 ⊂ 8-26
Hence 3-6 ⊂ 8-26
and therefore 3-6 ∈ K(4-26)

(2) 3-6 ⊂ 5-35 & 5-35 ⊂ 6-32
Hence 3-6 ∈ Kh(6-32)

(3) 4-26 ⊂ 5-35 & 5-35 ⊂ 6-32
Hence 4-26 ∈ Kh(6-32)

Thus, all members of cardinal 3 are in the relation K with all members of
cardinal 4, while all members of cardinal 6 are in the relation Kh with all
members of cardinal 3 and cardinal 4.

Finally, for Kh about nexus sets of cardinal 6, all components are in the relation K only. It should be remarked that this does not exclude the possibility
that Kh may hold between some members. However, this cannot be deduced
for the general case by the procedures used above.

The preceding discussion is summarized schematically below in terms of
cardinal numbers.

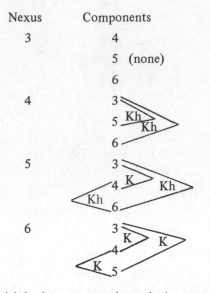

Thus, the only cases in which the set-complex relation extends to components of all cardinalities are those of Kh for nexus sets of cardinals 5 or 6. Only those set complexes possess the closure property. This suggests that set complexes about hexacords should be given special attention in the analytical application of the set-complex concept.

2.5 Invariance within the set complex

The purpose of the present section is to examine the correspondence between invariant subsets under some transformation (transposition or inversion followed by transposition) and set-complex membership (K or Kh).

What are perhaps the most significant problems can be approached by way of two questions. First, given an arbitrary set complex Kh, to what extent are its members invariant under transformation? Second, to what extent is the invariance (if any) reciprocal in a way analogous to the reciprocal property of the Kh relation itself (sec. 2.2)? That is, if B is an invariant subset of A, is $\overline{A}$ an invariant subset of $\overline{B}$? (Here and elsewhere in this section we exclude from consideration the invariant improper subset—that is, the "complete invariance" case.)

Before attempting to answer these questions, it may be useful to examine counts of invariant subsets by cardinal number in order to gain some idea of the magnitudes involved. Example 104 presents a summary of these, excluding cardinals 3 and 9, 2 and 10.

The counts shown in example 104 are arranged so that inverse-related cardinalities may be compared. A rough correspondence is evident, especially in the groupings at top and bottom, but there is no consistent regularity.

Certain special cases require comments. If a set is inversionally invariant—the

104. Counts of invariant subsets

Cardinal 8

1	3	4	5	6	13	16	17	18
8-28	8-9	8-25	8-21	8-1	8-19	8-2	8-4	8-11
			8-24	8-3		8-14	8-5	8-13
				8-6		8-22	8-12	8-Z15
				8-7			8-16	8-Z29
				8-8			8-18	
				8-10			8-27	
				8-17				
				8-20				
				8-23				
				8-26				

Cardinal 7

4	5	6	10	11	12	13	14	15	16
7-33	7-15	7-1	7-31	7-21	7-28	7-7	7-5	7-2	7-11
		7-8					7-13	7-3	7-16
		7-Z12					7-14	7-4	7-32
		7-Z17					7-19	7-6	7-Z36
		7-22					7-26	7-9	7-Z38
		7-34					7-30	7-10	
		7-35						7-11	
		7-Z37						7-Z18	
								7-20	
								7-23	
								7-24	
								7-25	
								7-27	
								7-29	

Cardinal 6

0	1	2	4	5	6	7	8
6-35	6-20	6-7	6-1	6-Z4	6-Z37	6-27	6-21
			6-30	6-Z6	6-Z48		6-22
			6-32	6-8			6-34
				6-Z13			
				6-Z23			
				6-Z26			
				6-Z28			
				6-Z29			
				6-Z38			
				6-Z42			
				6-Z45			
				6-Z49			
				6-Z50			

10	11	12	13	14	15
6-Z3	6-2	6-Z10	6-5	6-Z24	6-14
	6-Z12	6-Z33	6-9	6-Z39	6-15
	6-Z17	6-Z36	6-Z11	6-Z40	6-16
	6-Z25	6-Z43	6-18		6-Z19
		6-Z46	6-Z41		6-31
		6-Z47			6-44

cont'd.

Cardinal 4

0	1	2	3	4	5	6
4-28	4-9	4-1	4-6	4-4	4-2	4-Z15
	4-25	4-3	4-8		4-5	4-18
		4-7	4-19		4-11	4-27
		4-10	4-21		4-12	4-Z29
		4-17	4-24		4-13	
		4-20			4-14	
		4-23			4-16	
		4-26			4-22	

Cardinal 5

3	4	5	6	7	8	9
5-1	5-15	5-8	5-19	5-5	5-2	5-11
5-33	5-Z17	5-Z12	5-21	5-7	5-3	
5-35	5-34	5-22	5-28	5-10	5-4	
	5-Z37	5-31		5-14	5-6	
					5-9	
					5-13	
					5-16	
					5-Z18	
					5-20	
					5-23	
					5-24	
					5-25	
					5-26	
					5-27	
					5-29	
					5-30	
					5-32	
					5-Z36	
					5-Z38	

complete invariance situation discussed in section 1.12—then it has no inversionally invariant subsets, only transpositionally invariant subsets. These sets, such as 5-15 and 7-15 occupy the lower positions in the list of counts. The sets with both inversionally invariant and transpositionally invariant subsets tend to occupy the higher positions, although again there is not a consistent regularity there.

The reader will recognize the familiar cases in which no subsets are held invariant: 4-28 and 6-35. Less familiar perhaps are the few instances in which only one subset can be held invariant: 4-9, 4-25, 8-28, and 6-20. All these are prominent in the atonal repertory.

One final feature, not evident in example 104, deserves notice. There is a small number of sets that hold all subsets of a certain cardinal number invariant. Pc sets 4-4, 4-Z15, 4-18, 4-27, and 4-Z29 hold all subsets of cardinal 2 invariant. Pc set 5-11 likewise holds all subsets of cardinal 2 invariant, while pc set 5-21 holds all subsets of cardinal 4 invariant and 7-31 holds all subsets of cardinal 6 invariant. The latter two are perhaps of greatest interest.

To return now to the question stated at the beginning of this section concerning invariance within the subcomplex Kh, it must be said that invariance is not closely associated with membership in Kh. In general, members of a Kh often exclude subsets (or supersets) capable of invariance under transformation. Moreover, the reciprocal property, which was central to the second question, imposes a further limitation.

A specific example will clarify. Pc set 4-18 and its complement are members of Kh (5-22). Pc set 8-18 holds 5-22 invariant under transposition and under inversion followed by transposition. It also holds pc set 7-22 invariant under inversion, and, in fact, this is the only 7-element subset that is held invariant under 8-18. However, 5-22 does not hold 4-18 invariant, nor does 7-22 hold 4-18 invariant, and thus the reciprocal property is only partially realized.

Another brief example will suffice to illustrate. Pc set 5-7 and its complement are the only members of cardinals 5 and 7 of Kh(6-Z6,6-Z38). Both hexachords are invariant subsets of 7-7; neither, however, holds 5-7 invariant.

There are, nonetheless, exactly 11 cases in which the reciprocal property holds (among sets of cardinals 4, 5, and 6). These are listed below.

> 5-31 and 6-27*
> 5-35 and 4-23
> 5-35 and 6-32

---

*Recall that pc set 7-31 holds all its 6-element subsets invariant.

6-2 and 4-2
6-5 and 4-5
6-Z6/38 and 4-6, 4-8, 4-9*
6-8 and 4-10
6-18 and 4-16
6-33 and 4-22

From the foregoing discussion it can be concluded that invariance is not especially manifest in the subcomplex Kh, but instead belongs to the domain of the set complex K. This obviously does not render it any less important as a structural process. It does, however, imply that invariance combined with Kh membership has special importance, and should be regarded as exceptional rather than as routine.

In closing, it should be remarked that there is no simple correspondence between the number of invariant subsets of an arbitrary set S and the size of Kh(S). Nor is there a simple correspondence between the number of invariant subsets of S and the number of bips associated with S. All these counts represent structural attributes of S that may interact but which are not interdependent.

2.6 Similarity relations within the set complex

Just as the set complex can be considered from the standpoint of invariance, so can it be viewed in terms of similarity relations. Indeed, the similarity measures discussed in section 1.13 are of particular interest with respect to the set complex if only because they permit comparison of component sets to which the relations K and Kh do not apply, namely, sets of the same or inverse-related cardinality.

As might be expected, the similarity relations among set-complex members of the same or inverse-related cardinal do not form simple patterns. For example, one would like to find that for any set complex, any pair of components of the same cardinal is in one of the two maximal similarity relations R_1 or R_2. This, however, is not the case, and, in fact, there is often at least one pair in the relation R_0. Thus, viewed from the standpoint of internal similarity relations, a set complex may be far from homogeneous. Moreover, in the case of the unreduced set complex K, there may even be many sets which are in none of the defined relations to any of the others.

On the other hand, there are certain interesting regularities in the case of the reduced set complex Kh. For any Kh with nexus set of cardinal 6, every component of cardinal 5 is in some similarity relation with at least one other component of cardinal 5. This means that for any Kh with nexus set of cardinal 5, every component of cardinal 6 is in some similarity relation with at

*Only one 4-element member is excluded: 4-16.

least one other component. Further, for any Kh with nexus set of cardinal 5, every component of cardinal 4 is in some similarity relation, and for any Kh with nexus set of cardinal 4, every component of cardinal 5 is in some similarity relation.

Since similarity relations among pc sets exclude those of cardinal 3 (and 9), the Kh with nexus sets of cardinal 5 enjoy a special eminence: only in such Kh are all sets of cardinal 4 in some similarity relation and all sets of cardinal 6 in some similarity relation.

Example 105 illustrates the foregoing observations. Each entry in the triangular matrices specifies the relation that holds between the sets named at the head of column and row, as usual. Notice the empty entries, corresponding to the absence of a relation, in Kh(6-21) and in Kh(4-7), whereas there are no such lacunae in Kh(5-21).

Example 105 will serve as a useful reference for some additional comments. First, it is important to observe that the entry R_p means R_p *only*, and to recall that two sets of cardinal n are in the relation R_p if and only if both contain the same subset of n−1 elements. Thus, for Kh(5-21) all 6-element components have (at least) one common subset of 5 elements—viz., 5-21 (by definition of Kh)—and therefore any pair of 6-element components of the complex is at least in the relation R_p. Obviously this is general for the 6-element components of any Kh with nexus set of cardinal 5. Accordingly, the entry R_1 at the intersection of row 6-16 and column 6-15, for example, is to be interpreted as $\cdot(R_1, R_p)$. For the same reason R_p also holds for any pair of 5-element components of any Kh with nexus set of cardinal 4. It can also be shown that the relation holds over any pair of 5-element components of any Kh with nexus set of cardinal 6 and that it holds for any pair of 4-element components of any Kh with nexus set of cardinal 5.

From section 1.13 it will be recalled that the term *transitive tuple* was applied to a group of pc sets completely interrelated by means of at least one similarity relation. Formations of this kind are also of interest within the set complex.

Since a transitive tuple could only belong to a particular Kh if it were also transitive with respect to R_p, only those tuples marked by an asterisk in example 57 need be considered here. Now, it is remarkable that four of the five R_2 and R_p transitive triples of cardinal 6 belong to Kh(5-21) and are displayed in example 105. (The remaining one does not belong to any single Kh.) Furthermore, Kh(5-21) contains one of the five R_1 and R_p transitive triples: 6-15, 6-16, and 6-31. Of the remaining tuples, the R_2 and R_p transitive triples of cardinal 5 are in Kh(4-4) or in Kh(4-14), and the R_1 and R_p transitive triples of cardinal 5 are in Kh(4-19), Kh(4-24) or Kh(4-18). Thus, these sets have restricted and very special locations in the set-complex universe.

The R_1 and R_p triple, 6-21, 6-22, and 6-34 belongs to Kh(5-33). However,

Kh(5-21)

	4-7	4-17	4-19
4-17	R₁		
4-19	R₂	R₂	
4-20	R₁	R₁	R₃

	6-14	6-15	6-16	6-Z19	6-20
6-15	R₃				
6-16	R₂	R₃			
6-Z19	R₃	R₃	R₃		
6-20	R₂	R₁	R₃	R₁	
6-31	R₂	R₁	R₁	R₃	R₃

Kh(4-7)

	5-3	5-6	5-Z18
5-6	R_p	R₃	
5-Z18	R_p	R_p	R_p
5-21	R_p	R_p	R_p

	6-1	6-5	6-14	6-15	6-16
6-5	R_p				
6-14	R_p	R₃	R₂		
6-15	R₀	R_p	R₂	R₁	
6-16		R_p	R₂	R₃	R₃
6-Z19		R_p	R₂	R_p	R_p
6-20			R₂	R_p	R_p
6-31	R_p		R₂	R₃	R_p

	4-24	4-27
4-25	R₃	
4-27	R_p	R₂
(·)	R_p	R₀

Kh(6-21)

	4-2	4-5	4-11	4-12	4-Z15	4-19	4-21	4-24
4-5	R_p							
4-11	R₃	R_p						
4-12	R_p	R_p	R_p					
4-Z15	R_p	R₂	R₂	R₂				
4-19	R_p	R_p	R_z	R_p	R_p			
4-21	R_p	R_p	R₀	R_p	R_p	R₀		
4-24	R_p	R_p	R_p	R_p	R₀	R_p	R₂	R₃
4-25		R₁	R_p	R_p	R₁	R_p	R_p	R_p
4-27	R_p	R₂	R_p	R_p	R₂	R_p	R_p	R_p
4-Z29	R_p	R₂	R_p	R₂	R_p	R_p	R_p	R_p

	5-8	5-9	5-13	5-26	5-28
5-9	R_p	R₁			
5-13	R_p	R_p	R₁		
5-26	R_p	R_p	R_p	R₃	
5-28	R_p	R_p	R_p	R₀	R₃
5-33	R_p	R₀	R₀	R₀	R_p

the R_1 and R_p quintuple, 6-Z28, 6-Z29, 6-30, 6-Z42, 6-Z45 share common subset 5-31 but only one of these sets, 6-30, is in Kh(5-31). This is due to the single members of Z-related hexachords that, excepting 6-30, comprise the quintuple.

To complete this survey, it should be noted that the two R_1 and R_p tuples belong to Kh(3-4) or Kh(3-10). The triple also belongs to four hexachordal complexes, while the quadruple belongs to two hexachordal complexes.

With the exception of the hexachordal tuples and one tetrachordal, membership in Kh does not extend to complements. In the case of the 7-element complements of the 5-element tuples, either they are not R_p transitive or they are not in the relation Kh with their common 6-element subset—which is then necessarily of the Z type. The tetrachordal exception mentioned above is the quadruple, 4-12, 4-13, 4-18, 4-27. The complements of these sets are all members of Kh(7-31). The reader will recall from section 2.5 that 7-31 as well as 5-21 have unique attributes with respect to invariance in addition to the special roles they play in the transitive tuples under discussion.

Two samples from the atonal repertory will indicate how similarity and set-complex relations are associated in concrete instances. Example 106

106. Schoenberg, Three Piano Pieces Op. 11/2

Used by permission of Belmont Music Publishers, Los Angeles, California 90049.

shows 4-13 and 4-18, part of the R_1 and R_p transitive quadruple. These sets occur as successive verticals within 6-27, and of course they belong to Kh(6-27). They also occur as melodic strands in the same context, as indicated in example 106. Although R_p is not strongly represented here, it is of interest to note that the melodic forms of 4-18 and 4-13 have similar interval successions and bips (134 and 135). Also notice that 4-18 is again represented by its complement in the same passage.

107.   Webern, Six Pieces for Orchestra Op. 6/6

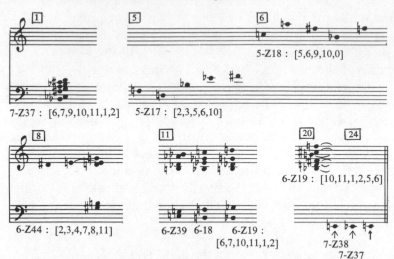

The example from Webern's Op. 6/6 (ex. 107) is more complicated and the relations span virtually the entire piece. The example is intended mainly to illustrate 5-Z17, 5-Z18 and 7-Z37, 7-Z38, each pair being part of a transitive triple. Pc set 5-Z17 and pc set 5-Z18 are successive melodic segments in the music. R_p is not strongly represented, but, as in example 106, the bips are similar (3345 and 3456). These two sets are Z-related to 7-Z37 and 7-Z38 and thus have the same vectors as the complements of the latter. The two occurrences of 7-Z37 shown here, one at the beginning of the movement and one at the end, are transpositionally equivalent, with t = 4, and the invariant subset for this maximum value is 5-Z17. There is no corresponding association of 7-Z38 and 5-Z18.

At the close of the movement 7-Z38 is formed when E is brought in in the lower register against the sustained sonority (6-Z19). The change from E to E-flat forms 7-Z37, as indicated in example 107. Thus, R_p is strongly represented here, by 6-Z19. The prior occurrence of 6-Z19 in measure 11 is of interest, since the two forms are inversionally related, with t = 0. As a result the form at measure 11 is a subset of 7-Z37 in measure 1 and thus corresponds to the immediate inclusion of 6-Z19 in 7-Z37 at measure 24. Since 6-Z19 is contained in 7-Z37 and 7-Z38, 5-Z37 and 5-Z38 are subsets of the complement of 6-Z19, 6-Z44, which is formed as a composite segment at measure 8.

From this it should be apparent that 7-Z37 and 7-Z38 are not members of Kh(6-Z19/44), although they are, of course, members of K(6-Z19) and K(6-Z44)

2.7 Set-Complex structures of small scale

The purpose of this and the following section is to demonstrate the value of set-complex theory and attendant systematics (e.g. invariants and similarity relations) in its practical application to the analysis of atonal compositions. In general, the set complex provides a simple model of relations among pc sets. For the particular vocabulary of pc sets used in a composition it should be possible to examine in very precise terms the set-complex relations exhibited.

The present section is concerned with structures formed by a complete section of a composition. In section 2.8, certain notions introduced here will be extended to the study of relations within and among the component parts of the complete composition.

It should be stressed at the outset that the analytical implementation of set-complex theory does not imply an exclusive concern for homogeneous structures. On the contrary, an adequate set-complex analysis will reveal the absence of relations and assist in the interpretation of those. For example, it may be that a particular section of a composition is not connected (to be defined below) with respect to set-complex structure. Or it may be that the components of a section reflect the interaction of more than one set complex.

The procedures of segmentation discussed in section 1.16 will be apparent in the examples that follow, and there will be no detailed explanation of them. In all cases a table of set-complex relations will be provided. This will be used to determine the nexus sets (if any) and will serve as a convenient and comprehensive display of all relations. As before, the entry at the intersection of column and row will either be empty, Kh, K, or K*. The latter, it will be recalled, is used in the case of a single member of a Z-related pair and indicates that the inclusion relation holds between the set actually listed, rather than its complement.

The determination of nexus sets for the particular vocabulary of pc sets used in a composition or section can present difficulties. If it were universally the case that every section of an atonal composition employed as its vocabulary of pc sets only sets drawn from the same set complex, there would be no problems. This is often not the case, however, and steps must be taken to provide an interface between theory and practice. The following rules for determining nexus sets are intended to do this.

Rule 1. Priority is given to hexachords, since they have the special internal properties discussed earlier, in particular the closure property (sec. 2.4). In the absence of qualified hexachords, sets of cardinal 5, then sets of cardinal

4 are candidates. Only in exceptional cases will a set of cardinal 3 qualify as a nexus set, since the set complexes with nexus sets of cardinal 3, even the Kh, are very large and the relations correspondingly diffuse and lacking in precise definition and interpretation.

Rule 2. The set with the greatest number of Kh and K* relations is designated provisionally as primary nexus set. If this set is related to all others, it is the only nexus set, and no further determination is required. And, if this situation exists, the set-complex structure is said to be *connected*—in the specific sense that the nexus connects all the other sets. If it is unrelated to some (or only in the relation K) then an attempt is made to find a secondary nexus set (rule 3).

Rule 3. A secondary nexus set of the same cardinal number as the primary nexus set must be in the set-complex relation to all sets not in the set-complex relation to the primary nexus set. And if the secondary nexus set is of the same cardinal number as the primary nexus set then an additional secondary nexus set must be found, such that it is in the set complex about the primary nexus set and in the set complex about the other secondary nexus set.

If by rule 3 there are primary and secondary nexus sets, the set-complex structure is said to be *connected,* as it would be if rules 1 and 2 were satisfied.

The notion of connectedness here, although somewhat more complicated where secondary nexus sets are required, is useful, since if a set-complex structure is connected, any pair of component sets is either in the same complex or is linked to a single complex through one of the nexus sets. In this sense, the distinction between a primary and secondary nexus sets is academic, and we can simply speak of nexus sets for a particular connected set-complex structure.

From the foregoing it will be evident that cardinal number is of singular importance. As an extreme example, suppose that the sets of a particular section were only of cardinal 6. It would then be impossible to analyze that section in terms of a connected structure.*

In the subsequent analyses the term *derivation* will often be used to refer to the array of processes by which one set is generated from another. More specifically, the derivational processes are complementation, inclusion, transposition, inversion, and the set-theoretic operations of union and intersection. All these are familiar to the reader from previous sections and examples.

As the first illustration of set-complex structure over a section of a larger work, we take the penultimate section of Stravinsky's *Le Roi des Étoiles* (1911), a little-known composition dedicated to Debussy. A condensed score, with segmentation and sets indicated, is provided in example 108.

---

*There is, in fact, a complete composition of this type: Schoenberg's Op. 23/4, which is comprised entirely of pc sets 6-14, 6-Z10/39, and 6-Z44/19.

108. Stravinsky, *Le Roi des étoiles*

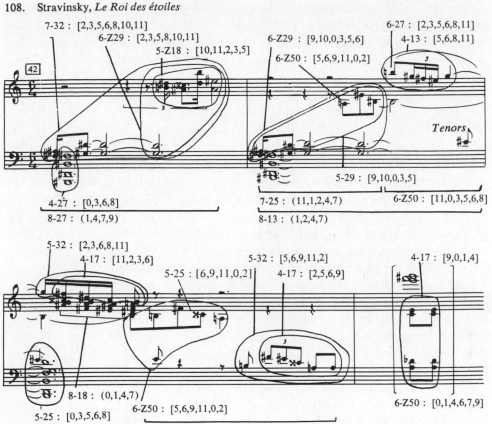

7-32 : [2,3,5,6,8,10,11]
6-Z29 : [2,3,5,8,10,11]
5-Z18 : [10,11,2,3,5]
6-Z29 : [9,10,0,3,5,6]
6-Z50 : [5,6,9,11,0,2]
6-27 : [2,3,5,6,8,11]
4-13 : [5,6,8,11]

Tenors

4-27 : [0,3,6,8]
8-27 : (1,4,7,9)
7-25 : (11,1,2,4,7)
8-13 : (1,2,4,7)
5-29 : [9,10,0,3,5]
6-Z50 : [11,0,3,5,6,8]

5-32 : [2,3,6,8,11]
4-17 : [11,2,3,6]
5-25 : [6,9,11,0,2]
5-32 : [5,6,9,11,2]
4-17 : [2,5,6,9]
4-17 : [9,0,1,4]

8-18 : (0,1,4,7)
5-25 : [0,3,5,6,8]
6-Z50 : [5,6,9,11,0,2]
8-28 : (1,4,7,10)
6-Z50 : [0,1,4,6,7,9]

Originally published by Musik Verlag Rob. Forberg, Bad Godesberg, Germany. Reprinted by permission of C. F. Peters Corporation, New York.

109. Stravinsky, *Le Roi des étoiles*
     Set-complex relations

| | 8-13 | | | | | 8-27 | | | | | |
	4-13	4-17	8-18	4-19	4-20	4-27	8-28				
5-Z18	K	K	Kh	K	K	K					
7-25/5-25	Kh	K	K			Kh	K				
5-29	Kh	K	K		K	Kh					
7-32/5-32	K	Kh	Kh	K	K	Kh	K	5-Z18	5-25	5-29	5-32
6-27	Kh	Kh	Kh			Kh	Kh		Kh		Kh
6-Z29/6-Z50	Kh	K	Kh			Kh	K	K	K	K	K

From the table of set-complex relations, example 109, it can be ascertained that the set-complex structure of the section is connected and that the nexus sets are 6-Z29/50 and 5-32/7-32. Pc set 6-Z50 is prominent throughout the composition, in fact, and its initial statement is shown at the far right of example 108.

At the beginning of the section under consideration, the complement of 6-Z50, 6-Z29, is formed as a composite segment. It is perhaps not insignificant that this form of 6-Z29 is the literal complement of the initial statement of 6-Z50, shown at the far right of example 108. Pc set 6-Z50 occurs in two overlapping forms in the music: as a melodic line that begins in measure 43 and extends into measure 44, and as a composite segment (comprising orchestra and chorus) over the last two beats of measure 43. In the latter context it intersects with the other hexachord shown in the table, pc set 6-27. Specifically, they intersect in the melodic segment that forms pc set 4-13: [5,6,8,11]. Here it should be remarked that since all sets in K(6-27) are also members of K(6-Z29/50) the two hexachordal complexes are firmly linked.

Two 8-element sets are formed in the first two measures: 8-27 and 8-13. Each contains its complement, as shown in example 108. Pc set 4-27 is the sustained sonority in the lower parts in measure 42, while 4-13 is the melodic figure connecting 6-Z50 and 6-27 in measure 43, as remarked above. Pc sets 4-13 and 4-27 (and their complements) form part of the R_1 and R_p transitive quadruple cited in section 2.6 (cf. 106).

Within 8-27 we find 7-32 and within 8-13 we find 7-25. Since pc set 6-Z29 is a subset of 7-32 and both 6-Z29 and 6-Z50 are contained in 8-13, these larger units are directly linked to the hexachordal nexus sets. The two 5-element melodic sets in these measures, 5-Z18 and 5-29, are both within 6-Z29. Whereas neither of these sets is represented more than once in the section, the complements of 7-32 and 7-25 both occur in the final measure. Pc set 5-25 is first formed by the E-sharp (tenors) and the sustained chord (4-27) of the orchestra, then by the melodic subsegment of 6-Z50, as indicated. Pc set 5-32 is the final melodic subsegment of 6-27 and then is the final melodic figure in the measure. (The two forms are transpositionally equivalent, with maximum invariance.) The set formed by the union of that melodic figure and the immediately preceding 5-25 is (perhaps trivially) 6-Z50.

Both statements of 5-32 contain 4-17, which is the set sung by the chorus in the initial statement of 6-Z50 shown at the far right of example 108. In both statements of 5-32, pc set 4-17 is formed as the last 4 notes, and the resulting bips, although not identical, are similar (133 and 135).

The two 8-element sets in the final measure require attention. The first of these, 8-18, is formed by a descending "chordal" configuration, a formation characteristic of *The Rite of Spring,* which was composed during the same period. It should be remarked, parenthetically, that in a section as cohesive as this and one, which is so clearly organized around a small number of sets, it

110.   Scriabin, Ninth Piano Sonata Op. 68

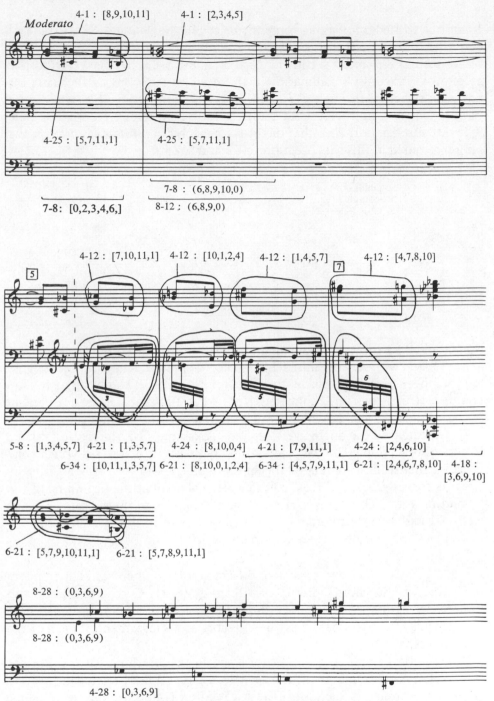

is curious to find anomalous components such as 4-19 and 4-20 within 8-18 here (the first two sixteenth-note chords).

The second 8-element set in the final measure, 8-28, has been cited earlier as one of Stravinsky's hallmarks. In this context it relates to the main set-complex structure through 5–32 and, of course, contains 5-25 as well. It will be recalled that the smallest set-complex Kh is that about 4-28/8-28. Thus, it is not surprising to find that of the six hexachords contained in 8-28, two are represented in this short section: 6-27 and 6-Z50.

111.   Scriabin, Ninth Piano Sonata Op. 68
       Set-complex relations

	4-1	8-12 4-12	4-18	4-21	4-24	4-25	8-28 4-28	
7-8	K	Kh		Kh	K	K		5-8
6-21		Kh		Kh	Kh	Kh	Kh	
6-34		Kh		Kh	Kh	Kh		

Example 110 shows the opening section of Scriabin's Op. 68, the *Black Mass* Sonata, with sets delimited and labeled. Despite the apparent simplicity and homogeneity of the music, the table (ex. 111) clearly shows that the set-complex structure is not connected. Note especially that two sets prominent in the section, 4-18 and 8-28, are quite unattached to the other sets.

As indicated by the dotted vertical line in example 110, the section divides into two subsections. The two successive statements of pc set 7-8 which comprise the first section are related transpositionally, with $t = 6$. The resulting invariants form 4-25:[5,7,11,1], and this is the vertical at the beginning of the second measure. This transposition obviously applies to the subsets of 7-8 as well, 4-1 and 4-25, but with a differential outcome. In the case of 4-25 complete invariance results, whereas in the case of 4-1 no pcs are held fixed between the two forms.

The second subsection consists of 4 hexachordal segments, in which pc set 6-34 (the mystic chord) alternates with pc set 6-21. Corresponding to this interchange is the alternation of the subsets 4-21 and 4-24. In contrast to these regular fluctuations, pc set 4-12 recurs as a subsegment of each of the hexachords.

It is significant that these hexachords are in the relations R_1 and R_p, for those relations are unique with respect to 6-21, and 6-34 relates in this way to only one other hexachord. (The R_p relation is not strongly represented here.)

Although the set-complex structure of the section as a whole is not connected, set-complex relations are of considerable importance. Notice that pc set 6-34 is formed by the union of 4-12 and 4-21, and that both tetrachords are members of Kh(5-8,7-8). Thus, although 6-34 and 7-8 are not in the set-complex relation—which would afford a direct connection between the two subsections—they are linked by means of the tetrachords. Both forms of 4-21 are subsets of 7-8 in the first subsection, although they are not represented as independent segments. Similarly, each form of 4-12 (as a subset of 6-34) is represented in one of the forms of 7-8 in the first subsection.

Just as pc set 6-34 is the union of 4-12 and 4-21, so is pc set 6-21 the union of 4-12 and 4-24. And those tetrachords are also members of K(5-8,7-8). This tetrachordal derivation of 6-21 from 7-8 is not quite as straightforward as was the derivation of 6-34 from 7-8, however, since no form of 4-24 or 4-12 is a subset of either form of 7-8, as it occurs in the first subsection.

The two tetrachords 4-21 and 4-24 are maximally similar to pc set 4-25 of the first subsection. This association is made quite explicit in terms of invariance, for both 6-21 and 6-34 hold forms of 4-25 invariant. Pc set 6-21 holds [2,4,8,10] and 6-34 holds [5,7,11,1]. The latter, of course, is identical to 4-25 as it occurs in the first subsection.

Not only is pc set 4-12 of the second subsection represented in 7-8 of the first subsection, as noted above, but its complement is formed by the final segment of the first subsection, and all forms of 4-12 in the second subsection except the last are contained in that segment.

It remains to discuss the two "unattached" sets, 8-28 and 4-18. Pc set 4-18 serves as a cadential harmony, delimiting the first section of the sonata. This function is pointed up by its R_0 relation to both 4-1 and 4-25, the melodic segments of the first subsection. It is vitiated to some extent, however, by the maximal similarity of 4-18 and 4-12. As indicated, 4-18 is preceded immediately by 4-12.

Pc set 8-28, although detached from the set-complex structure of this section, has an important role in the sonata as a whole, for it contains hexachords that subsequently are represented as thematic components. Here, locally, it forms an interesting substructure, as shown on the staves at the bottom of example 110. Two transpositionally equivalent linear statements of 8-28 are unfolded over the same time-span as the literal complement. The interval successions of the two 8-element sets are distinct. The upper consists of the pattern [1-4-1], etc.; the lower consists of the pattern [1-2-1], etc.

The last, and most complicated, of the small-scale structures to be examined in the present section is the transitional music preceding act 2, scene 3 from Berg's *Wozzeck* (ex. 112). All the sets in this transitional section are associated with one or more of the characters in the opera. Of these, perhaps the most important are: 4-Z29 (Doktor), 4-19 (Wozzeck and Marie), 5-5, 5-30, and 4-21 (Wozzeck), 6-22 (Andres),* 6-Z44 (Hauptmann), 4-Z15, 5-21, 4-16, and 5-9 (Marie), and 6-Z19 (Marie, Hauptmann, and Margret).

*And Wozzeck in act 3, scene 2, measure 89.

The prior knowledge of these motives simplifies to some extent what would otherwise be a difficult exercise in segmentation. Even so, there are problems, one of which is worth mentioning. Berg, like Schoenberg (and Webern to some degree) often composes melodic configurations that are not significant in themselves, but which combine with other contiguous components to form structural units. A good example of this is the horn line that begins in measure 370 (ex. 112). The entire line (a *Hauptstimme*) forms pc set 5-1, which is not a thematic set in the opera. Similarly, the descending chromatic lines in measure 372 are not in themselves structurally significant, but are entirely secondary features.

The set-complex table in example 113 summarizes the relations for the passage under consideration. Berg's command of the set-vocabulary of the opera is strikingly evident here. Note in particular the complementary pairs 5-9/7-9 and 4-Z29/8-Z29. Here, as throughout the opera, complementation is a fundamental process and one that gives rise to many large composite segments.

Although the set-complex structure is not connected, the table reveals a number of interesting links. Not all of these will be discussed, but only those involving the more prominent sets in the passage.

Let us begin with the set-complex relations for pc set 5-30, Wozzeck's motive, which is the culmination of the passage. The final melodic statement of 5-30 in measure 373 is a transposition of the first statement, measure 367, and the invariant pcs are [0,4,8]. These invariants are also contained in 4-19, the common subset in the statements of 5-30 at beginning and end.

The set-complex table informs us that 5-30 is a member of Kh(6-22), and

112. Berg, *Wozzeck* Op. 7
       act 2

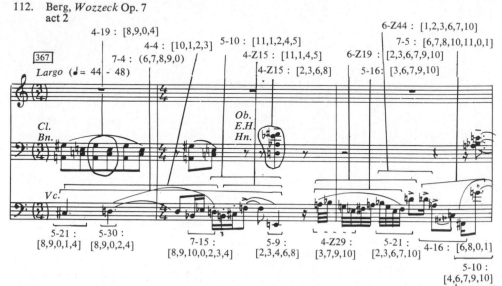

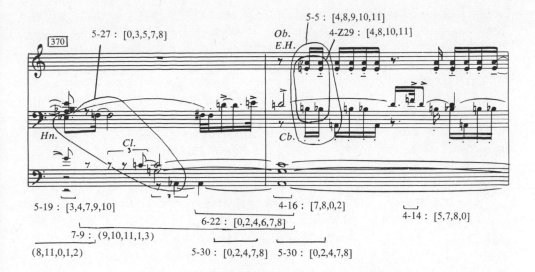

5-27 : [0,3,5,7,8]

5-5 : [4,8,9,10,11]

Ob.
E.H.

4-Z29 : [4,8,10,11]

Hn.

Cb.

Cl.

5-19 : [3,4,7,9,10]

4-16 : [7,8,0,2]

6-22 : [0,2,4,6,7,8]

4-14 : [5,7,8,0]

7-9 : (9,10,11,1,3)

(8,11,0,1,2)

5-30 : [0,2,4,7,8]   5-30 : [0,2,4,7,8]

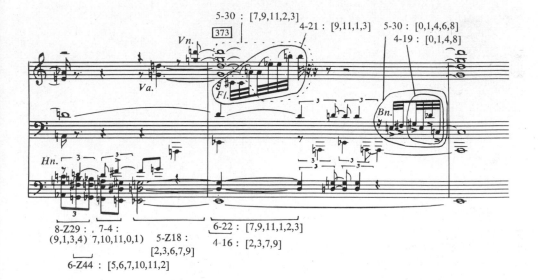

5-30 : [7,9,11,2,3]

373

4-21 : [9,11,1,3]

5-30 : [0,1,4,6,8]

4-19 : [0,1,4,8]

Vn.

Va.

Fl.

Bn.

Hn.

8-Z29 :   7-4 :

(9,1,3,4) 7,10,11,0,1)

5-Z18 :
[2,3,6,7,9]

6-22 : [7,9,11,1,2,3]

4-16 : [2,3,7,9]

6-Z44 : [5,6,7,10,11,2]

Hn.   Fl.

7-30 : [6,7,9,11,1,2,3]

examination of the first statement of 6-22, in measure 370, reveals a slightly concealed form of 5-30. This form of 5-30 contains 4-16 (Marie), which is sustained throughout measure 371 and remains a fundamental component of the music at the beginning of scene 3. (The two-note motive in measure 370, D-E, is a fixed pitch-reference in the opera—"Der Mann.")

The occurrence of pc set 5-30 within the first statement of 6-22 suggests that 5-30 might also be contained in the second statement of that set in measure 373. There is, in fact, such a form and it is indicated by dotted lines in measure 373. This helps to clarify the enigmatic three-note horn figure in measure 372. That figure, together with the subsequent flute motive (4-21) forms pc set 7-30, as shown at the bottom left in example 112.

The remaining set in Kh(5-30), 4-Z15, relates not to 5-30, but to 5-9 in the music. (Both 5-9 and 4-Z15 are associated with Marie.) The melodic statement of 4-Z15 in measure 368 is followed immediately by the vertical segment 5-9, within which 4-Z15 is set in relief by orchestration. Both 5-9 and 5-30 are in Kh(6-22), and this connection is evident in measure 370, where 7-9 contains 6-22 and 6-22 contains 5-30. This is an especially lucid illustration of set-complex relations in a small context.

113.   Berg, *Wozzeck* Op. 7. act 2, transition to scene 3
       Set-complex relations

	4-4	4-14	4-Z15	4-16	4-19	4-21	8-Z29 / 4-Z29						
7-4	Kh	K	K	K		K	K						
7-5/5-5	K	Kh	K	K		K	Kh						
7-9/5-9	K	K	Kh	K	K	Kh	K						
5-10	K	K	Kh			K	K						
7-15		K		Kh	K	K	K						
5-16	K		K		K		Kh						
5-Z18	K	Kh	K	Kh	K		K						
5-19	K	K	Kh		K		Kh						
5-21	K	K	K	K	Kh		K						
5-27	K	Kh	K	K	K								
7-30/5-30	K	K	Kh	Kh	Kh	K	K	5-9	7-15	5-16	5-Z18	5-21	5-30
6-Z19/6-Z44	K	K	K	K	Kh		K			K	K	Kh	
6-22			Kh	Kh	Kh	Kh	Kh	Kh	Kh				Kh

All the sets discussed above in connection with 5-30 belong to the set complex about 6-22. Let us now consider those members of the set complex about 6-Z19/44 which are not also members of Kh(6-22). Pc sets 6-Z19 and 6-Z44 first occur in measure 369, where they intersect in a melodic segment that forms 5-21. This is a detail, but not an insignificant one, since 5-21 is associated with the character of the Tambourmajor (act 2, scene 5, measure 800).

The opening melodic motive, 4-4, belongs to K(6-Z19,6-Z44) (and, in fact, is the same pc set as in its initial presentation in act 1, measure 9), as does 4-14, a motive associated with the child, which occurs briefly in measure 371. Both 4-4 and 4-14, as well as 4-19 are in the relation R_0 to pc set 4-21. The latter set, which is a member of Kh(6-22), occurs only in the final measure, where it is prominent as the ascending flute figure. The maximally dissimilar relation here is significant, since the only other similarity relations (both among sets of cardinal 4 and among sets of cardinal 5) are of the maximally similar types. The contrast of 4-21 and 4-19 is especially striking and cogent in the final measure because of the association of 4-21 with the character of the Hauptmann and the association of 4-19 with Marie and Wozzeck. (It will be recalled that the Hauptmann has dominated the close of the preceding scene.)

To return from this necessary digression concerning similarity relations to consider the remaining members of K(6-Z19,6-Z44), we observe that pc set 5-16, associated with Wozzeck, is formed by the 32nd-note figure in measure 368-369, and, as indicated in example 112, is contained within 6-Z19. The first reference to this hexachordal set complex is through 5-21 at the very beginning of the transition, in measure 367, and the occurrence of this set as the intersection of 6-Z19 and 6-Z44 in measure 369 has already been recorded. Pc set 5-Z18, which comes in at the end of measure 372, is the last reference to K(6-Z19,6-Z44).

Five sets of cardinal 5 belong neither to K(6-22) nor to K(6-Z19,6-Z44). However, all the sets of cardinal 4 relate to one of the two hexachordal complexes, and among these are four that serve to link the sets of cardinal 5 to the two hexachords: 4-4, 4-14, 4-Z15, and 4-Z29.

To sum up, the entire passage can be read in terms of the interaction of the two hexachordal complexes, in conjunction with the linking tetrachords listed above. The tetrachords, in general, have important functions in this music. In this regard, it should be remarked that although the hexachordal set complexes intersect in four 4-element sets, only one of those is in the relation Kh to both 6-22 and 6-Z19/44, viz., 4-19, the set which marks both the beginning and the end of the passage.

On the whole, the transformations involving equivalent sets are such that invariants are of no special significance. In fact, minimal or virtually minimal invariance appears to be the rule. (See 4-Z15 in measure 368.) The only exception is pc set 4-16 (Marie). This set first appears melodically in measure 369; subsequently it is an important component of measure 371 and measure 373, as already noted. The forms in measure 371 and measure 373 are transpositionally related, with $t = 7$, hence maximally invariant under T. And the resulting invariant pcs 2,7 are fixed pitch-references (to Marie) which occur in the final sonorities of acts 1 and 3.

2.8 Set-Complex structures of larger scale

In this final section the scope of the analytical procedures utilized in section 2.7 is enlarged to include more than the single section. In fact, four of the six musical samples to be investigated are complete movements.

This extension brings with it certain interesting and important questions that might be grouped under the general heading of form. For example, how are the various sections of a composition associated and how might these associations be described? Suppose that the set-complex structure of each section is connected, but that of the complete movement is not. How would such a construction be interpreted?

Before attempting to answer these and other questions, it seems essential to assume that form is not necessarily linear (sequential). That is, given consecutive sections A, B, and C, it is conceivable that whereas A may not be associated strongly with B, it may be closely related to C. It is also possible that a particular section cannot be explained with reference to any other single section, but only in terms of the structure of the entire movement. This implies that it may be necessary to examine not only relations among consecutive sections, but also relations among all combinations of sections up to and including the total movement.

Music by four composers (Berg, Schoenberg, Stravinsky, and Webern) will serve as material for analysis. It is hoped that the compositions, although not selected completely arbitrarily, are sufficiently diversified to demonstrate that the procedures and concepts can be generally applied and are essentially independent of a particular composer's style. This does not mean, however, that a rigid format will be imposed. On the contrary, for any particular work those structural aspects that seem most important and prominent will receive more attention than others.

As an initial and relatively uncomplicated example, let us consider the frequently cited Motto of Berg's Chamber Concerto and the opening section of the Thema scherzoso (ex. 114).

The first part of the Motto is a linear segment that forms pc set 8-14. This set, which is based on the letters of Schoenberg's name, divides into two tetrachords, 4-13 and 4-18. Pc set 4-13 is subsequently replicated to become Berg's part of the motto. The two forms of 4-13 which are transpositionally equivalent with t = 7, produce exactly one invariant, A. Webern's trichord, pc set 3-5, is also contained in Schoenberg's motto, as shown.

The table of set-complex relations for the Motto and the Thema combined, example 115, provides a convenient reference for the discussion that follows. Note that the structure is connected, with nexus sets 6-5 and 4-18.

The Thema relates directly to the Motto with respect to composite segments as well as to the more obvious motives. As shown in the sketch below the full notation, the largest sets formed in the Thema are 8-13 and 8-14. Pc set

114.   Berg, Chamber Concerto

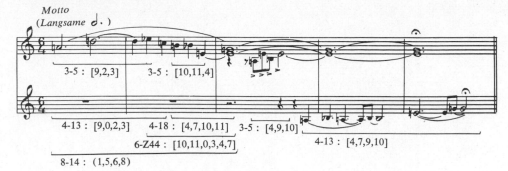

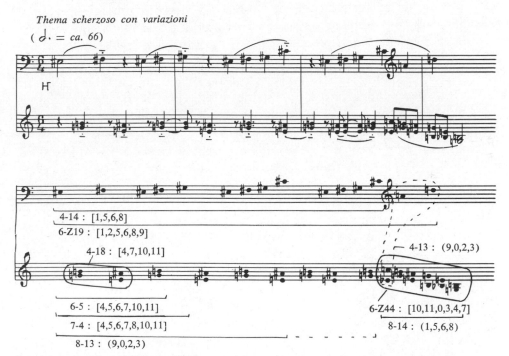

8-13, the first large segment, is the literal complement of 4-13, the first tetrachord in the Schoenberg motto. Pc set 8-14 is, of course, the same as the entire Schoenberg motto. The derivation of the melodic component of the Thema is not obvious, however. First 4-14, the literal complement of the Schoenberg motto, is unfolded, then, with the adjoining of A and D at the end, 6-Z19 is formed, the literal complement of the final hexachord in the Schoenberg motto. Accompanying the melodic component of the Thema is 4-18, which derives from the last tetrachord in the Schoenberg motto. Ob-

115.   Set-complex relations for example 114

	3-5				
4-13/8-13	Kh				
4-14/8-14	K				
4-18	Kh	4-13	4-14	4-18	
7-4	Kh	Kh	K	K	7-4
6-5	Kh	Kh	Kh	Kh	Kh
6-Z19/6-Z44	Kh		K	Kh	

serve the way in which the complement-related pairs are juxtaposed temporally. Pc set 4-14, a primary segment, is followed directly by its complement, a composite segment, and pc set 8-13, a composite segment, is followed by 4-13, also a composite segment. The statement of 4-13 (indicated by the dotted line in example 114) is especially interesting here since it is made up of the four new pitches introduced at the culmination of the passage. Thus, the composite segment 8-14 is the union of 4-18 and 4-13, just as it was in the linear statement of the Schoenberg motto.

There is only one similarity relation among the sets: 4-13 and 4-18 are in R_1 and R_p (part of the transitive quadruple discussed in section 2.6). Although the R_p relation is weakly represented, the two linear forms of the sets are so ordered that they yield the same interval succession (bip 136). Order relations are also of interest in the case of Webern's trichord, 3-5. Each occurrence presents a different bip, and the three occurrences taken together exhaust the possible bips for 3-5 (15, 16, and 56).

The third of Webern's Four Pieces for Violin and Piano Op. 7 is shown in example 116. From the table of set-complex relations, example 117, it can be ascertained that the structure is connected, with nexus sets 6-Z6/38, 6-Z13, and 4-9.

Excluding the trichords, every set but one relates primarily either to 6-Z6/ 38 or to 6-Z13. The sole exception is 4-9, which relates to both, thus linking two distinct hexachordal complexes. One might expect this feature of the total structure of the work to be reflected in the set-complex relations of the individual sections as well as in the set-complex relations of the sections combined.

And, indeed, this is clearly the case with respect to the individual sections. Pc set 6-Z13 is the nexus set for three of the four sections and, in section B, where it occurs together with 6-Z38, the two hexachords are connected in the most immediate fashion by 4-9, the violin figure which threads through the piano part, literally linking all the sets.

116.   Webern, Four Pieces for Violin and Piano Op. 7/3

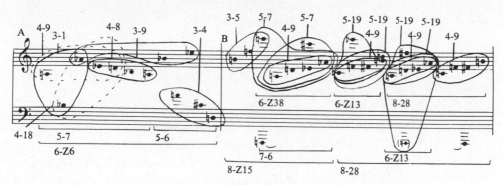

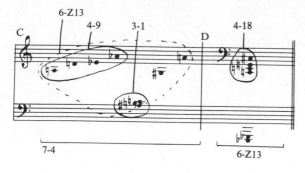

With the possible exception of C, the individual sections exhibit connected structures. Let us now consider the association of pairs of sections from the standpoint of their combined set-complex structure and from the standpoint of derivations, both explicit and implicit. Example 118 provides tables for all pairs.

Between A and B the strongest connection is afforded by the complement-related pair 6-Z6 and 6-Z38. Pc set 6-Z38 in B is derived from 6-Z6, the total content of A, as follows: 6-Z38 = T($\overline{6\text{-}Z6}$,9). The invariant subset consists of 5 pcs: [8,9,1,2,3], forming pc set 5-7. As can be seen in example 116, pc set 5-7 is both in A and in B. In B, both possible forms of 5-7 are explicit subsets (segments) of 6-Z38 and they intersect in 4-9. Moreover, the intersection of the two forms of 5-7 and 6-Z38 is again 4-9: [2,3,8,9]. Pc set 4-9 has an analogous linking function in A within 6-Z6 and 5-7, although it is not as strongly represented a segment here as it is in B.

Section B divides into two large composite segments: the first comprises 8-Z15, the second 8-28. In terms of the overall set-complex structure of the piece this represents a shift from the complex about 6-Z6/38 to the complex about 6-Z13. Thus, although there is minimal change at the surface level of the music, there is a pronounced change in the underlying structure. This change is evident, for example, in the exchange of interlocking forms of 5-7 for interlocking forms of 5-19, with pc set 4-9 remaining as the unifying component.

117. Webern, Four Pieces for Violin and Piano Op. 7/3
      Set-complex relations

	3-1	3-3	3-4	3-5	3-9	4-8	4-9	4-Z15	4-18	8-28	7-4	5-6	5-7	5-19
4-8	K	K	Kh	Kh	K									
4-9	K	K	K	Kh	K									
4-Z15/8-Z15	K	Kh	K	Kh	K									
4-18	K	Kh	K	Kh	K									
8-28		K		K		4-8	4-9	4-Z15	4-18	8-28				
7-4	Kh	Kh	Kh	Kh	K	K	K	K	K					
5-6/7-6	Kh	Kh	Kh	Kh	K	K	Kh	K	Kh	K				
5-7	Kh	K	Kh	Kh	Kh	Kh	Kh	K	K					
5-19	K	Kh	K	Kh	K	K	Kh	Kh	Kh	K	7-4	5-6	5-7	5-19
6-Z6/6-Z38	Kh	K	Kh	Kh	Kh	Kh	Kh	K				K	Kh	
6-Z13	K	Kh	K	Kh			K*	K*	K*	K*	K*			K*

To sum up the foregoing, the first part of B is derived from A through explicit sets in the latter. The second part of B, however, introduces a new set complex. It is remarkable that this is done with minimal change in pc content —in fact, only through the agency of three notes in the piano: E-flat, D, and F-sharp.

To a large extent, section C may be regarded as a continuation of B. Pc set 4-9 occurs again, and the additional components form the large composite segment, 7-4, which contains 6-Z13, the latter indicated by dotted lines in example 116.

Of the three pairs of non-adjacent sections only two are closely associated. Section A is associated with C through pc set 4-9, as in A + B. With respect

118.   Webern, Four Pieces for Violin and Piano Op. 7/3
      Set-complex relations for pairs of sections (trichords omitted)

A + B

	4-8	4-9	8-Z15 / 4-Z15	8-28	5-6	5-7	5-19
5-6/7-6	Kh	K	Kh				
5-7	Kh	Kh	K				
5-19	K	Kh	Kh	K			
6-Z6/6-Z38	Kh	Kh	K		K	Kh	
6-Z13		K*	K	K*			K*

A + C

	4-8	4-9	7-4	5-6	5-7
7-4	K	K			
5-6	Kh	K			
5-7	Kh	Kh			
6-Z6	Kh	Kh		K*	Kh

A + D

	4-8	4-18	5-6	5-7
5-6	Kh	K		
5-7	Kh	K		
6-Z6	Kh		K*	Kh
6-Z13		Kh		

B + C

	4-9	8-Z15 / 4-Z15	8-28	7-4	7-6	5-7	5-19
7-4	K	K					
7-6	K	Kh					
5-7	Kh	K					
5-19	Kh	Kh	K				
6-Z13	K*	K*	K*	K*			K*
6-Z38	Kh	K			K*	Kh	

B + D

	4-9	8-Z15 / 4-Z15	4-18	8-28	7-6	5-7	5-19
7-6	K	Kh	K				
5-7	Kh	K	K				
5-19	Kh	Kh	Kh	K			
6-Z13	K*	K*	Kh	K*			K
6-Z38	Kh	K			K*	Kh	

C + D

	4-9	4-18	7-4
7-4	K	K	
6-Z13	K*	Kh	K*

to register and pitch class, pc set 4-8 in A matches the implicit form of 4-8 in C, as shown in example 116. The most immediate association is provided by 3-1, the first composite segment in A and the piano part in C.

The total content of section D, 6-Z13, derives from the two forms of 6-Z13 in B by transposition, with t = 1 and t = 10. The resulting invariant subset is [0,3,6], from which pc3 and pc6 are singled out for special attention in the lowest register at the end of the section. This effects a partitioning of 6-Z13 and brings forth 4-18, apparently as a new set at the end of the piece. As indicated in example 117, pc set 4-18 is a member of K(6-Z13). This is

119.   Webern, Four Pieces for Violin and Piano Op. 7/3

4-Z15   4-18   4-18   4-8

Copyright by Universal Edition. Permission granted by Theodore Presser Company, sole representative in the United States, Canada, and Mexico.

not its first appearance. It occurs as an implicit set 8 times in the second part of section B, under 8-28 only. There are, however, only two contiguous forms, both within statements of 5-19, and these are displayed in example 119.

A graphic overview of the form of the piece, in terms of the association of sections, is given in example 120. The lower of the two graphs dramatizes the non-linear aspect of the form.

We now proceed to a composition of considerably greater duration and complexity, the second of Stravinsky's Four Studies for Orchestra. This composition is an orchestrated and somewhat revised version of the second of the Three Pieces for String Quartet (ex. 33). For the present purpose the orchestral version is preferred since the revisions it contains resolve a number of ambiguities in the earlier quartet version. A sketch-like representation of the score is provided in example 121.

As indicated, the composition consists of a succession of eight short sections, some of which are repeated, either intact or varied. These repetitions are interesting, in that they produce new successions of sections and hence new temporal relations. The sections are designated by letters, in the usual way. Subscripts indicate subsections of larger sections; superscripts indicate variants of a section or subsection.

Some 32 sets comprise the stock of pitch materials used in the work. Several of the sets are represented more than once, and repetitions within and among the eight sections are evident in example 121 and summarized at the bottom of example 122. Complement-related pairs are of considerable importance.

120.   Webern, Four Pieces for Violin and Piano Op. 7/3
       Association of sections

Notice in particular the sets of cardinals 4 and 8. In fact, sets of cardinal 4 predominate, whereas sets of cardinal 3 are not included at all in the analysis,
since they seem to be of no consequence in the music.

Examination of the table of set-complex relations for the entire movement
(ex. 122) will show that although the relations are by no means sparse the
set-complex structure is not connected. There are, however, connected structures for the individual sections and for the sections combined. Here, as in
the previous work, Webern's Op. 7/3, a main concern, in addition to the set-
complex relations, will be the derivational processes that provide links between sections and within sections.

In order to make this discussion as concise as possible, the set-complex
structure and some special aspects of the music of each section will be considered first. Then it will be ascertained whether for each pair of sections
there is an association. Two criteria will be invoked: (1) The sections have at

121.   Stravinsky, Four Studies for Orchestra (No. 2)

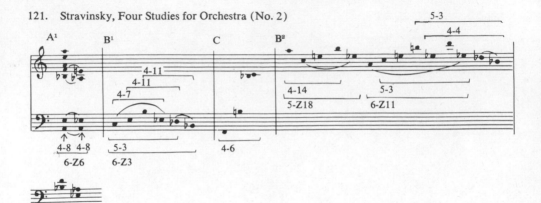

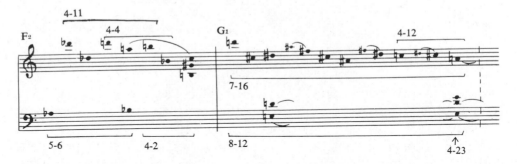

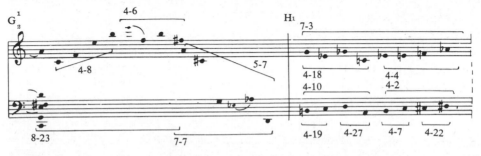

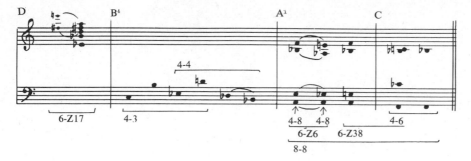

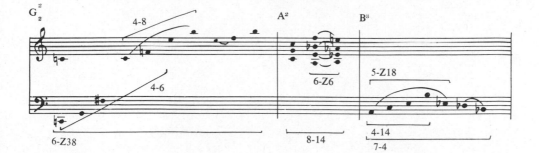

least one explicit set in common; (2) The combined set-complex structure is connected. The sets are regarded as associated if at least one of the criteria is met. If the first criterion is met, derivations involving explicit sets will be determined. If only the second criterion is met, implicit sets will enter into the analysis for derivations. Finally, by applying the rule of transitivity it will be determined if there are combinations of associated sections larger than the pair.

In the interest of economy the subscripts and superscripts designating subsections and variants of sections will often not be used; instead, the letter

	4-2	4-3	4-4	4-6	4-7	4-8	4-10	4-11	4-12	4-14	4-18	4-19	4-22	4-23	4-27	5-3	7-4	7-6	7-7	5-10	7-15	7-16	5-Z18	5-19	5-22	5-23
5-3	Kh	Kh	Kh	K	Kh	K	K	Kh	K	K	K	K	K	K	K		K*	K*	K	K*	K*	K*	K*	K*	K	K*
7-4	K	K	Kh	K	Kh	Kh	K	K	Kh	K	K	K	K		K	Kh		K	Kh	K	K	K		K	K	
7-6	K	K	Kh	K	Kh	K	Kh	K	Kh	K	Kh	K	K	K	K	K*	K		K	K*	K	K	K*	K	K	
7-7		K	K	Kh	K	Kh		K	K	K	K	K	K	K	Kh		Kh	K		K*		K	K	K	K	K
5-10	K	Kh	K	K		K	Kh	K	K	Kh	Kh	K	K		K	K*	K	K*	K*		K	K*	Kh	K*	K*	K*
7-15	K	K	K	Kh	K		K	K	K	K	Kh		Kh	K	Kh	K*	K	K		K		K	K	K	K	K
7-16	K	Kh	K		Kh		K	K	K	Kh	Kh	K	K		K	K*	K	K	K	K*	K		K	K		K
5-Z18	Kh		K	K	Kh	K	K	K	K	K	Kh	K		K	K	K*	K	K*	K	Kh	K	K			K*	K
5-19		K		K	K	K		K	K	K	Kh	Kh			K	K*	K	K	K	K*	K				K	K
5-22			K	K		Kh			K	Kh	K	Kh	K	K	K	K	K	K	Kh	K*	K	K	K*			K*
5-23	K	K			Kh		Kh	Kh	Kh	Kh	K	Kh	Kh	Kh	Kh	K*			K	K*	K		K	K		K
5-31										K		Kh			Kh											
7-32	K	K	K	K		K	K	K	Kh	K	K	K	Kh	K	Kh	K				K			K		K	K
6-Z3	Kh	K	Kh	K	K	K	K	K	K	K	Kh	K	Kh	Kh	Kh	K*	K	K	K	K*	K	K	K*	K	K	K
6-Z6/38			K	Kh	Kh	Kh	K	K*	K		Kh	K	K		Kh		Kh	K				K*	K			
6-Z11	Kh	K*	Kh	Kh	K*	K*	K	K	K*	Kh	Kh	K	Kh	K*	K	K*		K		K*			K*	K*	K	K*
6-Z17/43	K	K	K	K	K	Kh	K	Kh	K	K	Kh	K	Kh	K*	K	K*	K	K	K	K*	K	K	K	K	K	K*

Repetition of pc sets in sections A-H of example 121

Section		Section		Section	
4-2/8-2	E, F, H	5-3/7-3	B, H	6-Z3	B
4-3	B, E	7-4	B	6-Z6/38	A, G
4-4	B, F, H	5-6/7-6	E, F, H	6-Z11	B
4-6	C, G	5-7/7-7	G, H	6-Z17/43	D, E, H
4-7	B, H	5-10	H		
4-8	A, E, G	7-15	G		
4-10	H	7-16	F		
4-11	B, F	5-Z18	E		
4-12/8-12	G	5-19	D		
4-14/8-14	A, B	5-22	F		
4-18	E, H	5-23	E		
4-19	H	5-31	H		
4-22	A, F, G, H				
4-23	H				

123. Stravinsky, Four Studies for Orchestra (No. 2.)
      Association of pairs of sections; transitive tuples

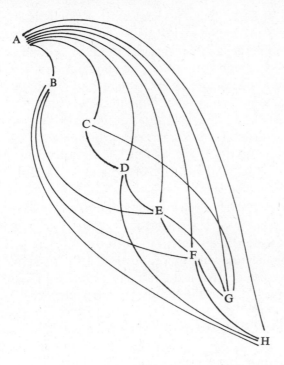

alone will refer to all subsections and variants of the section. Comments on the sets and relations of the individual sections follow.

A. In this opening section we find the invariant pcs 4 and 9 between the two forms of 4-8, as discussed earlier in connection with example 33. Also listed here is the set 4-23:[3,5,8,10], which is formed by the non-invariant pcs between the two forms of 4-8. The importance of this set in the derivational process will be evident as we proceed. With regard to set-complex structure, it is not difficult to ascertain that the section is connected, with nexus set 6-Z6.

B. Imbrication of 4-element sets within 5-element sets is characteristic of this section, which has four variants. The two-note figure that concludes each variant is puzzling. To be sure, it is imitated in the upper part of E, and the pitches B-flat–D-flat occur in F_1, framing the ostinato figure in the lower part, but the motive lacks other references, insofar as can be determined. Again, the set-complex structure is straightforward and connected. Here the nexus set is 6-Z3.

C. This section is also the last one in the piece, and only there, when it is combined with A, is its structural meaning made apparent.

D. Pc set 6-Z17 is important in the composition. Its 5-element subsets, 5-22, occurs only in D and has no further implications in the movement. It is, however, the opening sonority of the subsequent movement. Pc set 6-Z17 is obviously the nexus set here.

E. The set-complex structure is connected, with nexus sets 8-18/4-18 and 5-6/7-6. Pc set 8-18 is predominant in this section, and the two 5-element sets, 5-19 and 5-31, are perhaps best regarded merely as subsets of 8-18, since they do not occur elsewhere in the music. The emergence of 4-8 (from A) in the first vertical is due to one of the revisions mentioned at the outset.

F. The set-complex structure is not connected. A number of interesting features become evident when this section is combined with others.

G. The set-complex structure is connected, with nexus sets 4-8 and 5-7/7-7. With the exception of 4-23, the sets in G_1 do not occur elsewhere in the music; but in the subsequent subsection G_2^1 and its variant G_2^2, sets derived from other sections do occur.

H. The set-complex structure is not connected. This is perhaps the most complicated of all the sections. The orchestral version is particularly enlightening here since it provides H_1 as a separate introductory subsection, whereas the quartet version begins with the equivalent of H_2. Seven sets occur only in H, and, as can be seen from the table in example 122, they relate to one or more of the hexachords in the movement, with the exception of 7-32, which relates only to 4-18.

Before continuing to a discussion of the sections in pairs, the reader's attention is directed to example 123, a graph that shows the associated pairs of sections as well as the transitive tuples.

A+B. The set-complex structure of these sections combined is connected, but only with the aid of all the hexachords together with 4-4. No explicit association is effected between them, however, until the occurrence of the adjacent pair A^2 and B^3. As can be seen in example 121, A^2 differs from A^1 only with respect to pcs 0 and 7, which may be regarded as the transposition of pcs 4 and 9 in A^1 (the invariants). This simple transformation has a remarkable consequence, for A^2 then has as its total content pc set 8-14, and the first four notes in B^3 form the complement, 4-14. Additional associations between A^2 and B^3 are provided both by the invariants between 8-14 and 4-14, pcs 0, 4, and 9, which are also the first three notes in B^3, and by the obvious pitch-references, A and E.

A+C. The nexus set of this connected structure is 6-Z6, the same as the nexus set of A alone. As in the case of A+B, however, their close association is made apparent only at the close of the composition, where C follows A^1. The union of those two sections is pc set 8-8, the complement of the initial sonority of the composition. Perhaps even more extraordinary is the union of the second form of 4-8 in A^1 with 4-6, the total content of C. This union forms the set 6-Z38 which is also the complement of 6-Z6, the total content of A^1. In this way, the derivation of 4-6 from 6-Z6 is rendered precise and the closing function of C is evident. From this and the previous discussion of A+B it should be clear that the composer's reordering of the small sections is far from arbitrary.

A+D. The nexus sets are, perhaps trivially, the hexachords and 4-8. Section A is associated with D only through 4-8, in fact. Although this set is contained in 6-Z17 (the total content of D), it is made explicit as a segment only at the beginning of E, as remarked above.

A+E. The set-complex structure is not connected, and although the sections have a set in common, pc set 4-8, they are not strongly associated.

A+F. Again, the set-complex structure is not connected. However, the sections are associated in a most interesting way through pc set 4-23. It will be recalled that 4-23 in A consists of the non-invariant pcs formed by the successive statements of 4-8:[3,5,8,10]. In F_1 4-23 is formed by the ostinato figure in the lower register. This form of 4-23, which is transpositionally equivalent to 4-23 in A^1 with $t = 5$, effects three invariants. Pitch association is further strengthened by the dyad G-sharp-A-sharp, held throughout F_1, which corresponds to B-flat-A-flat in the same register in A^1.

A+G. The nexus sets are 6-Z6/38 and 4-8. A specific link from A to G is provided not only by 4-8, but also by 4-23. These sets, which are maximally dissimilar (R_0), are closely intertwined, as follows. Pc set 4-23 closes G_1 and is then followed by its complement in G_2^1. This large composite segment contains 4-8: [11,0,4,5]. Now, with respect to 4-23 in A, the transposition here effects nil invariance. In the case of 4-8, however, pcs 4 and 5 are held fixed between the two forms of that set which appear in A and in G. Comparison of G_2^1 with G_2^2 reveals an even closer connection between A and G. In G_2^2, 8-23 has been reduced to 6-Z38, the complement of 6-Z6 in A. The derivation is 6-Z38 = $T(I(\overline{6\text{-}Z6}),6)$. Again pcs 4 and 5 are held fixed by this transformation, and these are precisely the pitches of the upper moving voice in A. In G they are made prominent as a repeated dyad.

A+H. Although the set-complex structure is not connected, the two sections are linked by 4-23. Here 8-23, the upper part of H_2, is the transposed complement of 4-23 in A. The single invariant, pc8, is the terminal note in the melodic configuration.

B+C. The set-complex structure of this pair is connected but trivial in the sense that the nexus sets are the same as those for B alone. Although 4-6 is in Kh(6-Z11), there is no explicit derivation, and therefore the pair is not regarded as associated.

B+D. The set-complex structure is not connected and there are no sets in common. This lack of association is particularly apparent in the closing part of the movement, where D stands between B^3 and B^4.

B+E. The nexus sets for this pair are 6-Z3, 6-Z11, and 4-18. The latter is an explicit set only in E. Derivation of the common set is by transposition, with $t = 9$, and results in the invariant dyad 11, 0. The melodic prominence of these pcs in B (especially in B^1 and B^4) suggests that there may be further implicit or at least somewhat concealed associations of the two sections. Observe that that form of 8-18 in E which results from the combination of moving lines, as shown in the small notes below E in example 121, can be decomposed into two tetrachords, 4-3 followed by 4-7. And 4-7 here is the untransposed equivalent of 4-7 in B^1 and B^2:[11,0,3,4].

B+F. Section F alone exhibits a weak set-complex structure. Combined with B, however, it is connected, with nexus sets 6-Z3, 6-Z11, and 4-4. Since these are the same as the nexus sets of B alone, every set in F can be derived from B. Here we cite only the derivations of the common sets. Pc set 5-Z18 in F is derived by transposition from 5-Z18 in B, with t = 11. Pc set 4-11 in F derives from two forms of that set in B by transposition, with t = 10 and by inversion, with t = 0. The collection of invariants under these transformations forms pc set 5-3:[10,11,1,2,3], which is an explicit set in B.

B+G. These sections are not associated.

B+H. This pair exhibits a connected set-complex structure and three pc sets in common. The nexus sets are the hexachords and 4-18. No other pair with H as a member meets both criteria of association; therefore, it seems reasonable to claim that the primary derivation of H is from B. Invariants strengthen the association, as can be seen from the list below.

$$
\begin{array}{lll}
\text{4-4 in H:} & [3,4,5,8] & \\
\quad \text{in B:} & [10,1,2,3] & IT_6 \\
\text{4-7 in H:} & [11,0,3,4] & \\
\quad \text{in B:} & [11,0,3,4] & T_0 \\
\text{5-3 in H:} & [11,0,2,3,4] & \\
\quad \text{in B:} & [11,0,2,3,4] & T_0 \\
& [11,0,1,3,4] & IT_3 \\
& [10,11,1,2,3] & T_1 \\
\end{array}
$$

Complementation of each of the three forms of 5-3 listed above will produce 7-3 as it occurs in H, under the operations T_{10}, IT_0, and IT_1, applied to the sets in the order listed.

C+D. These sets have a connected set-complex structure, with 6-Z17 as nexus set. As in the case of A+C, the catenated sections form a large set that is structurally significant. Example 121 shows that C+D forms 8-18, which is followed immediately in section E by 4-18 and by two forms of 8-18.

C+G. Of the remaining combinations with C, only C+G is of interest. Section G_2^1 contains 4-6 (IT_4), and G_2^2 again contains 4-6 (T_7). The union of invariants is [0,5,11], thus effecting a strong pitch association as well, although the sections are some distance apart in the music. Pc set 4-8 is in the relations R_1 and R_p to 4-6, and here R_p is strongly represented.

D+E. Pc set 6-Z17 (all of D) is the first set in E.

D+F. These sections are not associated.

D+H. These sections are associated only through the pair 6-Z17/6-Z43. Pc set 6-Z43 (in H) = $T(\overline{6\text{-}Z17},1)$. Invariants are not significant.

E+F. Pc set 5-6 is in both sections, and the forms in F derive by transposition from the one in E.

E+G. The basis of association is the common set 4-8. The transposition level ($t = 2$) is such that no invariants are produced.

E+H. These sections are associated through the pair 6-Z17/6-Z43, and the derivation was described above in connection with D+H. Two additional sets in H derive from E, 4-18 (T_4) and 5-6 (IT_9). The invariants are inconsequential.

F+G. Pc set 4-23 occurs as the lower component of F_1 and as the final vertical in G_1. The two forms are transpositionally equivalent, with $t = 6$, but no invariants are produced. Pc set 8-23 in G_2^1 is the literal complement of 4-23 in F, an especially significant derivation.

F+H. Four sets in H derive from section F, 4-2, 4-4, 8-23, and 5-6. Invariance is unimportant.

G+H. Pc set 7-7 in H is a transposition of 7-7 in G_2^1. This operation leaves only two pcs invariant, 3 and 6. More significantly, perhaps, 7-7 in H is the literal complement of 5-7 in G_2^1. Finally, pc set 8-23, the upper part of H_2, derives from 8-23 in G_2^1 by transposition, with $t = 2$.

It is now appropriate to state some general conclusions concerning the form of the entire movement in terms of the association of sections according to the rule of transitivity. These associations can be discerned from the graph, example 123, but for convenience are listed below. There are two quintuples, one quadruple, and one triple:

A+B+E+F+H   (nexus sets: the hexachords and 4-14)
A+C+G   (nexus sets: 6-Z6/38 and 4-8)
A+D+E+H
A+E+F+G+H

No set is common to all the members of any of these combinations. Moreover, only the first two exhibit connected set-complex structures. Thus, as has already been said, the set-complex structure for the composition as a whole is not connected, and the structural coherence of the work is dependent upon the individual sections, the pairs, and the few larger combinations of components. Whereas it was not difficult to describe the overall structure of Webern's Op. 7/3 in terms of derivations involving the members of two set complexes, the situation here is more complicated and diffuse: every section is associated with at least one other section, but the derivations do not make reference to a single and interconnected system of relations.

Turning now to a shorter and perhaps simpler composition, let us consider the third of Berg's orchestral songs Op. 4, on picture postcard texts by Peter Altenberg. A condensed representation of the music is given in example 124.

124. Berg, "Altenberg Lieder" Op. 4/3

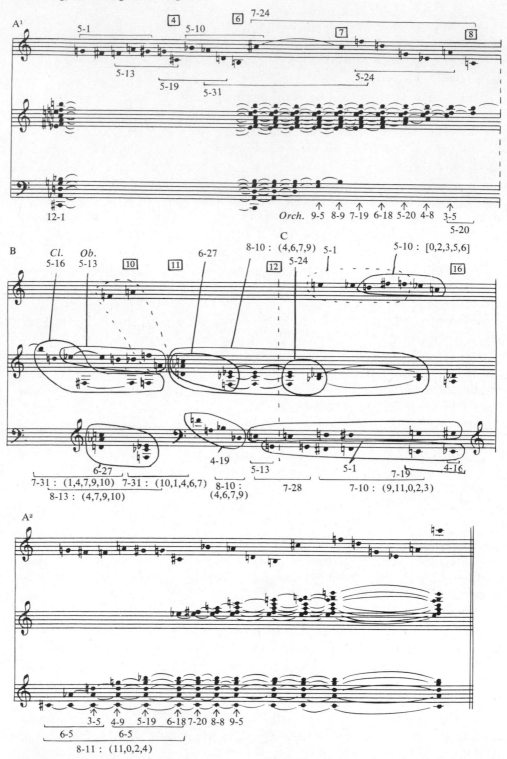

Copyright by Universal Edition. Permission granted by Theodore Presser Company, sole representative in the United States, Canada, and Mexico.

125. Berg, "Altenberg Lieder" Op. 4/3
Vocal line and segmentations

Ü – ber die Gren - zen des All blick – test du sin – –

a) *Text - dependent segmentation*

6-Z37 : [5,6,7,8,9,1]   3-8   6-21 : [11,1,2,3,5,7]
8-21 : (4,6,8,10)

b) *Text - independent segmentation* 5-19   5-10   5-10

5-1
5-1
5-13   5-31   7-24

4-13
4-13   4-13

– – nend hin - aus;   Hat-test nie Sor-ge um Hof und Haus!

a)
2-3

b)
5-24

4-11

Le - ben und Traum vom Le - ben.

5-10 : [0,2,3,5,6]
6-2 : [0,2,3,4,5,6]

5-1
5-10

126. Berg, "Altenberg Lieder" Op. 4/3
      Set-complex relations

	4-8	4-9	8-10	4-11	4-13	4-16	4-19
5-1	K		K	K	K		
5-10			Kh	K	Kh		
5-13	K			K		K	Kh
5-16	K		K	K	K		K
5-19	K	K			Kh	K	
5-20	Kh	K			K	Kh	K
5-24			K	Kh	K	Kh	K
7-28	K	K		K	K	K	K
5-31		K	K		Kh		
6-5	Kh	Kh			Kh	Kh	
6-18	Kh	Kh			Kh	Kh	
6-27			Kh		Kh		

	5-10	5-16	5-19	5-20	5-31
6-5			Kh		
6-18			Kh	Kh	
6-27	Kh	Kh			Kh

Ostensibly, the song divides into four sections, corresponding to the lines of the poem, but since the music for the last line is a variant of that for the first, it seems more reasonable to speak of a three-part division.

Section A^1 has an unusual feature. A 12-note sonority is sustained by the orchestra from the beginning of the song up to the middle of measure 6. At that point, one note at a time is relinquished, from the bottom up, until only the topmost note, B, remains. This process creates the series of verticals indicated below the staff. In section A^2 the 12-note sonority is reconstituted, from the bottom up, thus producing an ordered series of verticals consisting of the complements of those in A^1.

Before discussing set-complex and other relations, it is necessary to say a few words about the segmentation of the vocal part. This is composed in a very intricate way, so that there is very little correspondence between the grouping of words in the text and the set structure of the line. In example 125 the distinct components of the vocal line are displayed on the top stave. Immediately below this is shown a segmentation that is entirely dependent upon the text and that does not take into account other features of melodic structure—imbrication, in particular. This produces very strange results, indeed. With the exception of pc set 5-10, none of the sets occurs elsewhere in the music. The clue to the underlying structure is found in the melodic line at measure 13. There, the first five notes form 5-1, an ordered transposition of the opening five notes at measure 2. This interlocks with 5-10, as shown in example 124. The text-independent segmentation, shown in example 125 at b, which utilizes imbrication, reveals that the melodic line is made up of intersecting forms of sets that do occur elsewhere in the music. The lower stave shows the tetrachordal imbrication, including two circular permutations of 4-13, which is one of the most important sets in the composition. It should be added that there are also circular permutations in the case of 5-1 and 5-10, as evident in example 125.

The set-complex relations for the entire song are shown in example 126. Even a cursory inspection will confirm the fact that the structure is not connected. In addition, many of the sets are sparsely related—for example, 5-1. One tetrachord, 4-13, however, has abundant relations. It is perhaps not surprising that this is Berg's motto (cf. ex. 114).

Relations among the sets formed by the orchestral part in A can be read directly from example 124. All are members of Kh(6-18). With one exception, pc set 5-13, all the sets in the vocal line of A are members of K(4-13). Pc set 5-13 is in Kh(4-19), a set which occurs only in B. Since 4-19 is not a member of Kh(6-18), the set-complex structure of A is not connected.

Of the sets only in A (and these are all in the orchestral part), perhaps two require comment. Pc set 5-20 occurs twice, first as a vertical, then as the final composite segment. This, of course, refers to A^1. In A^2, 5-20 is represented by its complement, which occurs only once. Section A^2 also differs significantly from A^1 with respect to pc set 6-5, which is formed twice in succession as a composite segment between orchestra and voice. The invariant subset that results is 4-9:[7,8,1,2], which is the first vertical in the second form of 6-5. Note also that both forms of 6-5 are subsumed by a large composite segment, 8-11. This is the complement of a prominent tetrachord in the vocal line as shown on the lower staff of section b) in example 125. Pc set 6-5 is in the relations R_1 and R_p to 6-18, which overlaps the second statement of 6-5. Moreover, R_p is strongly represented as the vertical segment 5-19. Section B begins with a large composite segment, pc set 8-13, the complement of the two forms of 4-13 in the vocal line of A (ex. 125). The successive statements of 7-31 below 8-13 are also derived from the vocal line of A, by complementation of 5-31, with t = 8 and t = 5. In addition, the two forms of 7-31 are transpositionally equivalent, with t = 9, and the invariant subset is 6-27, which occurs twice as a segment in B (example 124).

Section B is also associated with A through pc set 5-13. This set is a subsegment of the vocal line in A and occurs twice in B, as a melodic line played by the oboe and as the final composite segment. The derivation of the melodic line from the vocal subsegment is such that three pcs are held fixed, and these are represented by the pitches D-flat, F, and A in measure 10 (oboe). This detail is quite prominent in the music at that point, since the sole pitch content of the vocal line is F-A. Further, those notes are taken up in the melodic segment, 4-19 in measure 11. It should also be remarked that the two melodic forms of 5-13 have similar bips (1146 and 1144).

Three sets occur only in B: 5-16, 8-10, and 6-27. Both 5-16 and 8-10 are members of Kh(6-27), as are 7-31 and 8-10. Thus, this set complex can perhaps be regarded as the predominant one in section B. From the table (ex. 126) it can be seen that pc set 5-10 is also a member of Kh(6-27). This set is a subsegment of the vocal line in A and in C. It is also in the relations R_1 and R_p with 5-16, the clarinet melody in B. R_p is strongly represented in 5-10 as it occurs, transposed, in the vocal line in C.

One set is unique to section C, pc set 4-16, which marks the end of the section. This set is a member of Kh(6-5), and 6-5 follows at the beginning of A^2. It is also a member of Kh(5-20), and 5-20 also has a closing function at the end of A^1.

Apart from pc set 4-16, the sets in C are derived from A. The two forms of 5-1 in the orchestra (in ordered inversion) derive from the opening 5-note segment of the vocal line of A. Pc sets 5-10 and 7-10 derive from the vocal line of A as well, as does pc set 5-24. Pc set 7-19, the final large segment in C, derives from 5-19 and 7-19 in A by complementation and transposition, under conditions of minimal invariance. It should be remarked in this connection that 7-19, the vertical in the orchestra in A, is the literal complement of 5-19, which precedes it as a subsegment of the vocal line.

Sections B and C are associated through the melodic components 5-16 and 5-10, as mentioned above, and are joined by 8-10, which is partitioned into 6-27 (in B) and 5-24 (in C). Otherwise the two sections are not closely linked.

Thus, although the set-complex structure of the song as a whole is not connected, the relations within the sections and the derivations between sections effect concise and cogent linkages.

In previous sections, extracts from Stravinsky's *The Rite of Spring* have served to illustrate some of the general relations between pc sets. Now we will undertake the analysis of a long span of music from that work, the first two sections of the final movement entitled "Sacrificial Dance." A condensed score is given in example 127.* The sketch-like representation in example 128 is intended to provide a still more concise overview and to indicate segments and sets. By omitting repetitions it is possible to show the main components in the succession in which they occur.

*This score was made from the 1943 revision of the "Sacrificial Dance," which contains some significant changes in detail. The rehearsal numbers given here correspond to those in that edition.

127. Stravinsky, "Sacrificial Dance" from *The Rite of Spring*

A

B

128. Stravinsky, "Sacrificial Dance" from *The Rite of Spring*

129.

130.

7-16 : [9,10,0,1,2,3,6]

We begin with a descriptive survey of the sections. This also provides an opportunity to explain some of the less obvious segments. The movement begins with the vertical, 6-Z42, repeated four times. At the fourth repetition a new succession is initiated, incorporating 6-27 and a transposition of 6-Z42. In this portion the upper voice forms pc set 4-2, and within 4-2 is 3-3. These structures are but part of the complete melodic line, which is unfolded over the span of the entire section and only completed with the accented B-flat two measures before the end of the section. Example 129 shows the entire line, with subsegments forming 3-11 and 4-20 at the close.

At rehearsal no. 3 new verticals are introduced, beginning with 6-Z29. At the same time, a composite segment is formed, pc set 7-32. It will be recalled that this is one of the basic sets in *The Rite of Spring*. All the individual vertical sets in the two measures beginning at rehearsal no. 3 are represented in section B as well. These and other repetitions will be discussed further on. In addition to the verticals, there is another substructure of importance in the passage, the segment formed by the outer voices shown in example 129. These voices form pc set 6-Z23, and at the accented point in the passage, with A in the upper voice, the vertical is the Z-correspondent of 6-Z23, 6-Z45.

The two passages just discussed are then repeated with minor variations not affecting pc content. At rehearsal no. 5 a new composite segment is formed solely by the placement of the bass note F. This set, 7-16, is another prominent set in *The Rite of Spring* and is often associated with 7-32. In fact, in the original version it is the first composite segment, incorporating 6-Z28 and 6-Z42 as component sets (example 130).

The final passage of the first section, beginning at rehearsal no. 7, carries the upper voice to the high B-flat mentioned above and introduces new pc sets, notably the verticals 6-Z43 and the composite segments forming 7-25

131. Stravinsky, "Sacrificial Dance" from *The Rite of Spring*
Set-complex relations

	8-1	4-2	4-Z15	8-18	4-20	8-23	8-28	5-10	7-16	5-19	5-20	5-22	5-23	5-25	7-27	5-28	7-29	7-30	7-31	5-32	7-35	7-Z37
5-10	K	K	Kh	K	K		K															
7-16	K	K	Kh	Kh	K	K	K	K														
5-19	K		Kh	Kh	K	K	K	K	K													
5-20		K	K	K	Kh	K		K	Kh													
5-22								Kh	K	K												
5-23	K	K	Kh	K	K	Kh	K	K	K	K*												
5-25	K	K	K	K	K	K		K	Kh													
7-27	K	K	Kh	K	Kh	K	Kh	K	K	K		K										
5-28	K	K	Kh	K	K	K		K	Kh	K		Kh	K*	K								
7-29	K	K	K	K	K	Kh		K	Kh	K				Kh		Kh						
7-30	K	K	Kh	K	K		Kh	K		Kh												
7-31		K	Kh		K	Kh	K						Kh	Kh	Kh	Kh	K	Kh	K			
5-32		K	Kh		K	Kh								K	K		K			K		
7-35																					K*	
7-Z37								K	K	K	K*	Kh	K	K	K	K	K	K	K	K	K*	K*
6-Z19	K			K	K	K	K			K		Kh							K			
6-Z23/45	K	K	K	K	K	Kh	K	K	Kh	Kh	K*		K*	K*	K	Kh	K	K	Kh	K	K*	
6-Z24/46	K	K	K	K	K	K	K	Kh	K	K				Kh	K		Kh		Kh	Kh		
6-Z25	K	K	K	K*	K	Kh	Kh	Kh	K	K*			Kh	K	K	Kh	Kh		K	K		
6-27			Kh	Kh	K	K	K	K	Kh	K		K	Kh	Kh		K*	Kh		K	Kh	Kh	
6-Z28/49			K	K	K	K	K	K	K	K	K*		K		K	K	K		K	K		
6-Z29			Kh	Kh	K	Kh	K	K	K	Kh	Kh		Kh	Kh	Kh	Kh	Kh		Kh	K	Kh	
6-30						Kh	K	K		K	K*	K		K					K		Kh	
6-33	K							K	K*	K	K*	K	Kh	Kh	K	K	Kh	K*	K	K	Kh	
6-Z42		K	K	Kh	K*			K	K*	K	K*	K										
6-Z43	K*	K*	Kh	Kh	K*																	K*

and 7-28. It is perhaps worth mentioning that both occurrences of 6-Z43 are replaced by 5-28 in the published piano score.

The second section begins at rehearsal no. 8 with a marked change in rhythm and sonority. With the introduction of the 3-note motive 3-1 one measure before rehearsal no. 11, the sonority becomes denser and we find the hexachord 6-Z25 at the end of the motion, within the composite segment forming 8-23. At rehearsal no. 12 a transposition of the motive 3-1 appears as a tremolo figure over 5-23 and forms pc set 7-29. As can be seen from the set-complex table, example 131, this set still contains 6-Z25, as well as its complement.

At rehearsal no. 15 the 3-note motive is brought in at still another level. The larger composite segment here is 6-Z43, which occurred at the end of section A, while the accompanying chord is 5-20, a vertical in A at 3+1. Thus, here for the first time in B, there are specific repetitions of sets introduced in A. This merging of the materials of the two sections is continued in the passage beginning at 16+3, where we find 6-27, 5-28, 5-10, 5-25, and 6-Z43, all of which have occurred in A. The composite segment formed in 16+5 at the stretto is the 8-note set 8-18, which is of considerable importance to the set-complex structure of the sections combined. It is an important set throughout *The Rite of Spring,* occurring, for instance, in "Ritual of the Two Rival Tribes," together with its complement.

Beginning at 17+2 there is a repetition of the passage just discussed, with a change only at the onset where 5-19, embedded in its complement replaces 5-28, the set appearing in an equivalent position in the first statement of the passage. A change of one note is involved (A replaces F-sharp) and the common subset is 4-18. There is no apparent reason for this change other than to point up the new beginning. In the first version the sonority at this point is 6-Z12, which does not occur at all in the revision.

At 19+1 the alternation of 6-Z19 and 6-27 becomes the point of departure for the progression that begins at 20. In addition to the verticals and to the composite segments formed by the verticals, there is again an important substructure formed by the outer voices. This pattern is shown in example 132. Observe that the unfolding of the hexachord, 6-Z24, in the lower voice is followed immediately by the vertical 6-Z46, its Z-correspondent. These, as well as the upper voice hexachord, 6-33, are associated with the initial sonority of the section, 5-23, as can be seen from the set-complex table, example 131, and indeed there follows at rehearsal no. 21 a return to the opening passage, now transposed, with t = 10.

Concluding the B section is the two measure passage that begins at 24+3. New sets introduced here are 7-30, the ascending melodic figure at the end, and the final vertical, 6-Z49. Pc set 6-Z49 in this cadential capacity can be understood only with reference to the original version, where, as remarked

132.

133.

134. Stravinsky, "Sacrificial Dance" from *The Rite of Spring*
Outer voices in section B

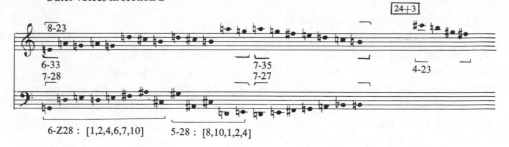

135. Stravinsky, "Sacrificial Dance" from *The Rite of Spring*
Set-complex relations (sections)

A

	4-2	4-20	5-10	7-16	5-20	5-22	7-25	7-28	7-32	7-Z37
5-10	K	K								
7-16	K	K	Kh							
5-20	K	Kh								
5-22		K								
7-25	K									
7-28	K									
7-32										
7-Z37	K	K								K*
6-Z19		K								
6-27		Kh	Kh	Kh			Kh			
6-Z29										
6-Z42	K	K	K	K*	K*	K	K	K*	K	
6-Z43	K	K*	K	K*		K	K*	K*	Kh	
6-Z45			K		Kh		K*		K	

B

	8-1	4-2	4-Z15	8-18	8-23	8-28	5-10	7-16	5-19	5-20	5-23	5-25	7-27	5-28	7-29	7-30	7-31	5-32	7-35
5-10	K	K	Kh	Kh															
7-16	K	K	Kh	Kh	K	K													
5-19	K	K	Kh	Kh	K														
5-20	K	K	Kh	Kh	K	K													
5-23		K	Kh	Kh	Kh	K													
5-25	K	K	Kh	Kh	Kh	K													
7-27		K	Kh	Kh	K	K													
5-28		K	Kh	Kh	K	K													
7-29			Kh	Kh	Kh	K													
7-30			Kh	Kh	Kh														
7-31			Kh	Kh	Kh	Kh													
5-32			Kh	Kh	Kh	Kh													
7-35			Kh	Kh	Kh	Kh													
6-Z19		K	K	K	K	K	K°	K	Kh	K*	K°	K*	K	K*	Kh	K	K*	K	K*
6-Z23		K	K	Kh	K	Kh	K	K	K	K*	K*	K*	K	K	Kh		Kh	K	K
6-Z24/46		K	K	Kh	Kh	Kh	Kh	Kh	K	Kh	Kh	Kh		Kh			K	Kh	Kh
6-Z25			Kh	Kh	Kh	Kh	Kh	K		K		Kh		K			K	Kh	
6-27			K	Kh	Kh	Kh	Kh	K	K	Kh	Kh	Kh		K°			Kh	Kh	Kh
6-Z28/49			K	Kh	K	K				Kh									
6-30			Kh	Kh		Kh			K	Kh									
6-33						Kh													
6-Z43		K*	K°	Kh	K	K*	K°		K	K*				K°		K*			Kh

above (ex. 130), the first sonority in the "Sacrificial Dance" is 6–Z28, the complement of 6–Z49.

At 24+3, as at rehearsal nos. 3 and 19+1, the outer voices (of the two lower staves) combine to form an important substructure. Example 133 shows pc set 4–23 in the upper voice moving against 4–Z15 in the bass.*
As shown in example 134, the upper voice pattern at 24+3 is the complement of the total upper voice motion from the beginning of the section through 20+1—with the return at 21 to the opening music regarded as a kind of interruption.†

The pattern of outer voices indicated in example 134, of the entire B section is remarkable in another way. The lowest voice is segmented according to the subdivisions of the section, into 6–Z28 followed by 5–28, the latter thus embedded in its complement. All the instances of important outer voice substructures suggest strongly that sets occurring over short spans of the music as verticals and composite segments formed by verticals also control larger patterns of motion in a way that is not immediately obvious.

The preceding narrative account may serve as a point of departure for a more detailed examination of the structure of this music, beginning with set-complex relations. Tables of those relations for A and B, both separately and combined, are provided in example 135.

The set-complex structure of A is not connected and is noticeably sparse. Among the hexachords of that section, 6–Z49 has the greatest number of relations, but it is not linked up in any simple way with the other hexachords, and, in fact, is completely detached from 6–Z45. This distinction is maintained in the relation R_0 between 6–Z19 and 6–Z45, and the extreme fluctuation of interval content reinforces the metrical accentuation that always accompanies the succession of the two chords. 6–Z19 is, however, the only hexachord represented here that contains 7–Z37, hence the only set-complex link between the verticals and the large-scale melodic motion shown in example 129.

In B as in A, the large number of hexachords virtually rules out a hexachordal nexus set. In B, however, as well as in the combined sections, pc set 8-18 is a likely candidate. Indeed, 8-18, together with 5-23 and 5-25 would connect the set-complex structure if it were not for the anomalous sets 7-30 and 7-35. It will be recalled that these are melodic sets in the upper part, and that 7-35 contains 6-33, which links to 8-18 through 5-23 and 5-25. Pc set 7-30, the final melodic pattern in the section, remains isolated from the main set-complex structure.

It should also be pointed out that pc set 8-1, which results from the

---

*In the sketchbook this passage as well as the one beginning at 20 are sketched in red ink as separate, and probably special, components (Stravinsky 1969).

†This way of combining units, so characteristic of Stravinsky, is documented by Edward T. Cone (1962).

136.

6-Z42 : [0,1,2,3,6,9]   6-Z42 : [11,0,1,2,5,8]

8-23 : [1,3,6,8]   8-23 : (11,1,4,6)

137.

A

5-10 : [11,0,2,3,5]

B

5-10 : [8,10,11,1,2̇]

138.

A   B

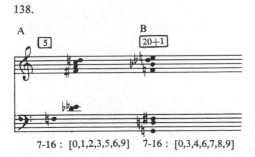

7-16 : [0,1,2,3,5,6,9]   7-16 : [0,3,4,6,7,8,9]

139.

A   B

5-20 : [10,11,3,5,6]   5-20 : [9,10,2,4,5]

140.

A   B

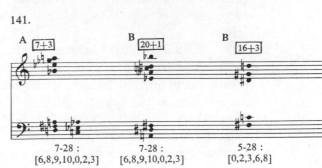

7-25 : [3,5,6,8,9,10,0]   5-25 : [8,11,1,2,4]

141.

A   B   B

7-28 : [6,8,9,10,0,2,3]   7-28 : [6,8,9,10,0,2,3]   5-28 : [0,2,3,6,8]

142.

A   B

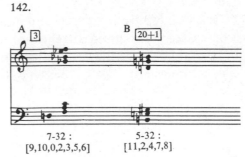

7-32 : [9,10,0,2,3,5,6]   5-32 : [11,2,4,7,8]

cumulative motion of the motive 3-1, is very weakly related to the remaining sets in B. Thus, there is maximum contrast between the "chordal" component (and its outer voices) and the recurrent and striking theme.

Two additional aspects of structure are of interest here: derivations among recurrent sets and similarity relations—in particular among the hexachords, which are so abundant in both sections.

Example 136 shows the two sets which recur only in A or in B, but not in both. The first of these, 6-Z42, has already been mentioned. The transposition here, t = 11, is extended to the subsequent repetition of section A. The three invariants form pc set 3-1, the set which will become the melodic motive of B. Pc set 8-23, which occurs only in B, is transposed, with t = 11, at 22+3.

Equivalent and complement-related sets occurring in A and B are displayed in examples 137 through 146. These recurring sets of course serve to unify the two sections, even though they do not seem to be arranged in any systematic way between the sections. With the exception of 5-28/7-28, which are associated with 6-Z43 whenever they occur, there is no consistent retention of particular sonic environments. Similarly, the transformations are not consistently of special import. Some comments on each of the recurring sets follow.

Pc set 5-10 (ex. 137), which occurs in A as the important bass figure (ex. 129), recurs as a vertical in B, as indicated. The two forms are inversionally equivalent and the invariants are inconsequential. This melodic statement of 5-10 is carried to the upper parts in the final section of the Sacrificial Dance (at 194+1).

Pc set 7-16 (ex. 138) occurs twice, and in this case the invariant subset, 4-28, is the complement of the 8-note set that occurs in the same context as the second statement of 7-16. It will be recalled (ex. 130) that 7-16 is formed by the union of 6-Z28 and 6-Z42 at the opening of the movement in the original version.

Pc set 5-20 (ex. 139) is prominent as a vertical in section A, occurring twice in the passage introduced at rehearsal no. 3, and again in B, where it occurs at rehearsal no. 15 as the first change of harmony from the initial 5-23.

The complementary pair 7-25/5-25 (ex. 140) are of no special significance. Pc set 7-25, formed as a composite segment in A at 7+1, is secondary with respect to its subset there, 6-Z45, while 5-25 at 17 in B is under 6-27, which is of greater interest, as will be discussed below.

In example 141 the two occurrences of 7-28, both formed as composite segments, are of interest, since the sets are transpositionally equivalent, with t = 0. The complement, 5-28, occurs as a vertical. Pc set 7-28 occurs with embedded complement in the lower part of B, as shown in example 134.

Pc set 7-32 (ex. 142) occurs as a composite segment in A, and its complement occurs as a vertical under 6-Z46 at the end of the passage beginning at rehearsal no. 20.

143.

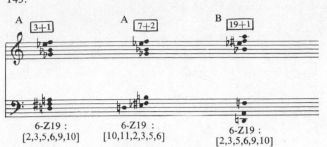

6-Z19 :
[2,3,5,6,9,10]

6-Z19 :
[10,11,2,3,5,6]

6-Z19 :
[2,3,5,6,9,10]

144.

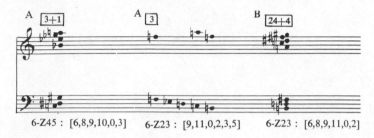

6-Z45 : [6,8,9,10,0,3]   6-Z23 : [9,11,0,2,3,5]   6-Z23 : [6,8,9,11,0,2]

145.

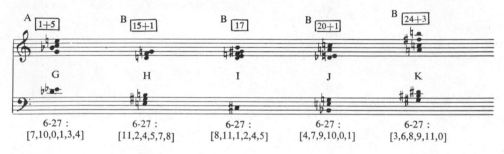

6-27 :
[7,10,0,1,3,4]

6-27 :
[11,2,4,5,7,8]

6-27 :
[8,11,1,2,4,5]

6-27 :
[4,7,9,10,0,1]

6-27 :
[3,6,8,9,11,0]

146.

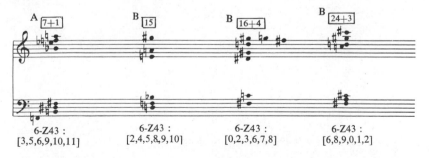

6-Z43 :
[3,5,6,9,10,11]

6-Z43 :
[2,4,5,8,9,10]

6-Z43 :
[0,2,3,6,7,8]

6-Z43 :
[6,8,9,0,1,2]

147. Stravinsky, "Sacrificial Dance" from *The Rite of Spring*
Similarity relations among hexachords

	6-Z19	6-Z23	6-Z24	6-Z25	6-27	6-Z28	6-Z29	6-30	6-33	6-Z42	6-Z43	6-Z45	6-Z46
6-Z19													
6-Z23	R_0												
6-Z24	R_p	R_p											
6-Z25	R_p	R_0	R_2,R_p										
6-27	R_p,R_p	R_2,R_p	R_p	R_p									
6-Z28	R_0,R_p	R_0	R_p	R_p	R_2,R_p								
6-Z29	R_p	R_1	R_p	R_p	R_2,R_p	R_1,R_p							
6-30	R_0	R_1,R_p	R_p	R_2,R_p	R_2,R_p	R_3,R_p	R_1,R_p						
6-33		R_p	R_0	R_0,R_p	R_p	R_0	R_p	R_p					
6-Z42		R_1			R_2,R_p	R_1,R_p	R_1,R_p	R_p	R_0				
6-Z43	R_p	R_p			R_2,R_p	R_1,R_p	R_1,R_p	R_p	R_p	R_p			
6-Z45	R_0				R_2,R_p	R_1,R_p			R_0	R_1,R_p	R_p		
6-Z46				R_2,R_p	R_p			R_p		R_0,R_p	R_p	R_1	
6-Z49	R_0,R_p	R_1,R_p			R_2,R_p	R_1,R_p				R_1	R_p	R_1	R_p

Of the hexachords, four occur both in A and in B. The two different forms of 6–Z19 shown in example 143 are inversionally equivalent, with t = 8. This operation yields 5 invariant pcs (more than obtainable under T alone) and the invariant subset is 5–Z17, a set that is not represented in the music here.

The complementary pair, 6–Z23/6–Z45, (ex. 144) has already been discussed (ex. 129). Pc set 6–Z23 occurs again as the penultimate chord in B, but the invariants involved are of no consequence, as is often the case in this music.

Pc set 6–27 (ex. 145), which is represented five times, offers an exception to the comment above concerning invariance. All the forms of 6–27 shown in example 145 are transpositionally equivalent. Maximum invariance under T is obtained for t = 3 and t = 9 only, and the latter value holds between G and J and between H and I. The resulting invariant set is 5–31, the complement of which occurs with J at 20+1.

Pc set 6–Z43 (ex. 146) occurs four times; invariance is not significant.

To sum up, the transformations of recurrent sets are such that, for the most part, maximum differentiation with respect to pc content is maintained, or invariance is not a significant structural feature.

In view of the large number (14) of hexachords represented in the music, it would seem worthwhile to examine similarity relations among them to ascertain if any additional light can be shed on important organizational factors. The table, example 147, summarizes the similarity relations for all hexachords in A and B.

Even disregarding the case of R_p alone, it is apparent that the sets are interrelated to a considerable degree. Closer study of the table reveals some rather remarkable facts. For instance, pc set 6–Z19 is maximally dissimilar to six other hexachords and maximally similar to none. Pc set 6–27, on the other hand, is in the relations R_2 and R_p to seven other hexachords and is maximally dissimilar to only one, 6–Z19. Indeed, 6–27 can only be in the relations R_2 and R_p to nine hexachords, seven of which are represented in this music.

As an additional indication of the extent to which similarity relations abound in this movement, it can be recorded that four of the eleven transitive quintuples (R_1) involving hexachords are represented (ex. 57).

The apparent complexity of the network of relations indicated in the table is of course greatly reduced if one considers only the local associations of hexachords. Example 148 summarizes the hexachordal successions as they occur and indicates the relations between pairs, as well as the common 5-element subset in the case of R_p.

In the opening succession we find the relations R_2 and R_p between 6–Z42 and 6–27. In the original version, which begins with 6–Z28, maximal similarity still holds, as can be ascertained from the table.

The second succession, beginning at rehearsal no. 3, features the relations R_1 and R_p, with one exception, the succession 6–Z19–6–Z45. As noted

148. Stravinsky, "Sacrificial Dance" from *The Rite of Spring*
Similarity relations for hexachord successions [common subset]

1	6-Z42	R_2,R_p [5-31]	6-27	R_2,R_p [5-31]	6-Z42				
3	6-Z42	R_1,R_p [5-31]	6-Z29	R_p [5-Z18] (5-20)	6-Z19	R_o	6-Z45	R_1,R_p [5-31]	6-Z42
7	6-Z19	R_o	6-Z45	R_2,R_p [5-20]	6-Z43	R_p [5-20]	6-Z19	(5-22) 6-Z45	6-Z43
15	6-Z43	R_p [5-20]	6-Z19	R_o,R_p [5-16]	6-27				
16+3	6-27	6-Z43							
19+1	6-Z19	R_o,R_p [5-16]	6-27						
20+1	6-30	R_2,R_p [5-31]	6-27	R_p [5-32]	6-Z46				
24+3	6-Z25	R_o,R_p [5-20]	6-Z43	R_2,R_p [5-10]	6-27	6-Z23	R_1,R_p [5-28]	6-Z49	R_1 (6-Z42)

149. Common subsets for R_p and R_o, R_1, R_2

	6-Z19	6-Z23	6-Z24	6-Z25	6-27	6-Z28	6-Z29	6-30	6-33	6-Z42	6-Z43	6-Z45	6-Z46
6-Z19	6-Z19												
6-Z23		6-Z23											
6-Z24			6-Z24										
6-Z25			5-23 5-29	6-Z25									
6-27	5-16	5-10			6-27								
6-Z28	5-22				5-31	6-Z28							
6-Z29					5-31	5-31	6-Z29						
6-30		5-28			5-31	5-31	5-31	6-30					
6-33									6-33				
6-Z42			5-23 5-29		5-31	5-31	5-31			6-Z42			
6-Z43			5-20		5-31	5-31	5-31			5-31	6-Z43		
6-Z45					5-31	5-31	5-31			5-31	5-31	6-Z45	
6-Z46		5-27			5-16 5-32						5-Z38		6-Z46
6-Z49	5-22	5-28											

150. Common subsets for R_p only

	6-Z19	6-Z23	6-Z24	6-Z25	6-27	6-Z28	6-Z29	6-30	6-33	6-Z42	6-Z43	6-Z45	6-Z46
6-Z19	6-Z19												
6-Z23		6-Z23											
6-Z24	5-Z17	5-10	6-Z24										
6-Z25	5-20			6-Z25									
6-27		5-10	5-25		6-27								
6-Z28		5-26	5-Z12			6-Z28							
6-Z29	5-Z18	5-29	5-29				6-Z29						
6-30								6-30					
6-33		5-23	5-29		5-25	5-29	5-31		6-33				
6-Z42										6-Z42			
6-Z43	5-Z18	5-28			5-Z18	5-28	5-31				6-Z43		
6-Z45	5-20						5-31				5-31	6-Z45	
6-Z46					5-32			5-34	5-34	5-28	5-34	5-38	6-Z46
6-Z49								5-34	5-28	5-34	5-29		5-32

earlier, this marked change effects a kind of structural accent corresponding to the metrical accentuation.

At rehearsal no. 7 R_p only and R_0 are represented among the three sets that comprise the hexachordal succession. Here for the first time R_p is strongly represented, with 5-20 invariant between 6-Z43 and 6-Z19.

In section B at 15 we find the relations R_p only and R_0 and R_p. Thus, with regard to similarity relations this succession resembles the one at the close of A.

At 16+3 there occurs the succession 6-27-6-Z43, and there is no similarity relation between these sets. In fact, pc set 6-Z43 is poor in similarity relations with respect to most of the other sets. In the context of this music it might be regarded as a kind of neutral sonority.

The catenation of 6-Z19 and 6-27 at 19+1 emphasizes the maximum dissimilarity of these sets. Further, the R_p relation through common subset 5-16 is weakly represented. This extreme contrast is followed at rehearsal no. 20 by a succession in which R_p only and R_2 and R_p are featured. Moreover, 6-Z24 and 6-33 in the outer voices of this passage (ex. 132) are in R_p, and in this case R_p is strongly represented in a contextually significant way. The common subset of 6-Z24 and 6-33 here is pc set 5-23:[2,4,6,7,9], and this set is immediately replicated at rehearsal no. 21, with the return to the opening music of the B section.

In the final succession in B, at rehearsal no. 24+3, all four similarity relations are represented, beginning with R_0 and R_p and ending with R_1 and R_p. The relation R_1 also holds between 6-Z49, the last chord of B, and 6-Z42, the first chord of A, which follows. Note that in this final succession there is again an instance of strong representation of R_p: between 6-27 and 6-Z23 the common 5-element subset 5-10 is preserved.

Examples 149 and 150 give the common 5-element sets for sets which are in R_p and in some other relation, and for sets which are in R_p alone. It is interesting to observe that in the case of the former all the common sets are either represented directly in the music by segments or are represented by their complements. Pc set 5-31, for example, is often the common subset, and its complement occurs in B.*

In the case of common 5-element sets for pairs of hexachords in R_p only, we find four sets that do not occur in the music. However, with the exception of 5-Z18 between non-consecutive sets 6-Z29 and 6-Z19 at rehearsal no. 3, none of these are involved in the actual successions of hexachords.

Because of the very few instances of strongly represented R_p, the tables in example 149 and example 150 are of interest only with respect to the deep-

---

*Pc set 7-31 is an important set in the complete work. Originally it was to be the climactic chord at the end of the "Sacrificial Dance" (201+1 in the original score). See Stravinsky 1969, p. 87 and p. 89.

151.   Schoenberg, Five Pieces for Orchestra Op. 16/3

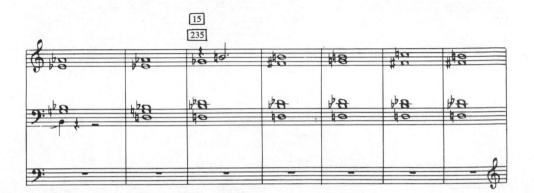

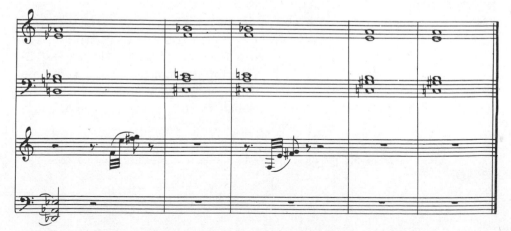

er structure of the music. But the sets which they display point to the strong link between similarity relations and the set-complex structure over the large span of music which has been examined.

The dearth of strongly represented R_p is analogous to the paucity of invariants among equivalent sets. From this we can conclude, perhaps trivially, that interval content, not pc content, is of prime importance for this music, and that similarity relations based upon interval content have a primary role within the set-complex structure.

A condensed score of the third of Schoenberg's Five Pieces for Orchestra Op. 16 is given in example 151. Although this is a correct representation of the pitch content of the music it does not show the orchestration. A good deal has been said about the latter, which is purportedly an actualization of the composer's *Klangfarben* idea, as set forth at the end of his *Harmonielehre* (1911).*

The present version of the score (prepared by the author), by omitting the complexities of orchestration, reveals clearly certain fundamental structural features of the composition which are not especially evident in the full score.†
In particular, this version shows important linear progressions of large scale which are concealed by the complicated orchestral tapestry. Most of these have gone quite unrecognized, if one can judge from the published literature on the work.

Example 152 is a sketch of the entire movement, and this will be the main illustration for the discussion that follows.

This remarkable work divides into three main sections, as indicated in example 152. In addition, it is organized into three distinct components each consisting of an initial formation and its development, which will be referred to as stratum 1, stratum 2, and stratum 3. Stratum 1 begins with the opening chord succession and forms the basic continuum of the music. Stratum 2 is initiated with the lower register formation beginning in measure 227 and is characterized by superimposed linear statements of the "whole-step" motive. The remaining component, stratum 3, first introduced in measure 240, contains several subparts, of which the most prominent are 4-19, 3-1, and 3-4. Some observations on each of these strata follow.

Stratum 1, ostensibly a succession of chords, exhibits a more primary structural feature: it is canonic. This can be seen in the upper voice motive A-B-flat-A-flat, replicated by the voices below it, in order, as E-F-E-flat, B-C-B-flat, G-sharp-A-G, and C-C-sharp, B. This imitative linear substructure continues throughout the movement at various pitch levels, and is systematically projected in stretto fashion even through the dense passage beginning in

*See, for example, Craft 1968.

†They are also not evident in the two-piano reduction prepared by Webern in 1913 (C. F. Peters Edition 3378).

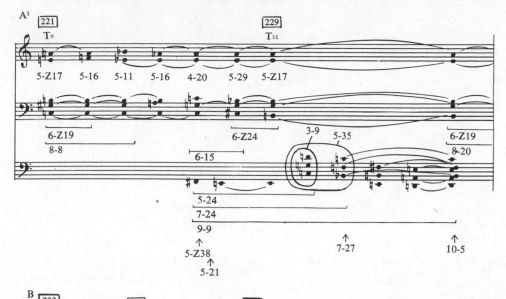

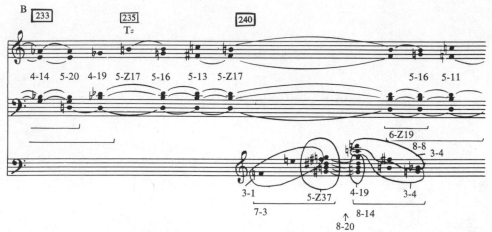

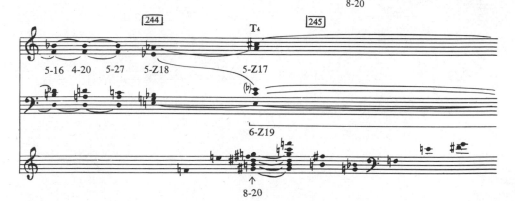

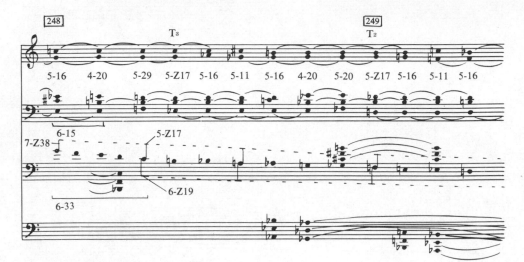

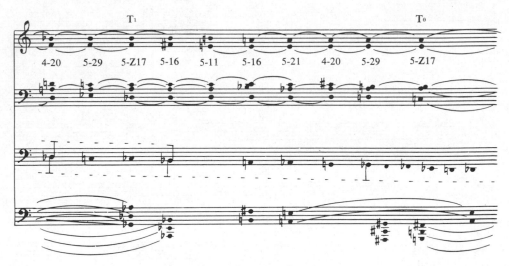

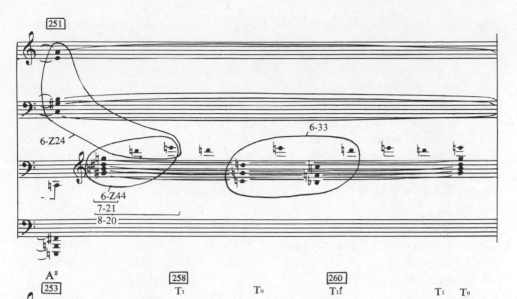

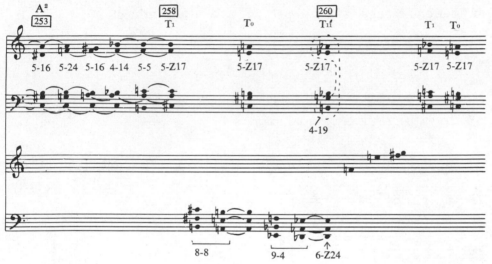

measure 248. In the final section of the piece, A^2, the canonic motive undergoes contour inversion and in measures 235-244 the motive is expanded by repetition of the first two notes, for example, B-C-B-C-B-flat. In the same section the lower voice does not complete the motive, as is always the case in one voice of a traditional canon not of the "infinite" type.

This canonic structure sheds considerable light on the chord succession of stratum 1. That is to say, if all the voices moved in the canonic pattern at the same time, beginning from the initial chord as given, the result would be a succession of verticals composed of the same set, pc set 5-Z17, as in the last measures, 259-263. Thus, with the exception of 5-Z17, the chords here result from the temporal displacement of the canonic motive in the various constituent voices and are not the determinants of motion in the most fundamental sense.* Pc set 5-Z17 therefore plays a basic role in the movement as a whole, and example 153 shows the set as it occurs throughout.

153.   Schoenberg, Five Pieces for Orchestra Op. 16/3
       Stratum 1

Note that both minimum and maximum invariance result from the values of t. More will be said about this substructure further along.

The verticals that result from the canonic "çoloring" of 5-Z17 comprise a

---

*According to an entry in Schoenberg's diary, quoted in Rufer 1959, p. 14, the title of this movement was to have been *Akkordfärbungen (technisches)*—chord coloring, technical. In this sense, the canon can be regarded as effecting the coloring of the initial sonority, 5-Z17.

more or less ordered sequence—especially in the stretto section, beginning at measure 248. Moreover, the composite segments formed by pairs of verticals within stratum 1 are of significance. In particular, the succession 5-Z17-5-16 yields 6-Z19 in each case, and this is the predominant hexachord in a texture otherwise made up mainly of sets of cardinals 4 and 5. Still larger composite segments within stratum 1 form 8-8 or 8-20 and (over the entire sequence) 9-4. Of these, 8-20 and 9-4 are represented by complements in the music at significant points. It should also be noted that pc set 4-19 (stratum 3) is contained in 9-4 nine times—more than any other tetrachord.

154.

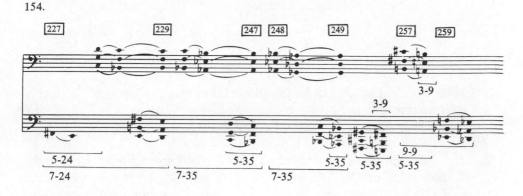

Turning now to stratum 2, the reader's attention is directed to example 154, which summarizes the motion of that component over the entire movement. The initial motive, F-sharp-E, derives of course from the last dyad of the canonic motive. Composite segments formed by this stratum are shown in example 154. Sets of three types are featured: 7-24, 7-35, and 3-9. In each case complement embedding occurs. Intervals of ic2 and ic5 are characteristically prominent in all these sets. Discussion of the long-range pattern shown in example 154 is postponed for the present.

Unlike strata 1 and 2, stratum 3 does not exhibit a long-range linear pattern, but its subparts remain unchanged at each occurrence. The components of stratum 3 are shown in detail in example 155. Note that the large set, 8-14, formed by the composite segment, as indicated in example 152, is the complement of the tetrachord at measure 233 in stratum 1. This is not the only link between the two strata. Pc set 4-19 is contained twice in 5-Z17 and is one of the three sets represented as subsets of 5-Z17 (4-14 being another, of course). Moreover, pc set 3-4 is the complement of stratum 1 over the entire first section of the music. And finally, pc set 3-1 here is the contour inversion (with octave displacement of the last two notes) of the canonic motive of stratum 1, just as it occurs in A². This detail has been misrepresented, perhaps understandably so.* The motive is not F-E-G, but F-E-F-sharp.

*Cf. Craft 1968. Webern made the same mistake.

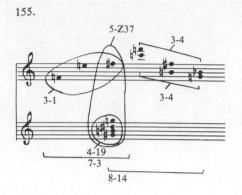

155.

The G (see ex. 151) is not part of the motive, but doubles the G at the top of 4-19 (reinforcing the composite segment 6-Z19 formed with 5-Z17 of stratum 1) and thereafter is retained with the F-sharp as a pc reference to both 4-19 and 6-Z19.

Pc set 5-Z37, the Z-correspondent of 5-Z17, plays an important part in the second movement of Op. 16, where it is stated initially as the consequent phrase of the opening theme. It is interesting to note that the antecedent phrase of that theme is 5-3, and that in stratum 3 of the present movement we find 5-Z37 embedded in 7-3.

Some indication of the distinctive structure of each of the three strata has been provided by the foregoing discussion. Let us consider now the composite segments formed between strata. Between strata 1 and 2 these segments do not seem to be significant, in the sense that they do not exhibit the structuring so evident in the strata taken separately. This is especially so in the case of measures 248-250, where the overall texture is so extremely dense. Nevertheless, some of the sets formed by these segments have been included in the set-complex analysis and are shown in example 152. In particular, notice 6-15, the hexachord formed at the onset of stratum 2 in measure 227, and 6-Z24, which closes two of the passages that combine the strata (at measure 250 and measure 260).

Between stratum 1 and stratum 3 there are three composite segments of interest. First, the large segment which forms pc set 8-20 in measure 240 and again in measure 244, and within that, pc set 6-Z19. Both these sets provide links to the opening music of stratum 1, as indicated above. The largest composite segment arising from the two strata is 10-5, and it is interesting to note that this set is the large vertical that ends the first section of the piece. Thus, even in this combination, the effect of stratum 2, with its emphasis on ic5, is made evident.

156. Schoenberg, Five Pieces for Orchestra Op. 16/3
Set-complex relations

	8-8	4-14	4-19	4-20
7-3		K	K	K
5-5	K	Kh		
5-11	K	Kh	K	K
5-13	K	K	Kh	K
5-16	K		Kh	K
5-Z17	K	Kh	Kh	K
5-Z18	K	Kh	K	K
5-20	Kh	Kh	K	Kh
5-21	K	K	Kh	Kh
5-24		K	K	Kh
5-27		Kh	K	K
5-29	K	Kh	K	K
5-35	K	K	K	K
5-Z37	K	K	Kh	Kh
7-Z38	K	K	Kh	Kh
6-15				
6-Z19	Kh	K	Kh	Kh
6-Z24		Kh	K*	Kh
6-33		Kh		K

	7-3	5-11	5-13	5-16	5-Z17	5-Z18	5-20	5-21	5-24	5-27	5-29	5-35	5-Z37	7-Z38
7-Z38	Kh		Kh	Kh	K*	K		Kh					K	
6-15														Kh
6-Z19		K*		K	K*	K	K	Kh		K*				K
6-Z24									Kh		K*			K*
6-33												Kh		

Strata 1, 2, and 3 are combined only in measure 251, at the beginning of the final section of the music. Composite segments resulting from this combination are shown in example 152. Again, as in the combination of strata 1 and 3, pc set 8-20 is formed, but now through the agency of the figure D-E, which belongs to stratum 2. Moreover, the figure D-E combines with 5-Z17 in stratum 1 to form 6-Z24, the set that closes the combined strata 1 and 2, as remarked above, and combines with 4-19 of stratum 3 to form 6-Z44, the complement of 6-Z19.

Finally, within pc set 8-20 we find 7-21, the complement of which occurs as a chord in stratum 1 (in measure 249) and, perhaps even more importantly, as the sonority that occupies the last three beats in measure 227.* This single measure (251) therefore synthesizes much of the music represented *in extenso* in the individual strata, and is an appropriate signal for the approaching close.

We come now to the large-scale linear progressions mentioned above. As a result of the successive transpositions of 5-Z17 (ex. 153), the controlling chord of stratum 1, the outer voice pattern formed by 5-Z17 over the span of the entire work consists of a motion traversing ic4. This is shown in example 153 by stemmed notes. A corresponding long pattern is formed by the lowest part of stratum 2, and this is shown in example 154. This pattern is the linear projection of 8-21, the 8-note complement of the "whole-tone" tetrachord. Thus, both the outer voices of stratum 1 and the lower voice of stratum 2 feature ic2. An abstraction of this combination is shown in example 157.†

157.

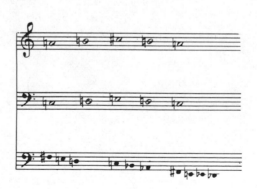

---

*Pc set 5-21 is the first theme of the first piece. See example 10.
†Long patterns of this kind are to be found elsewhere in the literature, of course. For example, the bass line of Berg's Op. 6/2 (*Reigen*) consists of an ascending chromatic pattern.

Perhaps the most extraordinary of the linear patterns, however, occurs in measures 248–250 with the descending line that begins on G (shown on the next to lowest stave in example 152). The rhythmic grouping of this line is such that the accented notes at the head of each group form 7-Z38. This, in turn, decomposes into two interlocking hexachords, 6-Z24 and 6-Z19, as indicated in example 152, and contains, as well, 5-Z17 as a contiguous subsegment. Thus, in this rapidly shifting texture, the line serves to unify stratum 1 and stratum 2.

The set complex table, example 156, reflects the associations as well as disassociations of the three strata, many of which have been discussed above.

158. Schoenberg, Five Pieces for Orchestra Op. 16/3
      Similarity relations

	8-8	8-14	4-19
8-8	8-8		
8-14		8-14	
4-19			4-19
4-20		R_2	R_2

	7-3	5-5	5-11	5-13	5-16	5-Z17	5-Z18	5-20	5-21	5-24	5-27	5-29	5-35	5-Z37
7-3	7-3													
5-5		5-5												
5-11	R_2		5-11											
5-13				5-13										
5-16					5-16									
5-Z17			R_2			5-Z17								
5-Z18			R_2		R_2	R_2	5-Z18							
5-20					R_1		R_2	5-20						
5-21			R_2			R_2			5-21					
5-24										5-24				
5-27	R_1		R_2						R_2		5-27			
5-29												5-29		
5-35				R_0	R_0			R_0					5-35	
5-Z37			R_2		R_2									5-Z37
7-Z38			R_2		R_2	R_1								R_2

	6-15	6-Z19	6-Z24	6-33
6-15	6-15			
6-Z19	R_2	6-Z19		
6-Z24			6-Z24	
6-33				6-33
6-Z44	R_2			

A further dimension is provided by the similarity relations displayed in the tables of example 158. Of the 5-note chords in stratum 1, 5-5, 5-13, and 5-24 are bereft of similarity relations, while each of the others has at least one such relation. Notice especially the multiple relations of 5-11, all of type R_2 and R_p. Another special aspect of the similarity relations among the 5-element sets is the number of transitive triples of types R_2 and R_p. Of the five possible triples, three are represented here. Pc set 5-35 (stratum 2) has only

R_0 relations with the other sets of cardinal 5, another indication of the distinctiveness of stratum 2 when compared with stratum 1 and 2.

Among the hexachords, again we find R_2 and R_p relations, here between 6-15 and the Z-correspondents 6-Z19/44, all belonging to stratum 1. In the table for sets of cardinal 4, pc set 8-14 is noteworthy for the large number of similarity relations, again of type R_2 and R_p. This set occurs both in stratum 1 and in stratum 3. Pc set 8-21, the long-range pattern discussed above, is maximally dissimilar to both 8-14 and 4-19.

159. Schoenberg, Five Pieces for Orchestra Op. 16/3
       Set-complex relations

Stratum 1

	8-8	4-14	4-20									
5-5	K	Kh										
5-11	K	Kh	K									
5-13	K	K	K									
5-16	K		K									
5-Z17	K	Kh	K									
5-Z18	K	Kh	K									
5-20	Kh	Kh	Kh									
5-21	K	K	Kh									
5-24		K										
5-27		Kh	Kh									
5-29	K	Kh	K	5-11	5-13	5-16	5-Z17	5-Z18	5-20	5-21	5-27	5-29
6-15		Kh		Kh					Kh			
6-Z19	Kh	K	Kh		K	K	K	K	Kh			
6-Z24		Kh	K	K*			K*				K*	K*

Stratum 2				Stratum 3		
	5-24	5-35			8-14	4-19
6-33	Kh	Kh		7-3	K	K
				5-Z37	K	Kh

Before giving attention to some further aspects of set-complex relations, it should be pointed out that the set-complex structure of the movement is not connected, reflecting the disassociation of strata 1 and 2. On the other hand, as shown in example 159, the set-complex structure for each stratum taken separately is connected.

For stratum 1 the main nexus sets may be regarded as 6-Z19/44, while 4-14 and 4-20 provide connections to the excluded sets. All the nexus sets are prominent in various configurations. Pc set 6-33, the nexus set of stratum 2, is not especially prominent in the music, but is strongly represented by its components, 5-35/7-35 and 5-24/7-24. For stratum 3, surprisingly enough, the nexus set is 5-Z37, the Z-correspondent of the chord of stratum 1.

The strata are, however, linked in very specific ways. Let us consider, first, the connections between strata 1 and 3. The derivation of 4-19 (in stratum 3) from 5–Z17 of stratum 1 has already been suggested. This derivation is made explicit in the music during the last statement of stratum 3 in measure 260, in the following way: if 4–19 in stratum 3, with fixed pcs [7,8,11,3] is derived from 5–Z17 as it is stated at the outset, then 4–19 in stratum 3 is a transposition of one of the representatives of 4–19 in 5–Z17, with t = 11. And this is exactly the transposition of 5–Z17 that occurs in measure 260 together with the truncated statement of stratum 3. This is shown by dotted lines in example 152.

Of the two 3-note motives in stratum 3, 3–1 has already been discussed with respect to the canonic motive of stratum 1. The corresponding pitches, E, F, F-sharp, occur in stratum 1 only in measure 249, in the voice immediately below the upper voice. The other 3-note motive, 3–4, is not as explicitly related to stratum 1. At each occurrence, however, the two forms of 3–4 in stratum 3 occur while 6–Z19 is being formed by the union of 5–Z17 and 5–16 in stratum 1, and 6–Z19 contains 3–4 four times. Also, it will be recalled that the total content of stratum 1 is pc set 9–4. Finally, note that two of the nexus sets of stratum 1, 4–14 and 4–20, are represented by their complements in stratum 3. In the case of 4–20, the connection is far more specific: the composite segment 8–20 beginning at measure 232 in stratum 1 is duplicated in the composite vertical formed in measure 240 between the two strata.

Since the links between strata 2 and 3 have already been discussed in connection with the formation of composite segments, it only remains to examine the links between strata 1 and 2 in somewhat more detail (see ex. 154). First, and perhaps obviously, the vertical statements of 3–9 which make up the initial appearance of 5–35 (measure 229) derive from 3–9 in 5–Z17, specifically from the three upper notes of the chord, by inversion, with t = 11. If we let 6–Z19 represent stratum 1 and 6–33 represent stratum 2, it is evident from the table, example 156, that the only set they share of cardinal greater than 3 is 4–14. There is no convincing link established by means of that set, from which we conclude, as indeed has been mentioned several times above, that the two strata are essentially detached from one another.

Appendix 1 Prime Forms and Vectors of Pitch-Class Sets

Name	Pcs	Vector	Name	Pcs	Vector
3-1(12)	0,1,2	210000	9-1	0,1,2,3,4,5,6,7,8	876663
3-2	0,1,3	111000	9-2	0,1,2,3,4,5,6,7,9	777663
3-3	0,1,4	101100	9-3	0,1,2,3,4,5,6,8,9	767763
3-4	0,1,5	100110	9-4	0,1,2,3,4,5,7,8,9	766773
3-5	0,1,6	100011	9-5	0,1,2,3,4,6,7,8,9	766674
3-6(12)	0,2,4	020100	9-6	0,1,2,3,4,5,6,8,10	686763
3-7	0,2,5	011010	9-7	0,1,2,3,4,5,7,8,10	677673
3-8	0,2,6	010101	9-8	0,1,2,3,4,6,7,8,10	676764
3-9(12)	0,2,7	010020	9-9	0,1,2,3,5,6,7,8,10	676683
3-10(12)	0,3,6	002001	9-10	0,1,2,3,4,6,7,9,10	668664
3-11	0,3,7	001110	9-11	0,1,2,3,5,6,7,9,10	667773
3-12(4)	0,4,8	000300	9-12	0,1,2,4,5,6,8,9,10	666963
4-1(12)	0,1,2,3	321000	8-1	0,1,2,3,4,5,6,7	765442
4-2	0,1,2,4	221100	8-2	0,1,2,3,4,5,6,8	665542
4-3(12)	0,1,3,4	212100	8-3	0,1,2,3,4,5,6,9	656542
4-4	0,1,2,5	211110	8-4	0,1,2,3,4,5,7,8	655552
4-5	0,1,2,6	210111	8-5	0,1,2,3,4,6,7,8	654553
4-6(12)	0,1,2,7	210021	8-6	0,1,2,3,5,6,7,8	654463
4-7(12)	0,1,4,5	201210	8-7	0,1,2,3,4,5,8,9	645652
4-8(12)	0,1,5,6	200121	8-8	0,1,2,3,4,7,8,9	644563
4-9(6)	0,1,6,7	200022	8-9	0,1,2,3,6,7,8,9	644464
4-10(12)	0,2,3,5	122010	8-10	0,2,3,4,5,6,7,9	566452
4-11	0,1,3,5	121110	8-11	0,1,2,3,4,5,7,9	565552
4-12	0,2,3,6	112101	8-12	0,1,3,4,5,6,7,9	556543
4-13	0,1,3,6	112011	8-13	0,1,2,3,4,6,7,9	556453
4-14	0,2,3,7	111120	8-14	0,1,2,4,5,6,7,9	555562
4-Z15	0,1,4,6	111111	8-Z15	0,1,2,3,4,6,8,9	555553
4-16	0,1,5,7	110121	8-16	0,1,2,3,5,7,8,9	554563
4-17(12)	0,3,4,7	102210	8-17	0,1,3,4,5,6,8,9	546652
4-18	0,1,4,7	102111	8-18	0,1,2,3,5,6,8,9	546553
4-19	0,1,4,8	101310	8-19	0,1,2,4,5,6,8,9	545752
4-20(12)	0,1,5,8	101220	8-20	0,1,2,4,5,7,8,9	545662
4-21(12)	0,2,4,6	030201	8-21	0,1,2,3,4,6,8,10	474643
4-22	0,2,4,7	021120	8-22	0,1,2,3,5,6,8,10	465562
4-23(12)	0,2,5,7	021030	8-23	0,1,2,3,5,7,8,10	465472
4-24(12)	0,2,4,8	020301	8-24	0,1,2,4,5,6,8,10	464743
4-25(6)	0,2,6,8	020202	8-25	0,1,2,4,6,7,8,10	464644
4-26(12)	0,3,5,8	012120	8-26	0,1,2,4,5,7,9,10	456562
4-27	0,2,5,8	012111	8-27	0,1,2,4,5,7,8,10	456553
4-28(3)	0,3,6,9	004002	8-28	0,1,3,4,6,7,9,10	448444
4-Z29	0,1,3,7	111111	8-Z29	0,1,2,3,5,6,7,9	555553
5-1(12)	0,1,2,3,4	432100	7-1	0,1,2,3,4,5,6	654321
5-2	0,1,2,3,5	332110	7-2	0,1,2,3,4,5,7	554331
5-3	0,1,2,4,5	322210	7-3	0,1,2,3,4,5,8	544431
5-4	0,1,2,3,6	322111	7-4	0,1,2,3,4,6,7	544332
5-5	0,1,2,3,7	321121	7-5	0,1,2,3,5,6,7	543342
5-6	0,1,2,5,6	311221	7-6	0,1,2,3,4,7,8	533442
5-7	0,1,2,6,7	310132	7-7	0,1,2,3,6,7,8	532353
5-8(12)	0,2,3,4,6	232201	7-8	0,2,3,4,5,6,8	454422
5-9	0,1,2,4,6	231211	7-9	0,1,2,3,4,6,8	453432
5-10	0,1,3,4,6	223111	7-10	0,1,2,3,4,6,9	445332
5-11	0,2,3,4,7	222220	7-11	0,1,3,4,5,6,8	444441

Name	Pcs	Vector	Name	Pcs	Vector
5-Z12(12)	0,1,3,5,6	222121	7-Z12	0,1,2,3,4,7,9	444342
5-13	0,1,2,4,8	221311	7-13	0,1,2,4,5,6,8	443532
5-14	0,1,2,5,7	221131	7-14	0,1,2,3,5,7,8	443352
5-15(12)	0,1,2,6,8	220222	7-15	0,1,2,4,6,7,8	442443
5-16	0,1,3,4,7	213211	7-16	0,1,2,3,5,6,9	435432
5-Z17(12)	0,1,3,4,8	212320	7-Z17	0,1,2,4,5,6,9	434541
5-Z18	0,1,4,5,7	212221	7-Z18	0,1,2,3,5,8,9	434442
5-19	0,1,3,6,7	212122	7-19	0,1,2,3,6,7,9	434343
5-20	0,1,3,7,8	211231	7-20	0,1,2,4,7,8,9	433452
5-21	0,1,4,5,8	202420	7-21	0,1,2,4,5,8,9	424641
5-22(12)	0,1,4,7,8	202321	7-22	0,1,2,5,6,8,9	424542
5-23	0,2,3,5,7	132130	7-23	0,2,3,4,5,7,9	354351
5-24	0,1,3,5,7	131221	7-24	0,1,2,3,5,7,9	353442
5-25	0,2,3,5,8	123121	7-25	0,2,3,4,6,7,9	345342
5-26	0,2,4,5,8	122311	7-26	0,1,3,4,5,7,9	344532
5-27	0,1,3,5,8	122230	7-27	0,1,2,4,5,7,9	344451
5-28	0,2,3,6,8	122212	7-28	0,1,3,5,6,7,9	344433
5-29	0,1,3,6,8	122131	7-29	0,1,2,4,6,7,9	344352
5-30	0,1,4,6,8	121321	7-30	0,1,2,4,6,8,9	343542
5-31	0,1,3,6,9	114112	7-31	0,1,3,4,6,7,9	336333
5-32	0,1,4,6,9	113221	7-32	0,1,3,4,6,8,9	335442
5-33(12)	0,2,4,6,8	040402	7-33	0,1,2,4,6,8,10	262623
5-34(12)	0,2,4,6,9	032221	7-34	0,1,3,4,6,8,10	254442
5-35(12)	0,2,4,7,9	032140	7-35	0,1,3,5,6,8,10	254361
5-Z36	0,1,2,4,7	222121	7-Z36	0,1,2,3,5,6,8	444342
5-Z37(12)	0,3,4,5,8	212320	7-Z37	0,1,3,4,5,7,8	434541
5-Z38	0,1,2,5,8	212221	7-Z38	0,1,2,4,5,7,8	434442
6-1(12)	0,1,2,3,4,5	543210			
6-2	0,1,2,3,4,6	443211			
6-Z3	0,1,2,3,5,6	433221	6-Z36	0,1,2,3,4,7	
6-Z4(12)	0,1,2,4,5,6	432321	6-Z37(12)	0,1,2,3,4,8	
6-5	0,1,2,3,6,7	422232			
6-Z6(12)	0,1,2,5,6,7	421242	6-Z38(12)	0,1,2,3,7,8	
6-7(6)	0,1,2,6,7,8	420243			
6-8(12)	0,2,3,4,5,7	343230			
6-9	0,1,2,3,5,7	342231			
6-Z10	0,1,3,4,5,7	333321	6-Z39	0,2,3,4,5,8	
6-Z11	0,1,2,4,5,7	333231	6-Z40	0,1,2,3,5,8	
6-Z12	0,1,2,4,6,7	332232	6-Z41	0,1,2,3,6,8	
6-Z13(12)	0,1,3,4,6,7	324222	6-Z42(12)	0,1,2,3,6,9	
6-14	0,1,3,4,5,8	323430			
6-15	0,1,2,4,5,8	323421			
6-16	0,1,4,5,6,8	322431			
6-Z17	0,1,2,4,7,8	322332	6-Z43	0,1,2,5,6,8	
6-18	0,1,2,5,7,8	322242			
6-Z19	0,1,3,4,7,8	313431	6-Z44	0,1,2,5,6,9	
6-20(4)	0,1,4,5,8,9	303630			
6-21	0,2,3,4,6,8	242412			
6-22	0,1,2,4,6,8	241422			
6-Z23(12)	0,2,3,5,6,8	234222	6-Z45(12)	0,2,3,4,6,9	
6-Z24	0,1,3,4,6,8	233331	6-Z46	0,1,2,4,6,9	
6-Z25	0,1,3,5,6,8	233241	6-Z47	0,1,2,4,7,9	
6-Z26(12)	0,1,3,5,7,8	232341	6-Z48(12)	0,1,2,5,7,9	
6-27	0,1,3,4,6,9	225222			

Name	Pcs	Vector		Name	Pcs	Vector
6-Z28(12)	0,1,3,5,6,9	224322		6-Z49(12)	0,1,3,4,7,9	
6-Z29(12)	0,1,3,6,8,9	224232		6-Z50(12)	0,1,4,6,7,9	
6-30(12)	0,1,3,6,7,9	224223				
6-31	0,1,3,5,8,9	223431				
6-32(12)	0,2,4,5,7,9	143250				
6-33	0,2,3,5,7,9	143241				
6-34	0,1,3,5,7,9	142422				
6-35(2)	0,2,4,6,8,10	060603				

Appendix 2   Similarity Relations

· (R_0, Rp) for sets of cardinal 4

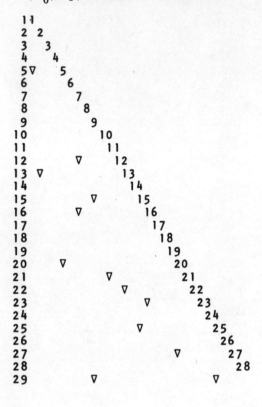

· (R_0, Rp) for sets of cardinal 6

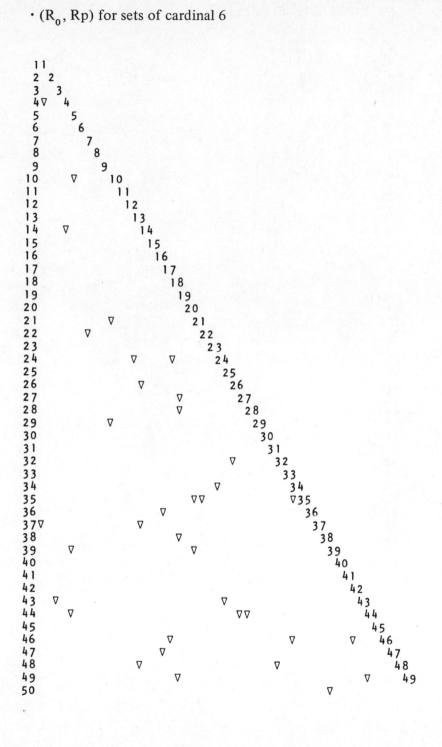

· (R$_1$, Rp) for sets of cardinal 6

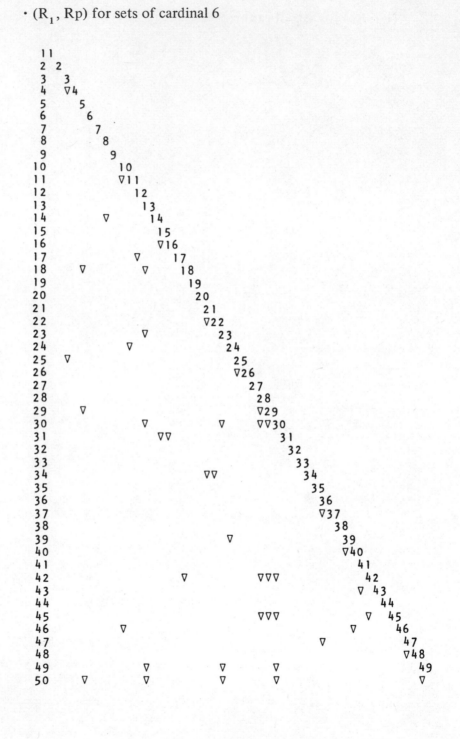

· (R$_2$, Rp) for sets of cardinal 6

```
1 1
2 ▽2
3   ▽3
4      4
5      5
6    ▽6
7      ▽7
8▽       8
9        ▽9
10    ▽▽      10
11    ▽    ▽▽ 11
12      ▽    ▽ ▽12
13             13
14             14
15        ▽    ▽15
16              16
17    ▽        ▽17
18     ▽     ▽   ▽18
19        ▽  ▽▽▽   19
20         ▽    20
21             21
22              22
23              23
24              24
25      ▽      ▽25
26             26
27       ▽       ▽  27
28               ▽28
29             ▽ 29
30             ▽  30
31        ▽    ▽    ▽    31
32     ▽            32
33             ▽    ▽33
34              34
35             35
36 ▽     ▽▽         36
37             37
38   ▽ ▽       ▽       38
39 ▽    ▽     ▽       ▽▽ 39
40 ▽   ▽▽  ▽        ▽    ▽ 40
41   ▽   ▽ ▽       ▽        ▽41
42                 ▽       42
43   ▽        ▽ ▽          43
44        ▽▽▽      ▽      ▽ 44
45              ▽           45
46           ▽▽    ▽         46
47     ▽       ▽      ▽      ▽      ▽47
48              ▽              48
49              ▽               49
50              ▽
```

R_0 for sets of cardinal 4*

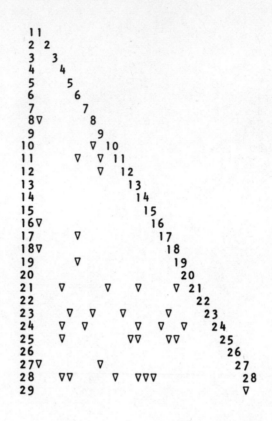

*Here and in the other matrices in Appendix 2 the single relation signifies that only that relation holds, i.e., not Rp as well.

R$_2$ for sets of cardinal 4

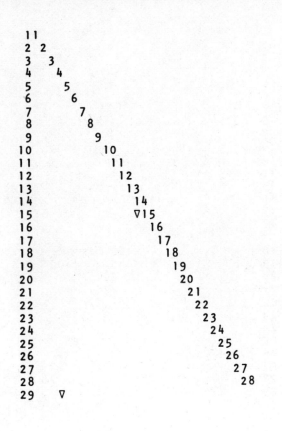

R₁ for sets of cardinal 4

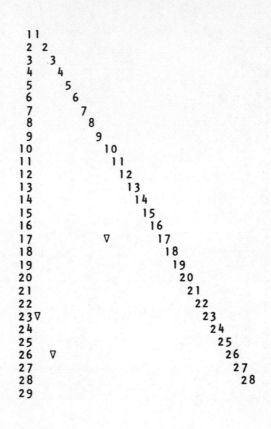

· (R_0, Rp) for sets of cardinal 5

```
1 1
2  2
3    3
4      4
5        5
6        6
7          7
8           8
9        ∇   9
10            10
11             11
12              12
13 ∇      ∇       13
14               14
15                15
16 ∇              16
17               17
18              18
19             19
20            20
21           21
22      ∇      22
23             23
24      ∇        24
25             25
26              26
27               27
28                28
29                 29
30      ∇            30
31        ∇          ∇      31
32                          32
33          ∇    ∇      ∇  ∇   ∇  33
34                          ∇   34
35                       ∇  ∇   35
36                              36
37                               37
38
```

· (R$_1$, Rp) for sets of cardinal 5

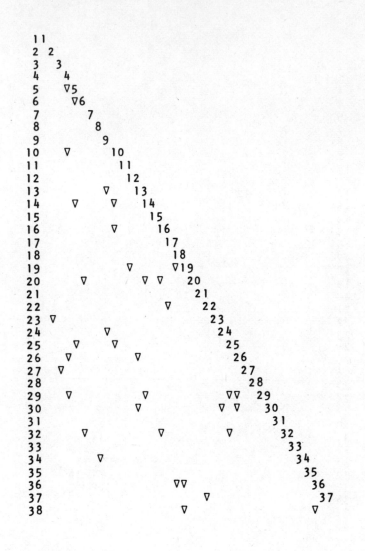

R_0 for sets of cardinal 6

```
11
2 2
3  3
4   4
5    5
6     6
7      7
8    ▽   8
9        9
10      ▽▽  10
11          11
12           12
13           13
14            14
15             15
16▽             16
17▽▽▽             17
18               18
19       ▽▽        19
20     ▽ ▽▽         20
21    ▽   ▽   ▽     ▽21
22          ▽      ▽ 22
23         ▽ ▽  ▽▽  23
24    ▽▽              24
25              ▽    25
26▽        ▽    ▽      ▽    26
27                ▽      27
28▽▽       ▽▽ ▽     ▽      28
29    ▽                 29
30             ▽▽        30
31                     31
32    ▽          ▽▽      ▽ 32
33              ▽      ▽ 33
34      ▽    ▽        ▽    ▽    34
35▽▽▽▽▽▽ ▽▽▽▽▽▽▽▽▽▽▽  ▽▽▽▽▽▽▽ ▽▽▽ 35
36                 ▽      ▽36
37      ▽          ▽      ▽  ▽  ▽ 37
38        ▽         ▽    ▽     ▽ 38
39    ▽▽                ▽      ▽39
40              ▽▽      ▽    ▽▽    40
41                          ▽   41
42                 ▽ ▽      ▽    42
43▽▽                 ▽▽  ▽▽    43
44      ▽           ▽       ▽   ▽  44
45          ▽  ▽  ▽▽              ▽45
46    ▽▽        ▽           ▽   ▽   46
47                      ▽▽       ▽ 47
48▽      ▽    ▽      ▽        ▽    ▽  48
49▽▽     ▽▽ ▽      ▽      ▽▽ ▽    ▽    49
50    ▽       ▽               ▽ ▽
```

· (R$_2$, Rp) for sets of cardinal 4

· (R$_1$, Rp) for sets of cardinal 4

R_0 for sets of cardinal 5

· (R$_2$, Rp) for sets of cardinal 5

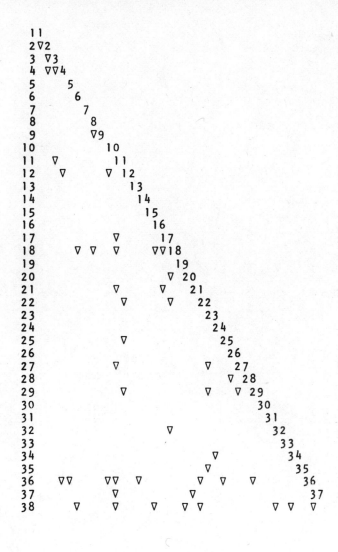

R$_2$ for sets of cardinal 6

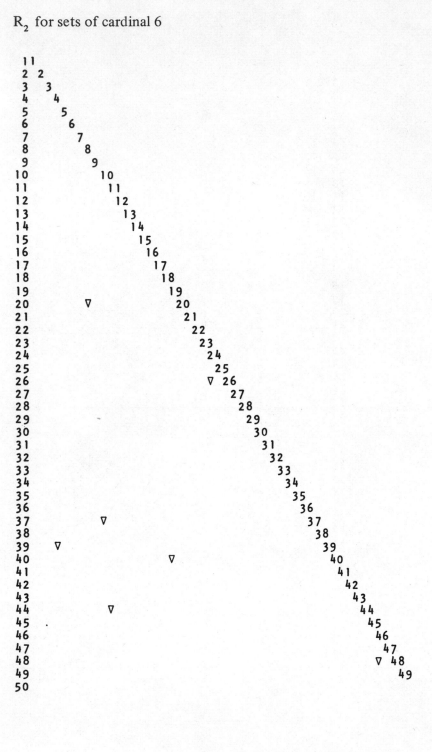

R₁ for sets of cardinal 6

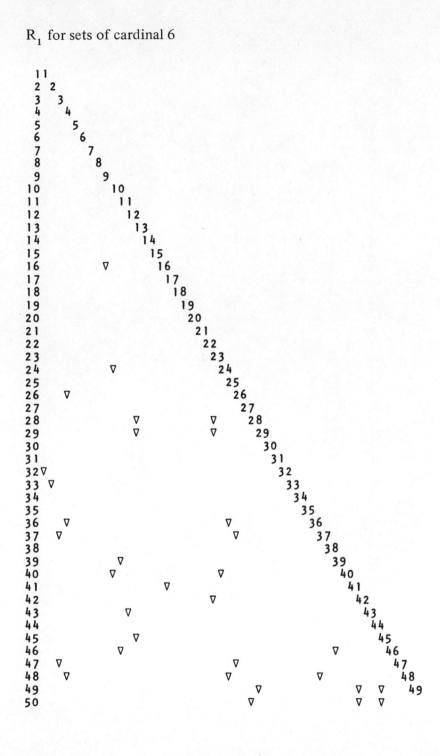

R$_1$ for sets of cardinal 5

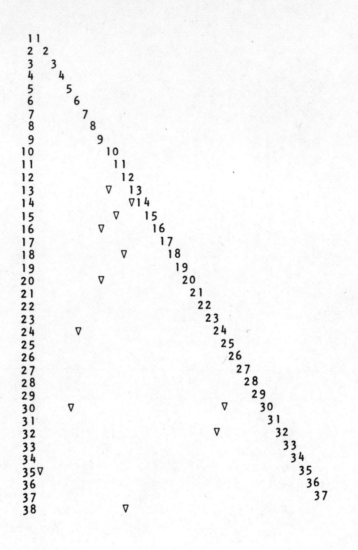

R$_2$ for sets of cardinal 5

```
 1 1
 2   2
 3     3
 4       4
 5         5
 6           6
 7             7
 8               8
 9                 9
10                  10
11                   11
12        ▽        ▽12
13                    13
14                ▽ 14
15                   15
16                    16
17                     17
18                      18
19                  ▽ 19
20                       20
21                        21
22                         22
23▽                         23
24                           24
25                            25
26                             26
27                              27
28      ▽                        28
29                                29
30                                 30
31                                  31
32                                   32
33                                    33
34                    ▽               34
35  ▽                                   35
36                                       36
37                      ▽▽                 37
38            ▽          ▽
```

Appendix 3   The Subcomplexes Kh

4-1 (12)
3. 1 2
5. 1 2 4 5
6. 1 2 Z3/Z36 5 8 9

4-2 (25)
3. 1 2 3 6
5. 1 2 3 8 9 11 13 Z36
6. 1 2 Z3/Z36 Z4/Z37 8 9 Z10/Z39 Z11/Z40 14 15 16 21 22

4-3 (14)
3. 2 3
5. 1 3 10 16 Z17
6. 1 2 Z3/Z36 Z4/Z37 14 15 27

4-4 (24)
3. 1 3 4 7
5. 2 3 4 6 11 14 Z37 Z38
6. 1 2 Z3/Z36 5 8 9 Z10/Z39 Z11/Z40 14 15 16 18

4-5 (26)
3. 1 4 5 8
5. 4 5 6 7 9 13 15 Z38
6. 2 Z3/Z36 Z4/Z37 5 Z6/Z38 7 9 Z12/Z41 15 16 Z17/Z43 18 21 22

4-6 (14)
3. 1 5 9
5. 5 7 14 Z36
6. 5 Z6/Z38 7 9 Z11/Z40 Z12/Z41 18

4-7 (14)
3. 3 4
5. 3 6 Z18 21
6. 1 5 14 15 16 Z19/Z44 20 31

4-8 (13)
3. 4 5
5. 6 7 20 22
6. 5 Z6/Z38 7 16 Z17/Z43 18 Z19/Z44

4-9 (8)
3. 5
5. 7 19
6. 5 Z6/Z38 7 18 30

4-10 (14)
3. 2 7
5. 2 10 23 25
6. 1 2 8 9 Z11/Z40 27 32 33

4-11 (26)
3. 2 4 6 7
5. 2 3 9 23 24 26 27
6. 1 2 8 9 Z10/Z39 Z11/Z40 14 15 21 22 Z24/Z46 31 32 33 34

4-12 (25)
3. 2 3 8 10
5. 4 8 10 16 Z18 26 28 31
6. 2 Z3/Z36 5 Z10/Z39 Z13/Z42 15 21 Z23/Z45 27 Z28/Z49 30 31 34

4-13 (25)
3. 2 5 7 10
5. 4 10 Z12 19 25 29 31 Z36
6. 2 Z3/Z36 5 Z11/Z40 Z12/Z41 Z13/Z42 18 Z23/Z45 Z25/Z47 27 Z29/Z50 30 33

4-14 (24)
3. 2 4 9 11
5. 5 11 Z17 Z18 20 23 27 29
6. 5 8 9 Z11/Z40 14 16 18 Z24/Z46 Z25/Z47 31 32 33

4-Z15 (26)
3. 3 5 7 8
5. 6 9 10 14 19 28 30 32
6. 2 5 9 Z12/Z41 16 Z17/Z43 18 21 22 Z24/Z46 27 30 31 34

4-16 (26)
3. 4 5 8 9
5. 7 14 15 Z18 20 24 29 30
6. 5 Z6/Z38 7 9 Z12/Z41 16 Z17/Z43 18 22 Z25/Z47 Z26/Z48 31 33 34

4-17 (14)
3. 3 11
5. 11 16 21 32
6. 8 14 15 16 Z19/Z44 20 27 31

4-18 (24)
3. 3 5 10 11
5. 16 Z18 19 22 31 32 Z36 Z38
6. 5 Z11/Z40 Z13/Z42 15 Z17/Z43 18 Z19/Z44 27 Z28/Z49 Z29/Z50 30 31

4-19 (20)
3. 3 4 11 12
5. 13 Z17 21 22 26 30 Z37
6. 14 15 16 Z19/Z44 20 21 22 31 34

4-20 (14)
3. 4 11
5. 20 21 27 Z38
6. 14 15 16 18 Z19/Z44 20 31 32

4-21 (14)
3. 6 8
5. 8 9 24 33 34
6. 2 9 21 22 33 34 35

4-22 (25)
3. 6 7 9 11
5. 11 23 24 27 30 34 35 Z36
6. 8 9 Z11/Z40 14 16 22 Z24/Z46 Z25/Z47 Z26/Z48 31 32 33 34

4-23 (12)
3. 7 9
5. 14 23 29 35
6. 8 9 18 Z25/Z47 32 33

4-24 (14)
3. 6 8 12
5. 13 26 30 33
6. 15 16 21 22 31 34 35

4-25 (10)
3. 8
5. 15 28 33
6. 7 21 22 30 34 35

4-26 (14)
3. 7 11
5. 25 27 32 35 Z37
6. 14 Z25/Z47 Z26/Z48 27 31 32 33

4-27 (25)
3. 7 8 10 11
5. 25 26 28 29 31 32 34 Z38
6. 15 18 21 Z23/Z45 Z24/Z46 Z25/Z47 27 Z28/Z49 Z29/Z50 30 31 33 34

4-28 (4)
3. 10
5. 31
6. 27 30

4-Z29 (26)
3. 2 5 8 11
5. 5 13 16 19 20 24 25 28
6. 5 9 Z10/Z39 Z12/Z41 15 16 Z17/Z43 18 21 22 27 30 33 34

5-1 (9)
3. 1 2 3 6
4. 1 2 3
6. 1 2

5-2 (15)
3. 1 2 3 4 6 7
4. 1 2 4 10 11
6. 1 2 8 9

5-3 (14)
3. 1 2 3 4 6 7
4. 2 3 4 7 11
6. 1 14 15

5-4 (16)
3. 1 2 3 4 5 7 8 10
4. 1 4 5 12 13
6. 2 Z3/Z36 5

5-5 (14)
3. 1 2 4 5 8 9 11
4. 1 5 6 14 Z29
6. 5 9

5-6 (13)
3. 1 3 4 5 7 8
4. 4 5 7 8 Z15
6. 5 16

5-7 (14)
3. 1 4 5 8 9
4. 5 6 8 9 16
6. 5 Z6/Z38 7 18

5-8 (11)
3. 1 2 3 6 8 10
4. 2 12 21
6. 2 21

5-9 (17)
3. 1 2 3 4 5 6 7 8
4. 2 5 11 Z15 21
6. 2 9 21 22

5-10 (13)
3. 2 3 5 7 8 10
4. 3 10 12 13 Z15
6. 2 27

5-11 (16)
3. 1 2 3 4 6 7 9 11
4. 2 4 14 17 22
6. 8 14 16

5-Z12 (7)
3. 2 4 5 6 7 10
4. 13

5-13 (18)
3. 1 2 3 4 5 6 8 11 12
4. 2 5 19 24 Z29
6. 15 16 21 22

5-14 (14)
3. 1 3 4 5 7 8 9
4. 4 6 Z15 16 23
6. 9 18

5-15 (10)
3. 1 4 5 8 9
4. 5 16 25
6. 7 22

5-16 (13)
3. 2 3 5 8 10 11
4. 3 12 17 18 Z29
6. 15 27

5-Z17 (10)
3. 2 3 4 9 11 12
4. 3 14 19
6. 14

5-Z18 (15)
3. 2 3 4 5 8 9 10 11
4. 7 12 14 16 18
6. 5 31

5-19 (15)
3. 2 3 5 7 8 10 11
4. 9 13 Z15 18 Z29
6. 5 18 30

5-20 (13)
3. 2 4 5 8 9 11
4. 8 14 16 20 Z29
6. 16 18

5-21 (14)
3. 3 4 11 12
4. 7 17 19 20
6. 14 15 16 Z19/Z44 20 31

5-22 (10)
3. 3 4 5 10 11 12
4. 8 18 19
6. Z19/Z44

5-23 (15)
3. 2 4 6 7 9 11
4. 10 11 14 22 23
6. 8 9 32 33

5-24 (17)
3. 2 4 5 6 7 8 9 11
4. 11 16 21 22 Z29
6. 9 22 33 34

5-25 (13)
3. 2 5 7 8 10 11
4. 10 13 26 27 Z29
6. 27 33

5-26 (18)
3. 2 3 4 6 7 8 10 11 12
4. 11 12 19 24 27
6. 15 21 31 34

5-27 (14)
3. 2 4 6 7 9 11
4. 11 14 20 22 26
6. 14 31 32

5-28 (15)
3. 2 3 5 7 8 10 11
4. 12 Z15 25 27 Z29
6. 21 30 34

5-29 (16)
3. 2 4 5 7 8 9 10 11
4. 13 14 16 23 27
6. 18 Z25/Z47 33

5-30 (18)
3. 3 4 5 6 7 8 9 11 12
4. Z15 16 19 22 24
6. 16 22 31 34

5-31 (14)
3. 2 3 5 7 8 10 11
4. 12 13 18 27 28
6. 27 30

5-32 (13)
3. 3 5 7 8 10 11
4. Z15 17 18 26 27
6. 27 31

5-33 (10)
3. 6 8 12
4. 21 24 25
6. 21 22 34 35

5-34 (11)
3. 6 7 8 9 10 11
4. 21 22 27
6. 33 34

5-35 (9)
3. 6 7 9 11
4. 22 23 26
6. 32 33

5-Z36 (15)
3. 1 2 3 5 6 7 9 10 11
4. 2 6 13 18 22
6. Z11/Z40

5-Z37 (10)
3. 1 3 4 7 11 12
4. 4 19 26
6. 14

5-Z38 (15)
3. 1 3 4 5 7 8 10 11
4. 4 5 18 20 27
6. 15 18

6-1 (16)
3. 1 2 3 4 6 7
4. 1 2 3 4 7 10 11
5. 1 2 3

6-2 (26)
3. 1 2 3 4 5 6 7 8 10
4. 1 2 3 4 5 10 11 12 13 Z15 21
5. 1 2 4 8 9 10

6-Z3/Z36 (17)
3. 1 2 3 4 5 6 7 8 10
4. 1 2 3 4 5 12 13
5. 4

6-Z4/Z37 (10)
3. 1 2 3 4 5 6 8
4. 2 3 5

6-5 (30)
3. 1 2 3 4 5 7 8 9 10 11
4. 1 4 5 6 7 8 9 12 13 14 Z15 16 18 Z29
5. 4 5 6 7 Z18 19

6-Z6/Z38 (11)
3. 1 4 5 8 9
4. 5 6 8 9 16
5. 7

6-7 (13)
3. 1 4 5 8 9
4. 5 6 8 9 16 25
5. 7 15

6-8 (20)
3. 1 2 3 4 6 7 9 11
4. 1 2 4 10 11 14 17 22 23

6-9 (30)
3. 1 2 3 4 5 6 7 8 9 11
4. 1 2 4 5 6 10 11 14 Z15 16 21 22 23 Z29
5. 2 5 9 14 23 24

6-Z10/Z39 (15)
3. 1 2 3 4 5 6 7 8 10 11
4. 2 4 11 12 Z29

6-Z11/Z40 (21)
3. 1 2 3 4 5 6 7 8 9 10 11
4. 2 4 6 10 11 13 14 18 22
5. Z36

6-Z12/Z41 (16)
3. 1 2 3 4 5 7 8 9 10 11
4. 5 6 13 Z15 16 Z29

6-Z13/Z42 (10)
3. 2 3 5 7 8 10 11
4. 12 13 18

6-14 (26)
3. 1 2 3 4 6 7 9 11 12
4. 2 3 4 7 11 14 17 19 20 22 26
5. 3 11 Z17 21 27 Z37

6-15 (31)
3. 1 2 3 4 5 6 7 8 10 11 12
4. 2 3 4 5 7 11 12 17 18 19 20 24 27 Z29
5. 3 13 16 21 26 Z38

6-16 (31)
3. 1 2 3 4 5 6 7 8 9 11 12
4. 2 4 5 7 8 14 Z15 16 17 19 20 22 24 Z29
5. 6 11 13 20 21 30

6-Z17/Z43 (16)
3. 1 2 3 4 5 7 8 9 10 11
4. 5 8 Z15 16 18 Z29

6-18 (30)
3. 1 2 3 4 5 7 8 9 10 11
4. 4 5 6 8 9 13 14 Z15 16 18 20 23 27 Z29
5. 7 14 19 20 29 Z38

6-Z19/Z44 (15)
3. 3 4 5 8 10 11 12
4. 7 8 17 18 19 20
5. 21 22

6-20 (9)
3. 3 4 11 12
4. 7 17 19 20
5. 21

6-21 (28)
3. 1 2 3 4 5 6 7 8 10 11 12
4. 2 5 11 12 Z15 19 21 24 25 27 Z29
5. 8 9 13 26 28 33

6-22 (28)
3. 1 2 3 4 5 6 7 8 9 11 12
4. 2 5 11 Z15 16 19 21 22 24 25 Z29
5. 9 13 15 24 30 33

6-Z23/Z45 (10)
3. 2 3 5 7 8 10 11
4. 12 13 27

6-Z24/Z46 (15)
3. 2 3 4 5 6 7 8 9 10 11
4. 11 14 Z15 22 27

6-Z25/Z47 (17)
3. 2 4 5 6 7 8 9 10 11
4. 13 14 16 22 23 26 27
5. 29

6-Z26/Z48 (10)
3. 4 5 6 7 8 9 11
4. 16 22 26

6-27 (23)
3. 2 3 5 7 8 10 11
4. 3 10 12 13 Z15 17 18 26 27 28 Z29
5. 10 16 25 31 32

6-Z28/Z49 (10)
3. 2 3 5 7 8 10 11
4. 12 18 27

6-Z29/Z50 (10)
3. 2 3 5 7 8 10 11
4. 13 18 27

6-30 (19)
3. 2 3 5 7 8 10 11
4. 9 12 13 Z15 18 25 27 28 Z29
5. 19 28 31

6-31 (31)
3. 2 3 4 5 6 7 8 9 10 11 12
4. 7 11 12 14 Z15 16 17 18 19 20 22 24 26 27
5. Z18 21 26 27 30 32

6-32 (16)
3. 2 4 6 7 9 11
4. 10 11 14 20 22 23 26
5. 23 27 35

6-33 (26)
3. 2 4 5 6 7 8 9 10 11
4. 10 11 13 14 16 21 22 23 26 27 Z29
5. 23 24 25 29 34 35

6-34 (28)
3. 2 3 4 5 6 7 8 9 10 11 12
4. 11 12 Z15 16 19 21 22 24 25 27 Z29
5. 24 26 28 30 33 34

6-35 (7)
3. 6 8 12
4. 21 24 25
5. 33

Glossary of Technical Terms

The glossary is intended to provide the reader with a convenient list of definitions. In some cases, however, it has not been possible to give a meaningful, yet concise definition. For a more complete explanation the General Index should be consulted for the relevant pages in the main text.

Basic interval pattern. A reduction of an interval succession to a normalized pattern. For example, if the interval succession of a pc set is [1-4-1-1], the resulting basic interval pattern (bip) is 1114.

Cardinal number. The number of elements in a set.

Closure property (of a set complex). This property holds for a set complex if every member of that complex is in the set-complex relation to every other member.

Connected (set-complex structure). A descriptive analytical term used to describe the situation in which all the sets formed by the segments of a particular unit of music are interrelated through one or more nexus sets.

Complement (of a pc set). If, for example, M is a pc set containing 4 elements (pc integers), then the complement of M, written $\overline{M}$, is the set of 8 elements (pc integers) not contained in M. Specifically, if M = [0, 1, 3, 4], then $\overline{M}$ = [2, 5, 6, 7, 8, 9, 10, 11].

Composite segment. A segment (other than a primary segment) formed by segments or subsegments that are contiguous or otherwise linked in some way.

Derivation. Refers to the processes by which one pc set is generated from another: complementation, inclusion, transposition, inversion, union, and intersection.

Imbrication. The analytical procedure of extracting, sequentially, subcomponents of some linear configuration.

Integer notation. The representation of pitch classes by the integers 0 through 11 (pc integers).

Intersection. For two sets A and B, the intersection C of A and B is the set of elements common to A and B. This is written C = · (A, B).

Interval. If a and b are pc integers, then the interval formed by a and b is the absolute (positive) value of the difference of a and b ($|a-b|$).

Interval class. One of the seven interval classes designated by the integers 0 through 6.

Interval content. Refers to total interval-content: the collection of interval-class representatives formed by taking the absolute value differences of all pairs of elements of a pc set.

Interval succession. The intervals formed by successive elements of an ordered pc set. If for example, the set is [0, 1, 6, 7], the interval succession is [1-5-1].

209

Interval vector.   An ordered array of numerals enclosed in square brackets that represents the interval content of a pc set. The first numeral gives the number of intervals of interval class 1, the second gives the number of intervals of interval class 2, and so on.

Invariant subset.   Whenever a set S undergoes a transformation (transposition or inversion), some subset T of S remains unchanged, or invariant. Possibly T is null (empty).

Inverse.   If a is a pc integer and a' represents the inverse of a, then $a' = 12 - a$ (modulo 12).

Inversion.   Refers to the process by which each element e of a pc set is replaced by $12-e$.

Inversional equivalence.   Refers to two pc sets related by the operation of inversion followed by transposition, such that the two sets are reducible to the same prime form.

Modulo 12.   In order to ensure that a pitch number j is reduced to a pitch-class integer, it is necessary to replace j by the remainder of j divided by 12 if j is greater than or equal to 12.

Nexus set.   A referential set for a particular set complex.

Normal order.   A particular circular permutation of a pc set in ascending order.

Ordered inversion.   This occurs when a pc set is inverted and transposed in such a way that the original order of the elements is unchanged.

Ordered set.   A pc set in which the order of the elements is regarded as significant.

Ordered transposition.   This occurs when a pc set is transposed in such a way that the original order of the elements is unchanged.

Order inversion.   If in a given ordering of a pc set, element a precedes element b, and in a reordering of the set element b precedes element a, an order inversion has occurred.

Pitch class (pc).   One of the 12 pitch-classes designated by the integers 0 through 11. Pitch-class 0 refers to all notated pitches C, B-sharp, and D-double-flat. Pitch-class 1 refers to all notated pitches C-sharp, D-flat, B-double-sharp, and so on.

Pitch-class set (pc set).   A set of distinct integers representing pitch classes.

Primary segment.   A segment determined by conventional means, such as a melodic configuration.

Prime form.   A set in normal order, transposed so that the first integer is 0.

Retrograde.   The complete reversal of the order of the elements of a set.

Segment.   A musical unit of fixed extent.

Segmentation.   The analytical procedure by which the significant musical units of a composition are determined.

Set complex (K).   A set of sets associated by virtue of the inclusion relation.

Set complex (Kh).   A special subcomplex of the set complex K.

Set name.   The name of a pc set, consisting of two numerals separated by a hyphen. The numeral to the left of the hyphen is the cardinal number of the set; the numeral to the right of the hyphen is the ordinal number of the set, its position on the list of prime forms.

Similarity relations.   Refers to ways in which two non-equivalent sets of the same cardinal number may be compared for structural similarity and difference.

Subset.   A set X is said to be a subset of a set Y if every element of X is an element of Y. X is a *proper* subset of Y if the cardinal number of Y is greater than the cardinal number of X and if every element of X is an element of Y.

Superset.   A set X is said to be a superset of a set Y if every element of Y is an element of X. X is a *proper* superset of Y if the cardinal number of X is greater than the cardinal number of Y and if every element of Y is an element of X.

Transitive tuple.   If each set in a set of n sets, where n is greater than 2, is in relation R with every other set, then the set of sets is called a transitive tuple.

Transposition.   Transposition of a pc set S consists of the addition (modulo 12) of some integer t to each element of S.

Transpositional equivalence.   Refers to two pc sets related by the operation of transposition such that the two sets are reducible to the same prime form.

Transposition operator.   The letter t is a variable, by convention, whose integer value is added to each element of a pc set to produce a transposition of that set. In this role, the variable t is construed as an operator.

Union.   For two sets A and B, the union C of A and B is the set of all the elements of A and all the elements of B. This is written $C = + (A, B)$.

Unordered set.   A pc set in which the order of the elements is regarded as insignificant.

Z-correspondent.   Designates one member of a pair of Z-related sets.

Z-related pair.   This refers to a pair of sets with the same interval vector, but which are not reducible to the same prime form.

References

Babbitt, Milton. 1960. "Twleve-Tone Invariants as Compositional Determinants," *The Musical Quarterly* 46, no. 2.

——. 1961. "Set Structure as a Compositional Determinant," *Journal of Music Theory* 5, no. 1.

——. 1964. "Remarks on the Recent Stravinsky," *Perspectives of New Music* 2, no. 2.

——. 1965. "The Structure and Function of Music Theory," *College Music Symposium* 5.

Berger, Arthur. 1964. "Problems of Pitch Organization in Stravinsky," *Perspectives of New Music* 2, no. 1.

Chrisman, Richard A. 1969. *A Theory of Axis-Tonality for Twentieth-Century Music.* Ph.D. dissertation, Yale University.

Cone, Edward T. 1962. "Stravinsky: The Progress of a Method," *Perspectives of New Music* 1, no. 1.

Craft, Robert. 1968. "Schoenberg's Five Pieces for Orchestra." In *Perspectives on Schoenberg and Stravinsky,* eds. B. Boretz and E. T. Cone. Princeton: Princeton University Press.

Forte, Allen. 1964. "A Theory of Set-Complexes for Music," *Journal of Music Theory* 8, no. 2.

——. 1972. "Sets and Nonsets in Schoenberg's Atonal Music," *Perspectives of New Music* 11, no. 1.

Gilbert, Steven E. 1970. *The Trichord: An Analytic Outlook for Twentieth-Century Music.* Ph.D. dissertation, Yale University.

Howe, Hubert. 1965. "Some Combinational Properties of Pitch Structures," *Perspectives of New Music* 4, no. 1.

Lewin, David. 1960. "The Intervallic Content of a Collection of Notes," *Journal of Music Theory* 4, no. 1.

Lewin, David. 1962. "A Theory of Segmental Association in Twelve-Tone Music," *Perspectives of New Music* 1, no. 1.

Martino, Donald. 1961. "The Source-Set and Its Aggregate Formations," *Journal of Music Theory* 5, no. 2.

Nüll, Edwin von der. 1932. *Moderne Harmonik.* Leipzig: Fr. Kistner & C. F. W. Siegel.

Perle, George. 1967. "The Musical Language of Wozzeck." In *The Music Forum,* 1, eds. W. J. Mitchell and F. Salzer. New York: Columbia University Press.

——. 1968. *Serial Composition and Atonality.* 2d ed. Berkeley and Los Angeles: University of California Press.

Redlich, Hans. 1957. *Alban Berg: The Man and His Music.* New York: Abelard-Schumann.

Rufer, Josef. 1959. *Das Werk Arnold Schoenbergs.* Kassel: Bärenreiter-Verlag.

Stravinsky, Igor. 1969. *The Rite of Spring: Sketches 1911-1913.* London: Boosey & Hawkes.

Teitelbaum, Richard. 1965. "Intervallic Relations in Atonal Music," *Journal of Music Theory* 9, no. 1.

Index 1   Musical Examples

Bartok, Bela
 Suite for Piano Op. 14, ex. 24, 25
Berg, Alban
 Chamber Concerto for Violin, Piano, and
  Thirteen Wind Instruments, ex. 114
 Five Songs with Orchestra (("Altenberg
  Lieder") Op. 4, ex. 11, 75, 124, 125, 126
 Four Pieces for Clarinet and Piano Op. 5, ex.
  6, 35, 36
 Wozzeck Op. 7, ex. 12, 15, 16, 26, 29, 55, 72,
  82, 112, 113
Busoni, Ferruccio
 Second Sonatina, ex. 13
Ives, Charles
 Second String Quartet, ex. 63
 Tone Roads No. 1, ex. 14
 The Unanswered Question, ex. 9, 48
Ruggles, Carl
 Angels, ex. 44
Schoenberg, Arnold
 Fifteen Poems from the Book of the Hanging
  Gardens by Stefan George ("George Lieder")
  Op. 15, ex. 1, 8, 38, 68
 Five Piano Pieces Op. 23, ex. 18, 40, 78
 Five Pieces for Orchestra Op. 16, ex. 10, 69,
  87, 151 through 159
 Die glückliche Hand Op. 18, ex. 50
 Pierrot Lunaire Op. 21, ex. 43
 Serenade Op. 24, ex. 86
 Six Short Piano Pieces Op. 19, ex. 100, 101,
  102
 Three Piano Pieces Op. 11, ex. 46, 95, 96,
  106
Scriabin, Alexander
 Ninth Piano Sonato Op. 68, ex. 110, 111
 Seventh Piano Sonata Op. 64, ex. 61
 Sixth Piano Sonata Op. 62, ex. 58
 Two Poems Op. 63, ex. 83
Stravinsky, Igor
 Cantata, ex. 74
 Four Studies for Orchestra, ex. 121, 122, 123
 Petrouchka, ex. 19
 The Rite of Spring, ex. 37, 39, 45, 59, 79, 80,
  88, 127, 128
 Le Roi des étoiles, ex. 108, 109
 Symphonies of Wind Instruments, ex. 11, 97
 Three Pieces for String Quartet, ex. 33, 81
 Three Poems from Japanese Lyrics, ex. 84
 Three Songs from William Shakespeare (No.
  1), ex. 76
 Two Poems by K. Balmont (No. 1), ex. 64
Varèse, Edgar
 Intégrales, ex. 22
Webern, Anton
 Cello Sonata 1914, ex. 65
 Five Movements for String Quartet Op. 5, ex.
  5, 27, 67, 98
 Five Pieces for Orchestra Op. 10, ex. 17, 56,
  93, 94
 Four Pieces for Violin and Piano Op. 7, ex.
  7, 116 through 120
 Four Songs for Voice and Piano Op. 12, ex.
  60, 70, 77
 Six Bagatelles for String Quartet Op. 9, ex.
  23
 Six Pieces for Large Orchestra Op. 6, ex. 2,
  49, 66, 107
 Six Songs for Voice, Clarinet, Bass Clarinet,
  Violin, and Cello Op. 14, ex. 71
 Three Short Pieces for Cello and Piano Op.
  11, ex. 21

Index 2   Pc Sets in Musical Examples

3-1
    94   Webern
   119 Webern
   128 Stravinsky
9-1
    94   Webern
3-3
   119 Webern
   129 Stravinsky
9-3
    40   Schoenberg
3-4
    93   Webern
   119 Webern
3-5
   114 Berg
   119 Webern
3-7
   100 Schoenberg
3-9
   100 Schoenberg
   119 Webern
3-11
   129 Stravinsky
9-11
    89   Stravinsky
3-12
    89   Stravinksy
4-1
    94   Webern
   110 Scriabin
8-1
   100 Schoenberg
4-2
    38   Schoenberg
    50   Schoenberg
    76   Stravinsky
   121 Stravinsky
   128 Stravinsky
   129 Stravinsky
4-3
    65   Webern
    86   Schoenberg
    89   Stravinsky
   121 Stravinsky
8-3
    89   Stravinsky
4-4
   100 Schoenberg

   112 Berg
   121 Stravinsky
4-5
    60   Webern
    66   Webern
    77   Webern
    94   Webern
8-5
    77   Webern
4-6
    94   Webern
   121 Stravinsky
8-6
    94   Webern
4-7
    86   Schoenberg
    87   Schoenberg
    94   Webern
   121 Stravinsky
4-8
    33   Stravinsky
   116 Webern
   121 Stravinsky
   124 Berg
4-9
    17   Webern
    27   Webern
    58   Scriabin
    90   Stravinsky
   116 Webern
   124 Berg
4-10
   121 Stravinsky
8-10
   124 Berg
4-11
    68   Schoenberg
    97   Stravinsky
   125 Berg
8-11
   124 Berg
4-12
    93   Webern
   110 Scriabin
   121 Stravinsky
8-12
   110 Scriabin
4-13
    50   Schoenberg

(Continued)

216

4-13 (*Continued*)
75	Berg
106	Schoenberg
108	Stravinsky
114	Berg
125	Berg

8-13
84	Stravinsky
108	Stravinsky
114	Berg
124	Berg

4-14
112	Berg
114	Berg
121	Stravinsky
152	Schoenberg

8-14
114	Berg
152	Schoenberg

4-Z15
1	Schoenberg
2	Webern
21	Webern
58	Scriabin
86	Schoenberg
95	Schoenberg
112	Berg
119	Webern
133	Stravinsky

8-Z15
94	Webern
100	Schoenberg
116	Webern

4-16
60	Webern
77	Webern
112	Berg
124	Berg

8-16
77	Webern
93	Webern

4-17
9	Ives
108	Stravinsky

4-18
8	Schoenberg
12	Berg
59	Stravinsky
86	Schoenberg
106	Schoenberg
110	Scriabin
114	Berg

8-18
106	Schoenberg
108	Stravinsky
128	Stravinsky

4-19
15	Berg
26	Berg
35	Berg
72	Berg
86	Schoenberg
112	Berg
121	Stravinsky
124	Berg
152	Schoenberg

8-19
81	Stravinsky

4-20
129	Stravinsky
152	Schoenberg

4-21
60	Webern
77	Webern
89	Stravinsky
110	Scriabin
112	Berg

8-21
77	Webern

4-22
121	Stravinsky

4-23
100	Schoenberg
121	Stravinsky
133	Stravinsky
134	Stravinsky

8-23
128	Stravinsky
134	Stravinsky

4-24
110	Scriabin

8-24
16	Berg

4-25
90	Stravinsky
110	Scriabin

4-27
59	Stravinsky
108	Stravinsky

8-27
108	Stravinsky

4-28
89	Stravinsky
110	Scriabin

8-28
   45 Stravinsky
  108 Stravinsky
  110 Scriabin
  116 Webern
  128 Stravinsky
4-Z29
    9 Ives
   21 Webern
   46 Schoenberg
   64 Stravinsky
  112 Berg
8-Z29
  112 Berg
5-1
  124 Berg
5-3
    7 Webern
   60 Webern
  121 Stravinsky
7-3
  152 Schoenberg
5-4
   60 Webern
   69 Schoenberg
7-4
  100 Schoenberg
  112 Berg
  114 Berg
  116 Webern
  121 Stravinsky
5-5
  112 Berg
  152 Schoenberg
7-5
  100 Schoenberg
  112 Berg
5-6
   86 Schoenberg
   93 Webern
  116 Webern
  121 Stravinsky
7-6
  116 Webern
5-7
    5 Webern
   67 Webern
   96 Schoenberg
  116 Webern
7-7
  121 Stravinsky

5-8
   60 Webern
  110 Scriabin
7-8
   63 Ives
  110 Scriabin
5-9
   49 Webern
  112 Berg
7-9
   89 Stravinsky
  112 Berg
5-10
   48 Ives
   75 Berg
   78 Schoenberg
  112 Berg
  121 Stravinsky
  124 Berg
  128 Stravinsky
  129 Stravinsky
7-10
   78 Schoenberg
5-11
  152 Schoenberg
5-Z12
   48 Ives
7-Z12
  100 Schoenberg
5-13
  124 Berg
  152 Schoenberg
5-15
   55 Berg
   94 Webern
7-15
  112 Berg
  121 Stravinsky
5-16
   61 Scriabin
   80 Stravinsky
   84 Stravinsky
  112 Berg
  124 Berg
  152 Schoenberg
7-16
   80 Stravinsky
  121 Stravinsky
  128 Stravinsky
5-Z17
   55 Berg

(Continued)

5-Z17 (*Continued*)
    86   Schoenberg
   152   Schoenberg
   107   Webern
5-Z18
   24   Bartok
   25   Bartok
   60   Webern
   70   Webern
   87   Schoenberg
   107   Webern
   108   Stravinsky
   112   Berg
   121   Stravinsky
   152   Schoenberg
7-Z18
   46   Schoenberg
5-19
   55   Berg
   112   Berg
   116   Webern
   121   Stravinsky
   124   Berg
   128   Stravinsky
7-19
   94   Webern
   128   Stravinsky
5-20
   93   Webern
   124   Berg
   128   Stravinsky
   152   Schoenberg
7-20
   93   Webern
5-21
   10   Schoenberg
   24   Bartok
   25   Bartok
   44   Ruggles
   86   Schoenberg
   112   Berg
   152   Schoenberg
7-21
   36   Berg
5-22
   121   Stravinsky
   128   Stravinsky
7-22
   86   Schoenberg
5-23
   121   Stravinsky
   128   Stravinsky

5-24
   49   Webern
   100   Schoenberg
   124   Berg
   152   Schoenberg
7-24
   100   Schoenberg
   152   Schoenberg
5-25
   108   Stravinsky
   128   Stravinsky
7-25
   108   Stravinsky
   128   Stravinsky
7-26
   83   Scriabin
5-27
   112   Berg
   152   Schoenberg
7-27
   132   Stravinsky
   134   Stravinsky
5-28
   90   Stravinsky
   128   Stravinsky
   134   Stravinsky
7-28
   100   Schoenberg
   124   Berg
   128   Stravinsky
   134   Stravinsky
5-29
   108   Stravinsky
   152   Schoenberg
7-29
   128   Stravinsky
5-30
   26   Berg
   112   Berg
7-30
   112   Berg
5-31
   11   Berg, Stravinsky
   43   Schoenberg
   121   Stravinsky
   124   Berg
7-31
   45   Stravinsky
   63   Ives
   84   Stravinsky
   128   Stravinsky

5-32
    58 Scriabin
    79 Stravinsky
    108 Stravinsky
    128 Stravinsky
7-32
    79 Stravinsky
    84 Stravinsky
    108 Stravinsky
    121 Stravinsky
    128 Stravinsky
5-33
    83 Scriabin
5-35
    152 Schoenberg
7-35
    13 Busoni
    134 Stravinsky
    132 Stravinsky
    152 Schoenberg
5-Z36
    89 Stravinsky
5-Z37
    152 Schoenberg
7-Z37
    89 Stravinsky
    107 Webern
    129 Stravinsky
5-Z38
    25 Bartok
    84 Stravinsky
7-Z38
    46 Schoenberg
    107 Webern
    152 Schoenberg
6-Z3
    74 Stravinsky
    121 Stravinsky
6-Z36
    84 Stravinsky
6-Z4
    23 Webern
6-Z37
    23 Webern
6-5
    87 Schoenberg
    98 Webern
    114 Berg
    124 Berg
6-Z6
    94 Webern
    116 Webern

    121 Stravinsky
6-Z38
    94 Webern
    116 Webern
    121 Stravinsky
6-9
    56 Webern
    94 Webern
6-Z10
    18 Schoenberg
    21 Webern
    22 Varèse
6-Z39
    21 Webern
    22 Varèse
    107 Webern
6-Z11
    121 Stravinsky
6-Z12
    100 Schoenberg
6-Z13
    61 Scriabin
    71 Webern
    116 Webern
6-Z42
    128 Stravinsky
6-15
    152 Schoenberg
6-16
    56 Webern
    93 Webern
6-Z17
    82 Berg
    121 Stravinsky
6-Z43
    82 Berg
    94 Webern
    121 Stravinsky
    128 Stravinsky
6-18
    107 Webern
    124 Berg
6-Z19
    39 Stravinsky
    61 Scriabin
    107 Webern
    112 Berg
    114 Berg
    128 Stravinsky
    152 Schoenberg
6-Z44
    6   Berg

(Continued)

6-Z44 (*Continued*)
    35 Berg
  107 Webern
  112 Berg
  114 Berg
6-21
  110 Scriabin
6-22
  100 Schoenberg
  112 Berg
6-Z23
  129 Stravinsky
6-Z45
  128 Stravinsky
  129 Stravinsky
6-Z24
   61 Scriabin
  132 Stravinsky
  152 Schoenberg
6-Z46
  128 Stravinsky
  132 Stravinsky
6-Z25
  128 Stravinsky
6-27
  106 Schoenberg
  108 Stravinsky
  124 Berg
  128 Stravinsky

6-Z28
   89 Stravinsky
   92 Stravinsky
  130 Stravinsky
  134 Stravinsky
6-Z49
   58 Scriabin
   61 Scriabin
  128 Stravinsky
6-Z29
  108 Stravinsky
  128 Stravinsky
6-Z50
   58 Scriabin
  108 Stravinsky
6-30
   19 Stravinsky
   58 Scriabin
  128 Stravinsky
6-32
   14 Ives
   37 Stravinsky
6-33
  132 Stravinsky
  134 Stravinsky
  152 Schoenberg
6-34
   29 Berg
   61 Scriabin
  100 Schoenberg
  110 Scriabin

Index 3　General Index

Addition modulo *12* (mod *12*), 6
All-interval tetrachord, 1, 18, 21
Association of sections, 131-33

Babbitt, Milton, 1*n*, 3*n*, 70*n*, 72*n*, 77*n*
Basic interval pattern: comparison of, 64; and similarity relation R$_p$, 66; and cardinal number of pc set, 67; and total interval content of pc set, 67; of sets of cardinal *4*, 67-69; number of for each cardinality, 70; and similarity relations, 70; and combinatorial properties, 70; and retrograde, 71; number of ways it can be formed, 71; and set-complex size, 101
Berger, Arthur, 43*n*
Bip. *See* Basic interval pattern

Cardinal number: defined, 3; and set name, 12; and interval content, 19
Chrisman, Richard, 14*n*
Closure (of a set complex), 101-04
Complement: defined, 73-74; notation, 74; and set names, 74; literal, 75; transformation of, 75; and set identification, 75; and invariance, 75, 82; and inclusion, 75, 78; and interval vector, 77-78; and Z-hexachords, 79; and similarity relations, 80
Composite segment, 84, 90
Cone, Edward T., 154*n*
Connectedness, 114
Correspondence (rule of), 8
Craft, Robert, 166*n*, 171*n*

Derivation, 114

Enharmonic equivalence, 2
Equivalence class, 14
Equivalence of pc sets, 5

Factorial function, 3
Form, 124. *See also* Association of sections

Gilbert, Steven E., 84*n*

Howe, Hubert S., 30*n*, 45*n*

Inclusion relation, 25. *See also* Subset
Imbrication, 83
Integer notation, 2-3
Intersection (set-theoretic), 29

Interval
—class: defined, 14; even and odd, 20
—content: total, 14-15; and cardinal number, 19
—succession, 63
—vector: defined, 15; unique entries property of, 16; maximum ic property of, 17; equal or near equal distribution property of, 18; and invariance under transposition, 30-31
Invariance: defined, 29; for subset of cardinal n-1, 37; within the set complex, 104-08
—under transposition: 28-37; maximum, 32-33; minimum, 33-34; more than two sets, 34; inverse-related values of t, 31-32, 35-36
—under inversion: structural basis of, 40-41; complete, 41, 44; less than complete, 41; sums of S, 41; sums of S in S, 41
Inverse, 8
Inversion: symbolic notation for, 10; ordered, 62-63
Inversional equivalence, 7-9
Irreflexive property, 52

K. *See* Set complex
Kh. *See* Set complex

Lewin, David, 21*n*, 45*n*

Mapping: onto, 7; double, 8, 40; inversion as, 9; transposition as, 9
Martino, Donald, 15*n*, 70*n*, 82*n*
Modulo *12*, 6

Nexus set: defined, 101; rules for determination of, 113-14
Non-equivalent sets with identical vectors. *See* Z-relation
Non-transitive property, 52
Normal order: determination of, 3-5; requirement *1*, 4; requirement *2*, 4; best, 4, 12-13
Notation class, 2
Nüll, Edwin von der, 30*n*

Octave equivalence, 2
Order inversion: defined, 65; and basic interval pattern, 66
Order relations: 60-73; and subsets, 66; and repeated pcs, 72. *See also* Basic interval

pattern; Order inversion
Ordered inversion, 62-63
Ordered set: defined, 3, 60*n*; notation of, 61
Ordered transposition, 62
Ordinal number, 12

Pascal's triangle, 27
Pc set. *See* Pitch-class set
Perle, George, 12*n*, 28*n*
Permutation: defined, 3; circular, 3-4, 72; as
    mapping, 61; after transposition, 61; after
    inversion and transposition, 61; and order
    inversions, 65
Pitch class, 2
Pitch-class integer, 3
Pitch-class set, 1, 3
Pitch combination, 1
Primary segment, 83
Prime form, 3, 5, 11-13

Redlich, Hans, 28*n*
Reflexive property, 52
Retrograde, 71
Rufer, Josef, 18*n*
Rule of correspondence, 8

Scriabin's mystic chord, 28*n*
Segment: primary 83; composite, 84, 90;
    large composite, 92. *See also* Segmentation
Segmentation: defined, 83; imbrication, 83;
    and union, 91; and intersection, 91; con-
    textual criteria, 91; and set-complex re-
    lations, 92
Set. *See* Pitch-class set
Set complex: K, 93-96; and inclusion, 93-94;
    and complementation, 94; symmetric
    property, 95, 97; and transposition, 95-96;
    and inversion, 95-96; Kh (subcomplex),
    96-97; and reciprocal complement relation,

96-97; graphic display of (tables), 100;
    sizes, 101; nexus set, 101; closure property,
    101-04; and transitivity, 102-04 passim;
    invariance within, 104-08; similarity rela-
    tions within, 108-13; structures of small
    scale, 113-23; structures of larger scale,
    124-77; and form, 124
Set name, 11-13
Similarity relations: pitch-class, 47; interval-
    class, 48; R_p, 47; R_1, 48; R_2, 48; R_0, 49;
    maximal, 48, 50; minimal, 49; summarized,
    49; pitch and interval class combined, 49;
    weak and strong representation of R_p, 50;
    properties of, 52-53; transitive tuples, 53-
    55; within the set complex, 108-13

Subset: defined, 24; proper, 26; unit, 26; null,
    26. *See also* Invariance
Sums of S. *See* Invariance
Sums of S in S. *See* Invariance
Superset, 25
Symmetric property, 52

Teitelbaum, Richard, 4*n*
Transitive tuple, 109.
Transitivity, 52, 102
Transposition: 2, symbolic notation for, 10;
    ordered, 62
Transposition operator, 6, 8
Transpositional equivalance, 5

Union (set-theoretic), 22
Unordered set, 3, 60*n*

Vector. *See* Interval vector

Z-relations: Z-correspondent in, 21-22; and Z-
    related pair, 21; and Z-hexachords, 79